THE LIBRARY
COMPENSATION
HANDBOOK

THE LIBRARY COMPENSATION HANDBOOK

A Guide for Administrators, Librarians, and Staff

David A. Baldwin

A Member of the Greenwood Publishing Group

Westport, Connecticut • London

LIBRARIES UNLIMITED
A Member of Greenwood Publishing Group, Inc.
88 Post Road West
Westport, CT 06881
1-800-225-5800
www.lu.com

Library of Congress Cataloging-in-Publication Data
Baldwin, David A. (David Allen), 1946-
    The library compensation handbook : a guide for administrators,
librarians, and staff / David A. Baldwin.
        p.   cm.
Includes bibliographical references and index.
    ISBN 1-56308-970-X (alk. paper)
    1. Library employees—Salaries, etc.—United States. 2. Librarians—
Salaries, etc.—United States. 3. Compensation management—United States.
I. Title.
    Z682.3.B35 2003
    023'.9—dc21   2002155401

CONTENTS

CONTENTS

CONTENTS

INTRODUCTION

The only thing we can predict with certainty is change.

—JAYNE SPAIN

Compensation policies and practices affect all library employees. Perhaps a few employees would work in libraries without being paid, but most would be doing something else if that paycheck were not forthcoming. When salary and compensation issues are dealt with effectively in an organization, it is an issue rarely discussed except at raise time. When library employees perceive that compensation is not handled fairly, it becomes a constant source of discussion, dissatisfaction, and discouragement. How often have you heard, "Our employees are our greatest assets"? Like any other asset, people can depreciate quickly if treated improperly. Creativity can be dulled by lack of challenge, and contentment can soon turn to resentment. People have tremendous value, and it is the library director's job to make sure the library's most important assets are being properly maintained. Employees must be encouraged with recognition, paid what they are worth, and given the tools they need to reach personal and organizational goals.

This book is intended to provide library managers with information to help them understand what is involved in establishing and maintaining a compensation system that meets the needs of library employees. It can also help library employees understand how their own compensation is determined.

Employee compensation consists of everything an employed person receives in return for work performed and includes all expenditures of valued resources by the organization for an employee. This definition relates to all employees—librarians, exempt and nonexempt staff, and student employees. Included in compensation are wages, salaries, and indirect compensation, or fringe benefits. Compensation is a major cost in libraries of all types. It is often the largest single portion of library budgets. Because libraries wish to use resources efficiently, compensation expenses must be controlled. Pressures to increase compensation expenditures come from employees who want more money or from supervisors who seek large raises for their employees. Pressures to reduce compensation expenditures come from governing bodies or administrators who are faced with other financial pressures.

If libraries could regard the compensation paid to employees like those expenditures for books, supplies, and furniture, management of compensation would be much less complex. However, compensation is not that simple. Perhaps the greatest difficulty is that a library cannot depend on a standardized unit for labor like other resources it acquires. When a library purchases books from vendors, damaged books or those ordered in error are replaced. However, when it hires individuals, it cannot be guaranteed of their performance, and if mistakes are made in hiring, the library must live with the consequences. To complicate matters further, the performance of employees varies over time; for example, an employee may behave one way during the probationary period and quite another way after gaining seniority and security.

The importance of compensation to employees is relatively clear. Pay is a central factor in inducing people to accept employment and can be an effective means of encouraging productivity. But pay can also be the greatest source of dissatisfaction for some employees. Pay dissatisfaction can result not only when individuals do not earn what is considered to be enough money but also when they do not know what their coworkers earn.

How is compensation established and distributed fairly? How are compensation decisions made? What part does job evaluation play in making salary decisions? How is compensation made competitive? How do you know if it is competitive? Once established and made fair and competitive, how is this maintained through assessment and merit systems? Libraries employ librarians, who perform a number of public, technical, and administrative duties, and a large number of staff members, who do everything from teaching classes to cataloging books to supervising student employees. There are catalogers, reference personnel, accountants, supervisors, and computer specialists. How is pay determined for these different jobs? Is a cataloger worth more than an accountant? Is a computer specialist worth more than a circulation-desk worker? How much more? What procedures are used to set pay rates, and who does it? How important are the characteristics of the employee versus the characteristics of the work? Who decides?

The answers are found in the organization's compensation policies and practices. The library's administrators and managers must have an understanding of compensation policy and be able to communicate those policies to library employees. All employees should know what the library is providing in direct and indirect compensation to obtain their services. They should know why they are receiving these payments, how they are determined, who makes the determinations, when payments are available, and what opportunities are available to each employee to influence the amount. This book is intended to help managers and employees understand all aspects of compensation for librarians and staff.

1 BASIC LIBRARY COMPENSATION MANAGEMENT

The secret of successful management is to keep the five guys who hate you away from the five guys who haven't made up their minds.

—CASEY STENGEL

COMPENSATION SYSTEM PHILOSOPHY

Managers of all compensation programs will be faced regularly with decisions that present several possible alternatives or solutions. Each of these alternatives, in turn, will have consequences for labor costs, employee satisfaction, and employee performance and will be examined by those who review those decisions. It is not possible to confidently say which of the alternatives will present the correct answer because each depends on the differences in the situations facing various organizations. Although policy may dictate most solutions, additional alternatives still must be considered. The alternatives will certainly be examined by the employees affected by those decisions. The decisions made by the compensation managers must be guided by a compensation policy that will aid in making salary decisions that are fair and equitable, as well as being perceived by nearly everyone else as fair and equitable.

There are four basic policies that any employer must consider in the management of compensation:

- internal consistency
- external competitiveness

- individual contributions
- the method by which the pay system is administered

Internal Consistency

Internal consistency refers to the comparisons among jobs or skill levels within an organization. Also called internal equity, its focus is on comparing jobs in terms of their relative contribution to the organization's objectives. Internal consistency becomes an issue both for individuals doing equal work and for those doing dissimilar work but at the same level. Determining what is an equitable difference in pay for employees performing different work is one of the key issues in compensation management.

Internal equity has two dimensions: 1) the relative similarities and differences in the content of the work or skills required, and 2) the relative contribution of the work or skills to the organization's objectives. To maintain internal equity, organizations must have an elaborate and reliable system of job analysis and job evaluation. This is extremely important for libraries, which are a part of larger organizations, such as colleges and universities, city, county, and state governments, and corporations. Those responsible for managing the organization's pay system must understand the work performed and the skills required to perform that work. Internal equity is often the source of employee compensation complaints. Internal equity decisions have a great impact on the library's ability to retain employees, have them invest time in retraining, and to have staff seek greater responsibility through promotions. Because internal equity is such an important pay policy issue, it is incumbent on library managers to understand how positions are classified by the organization and how those positions compare with others in the organization.

External Competitiveness

Library managers have to be aware of what competitors are paying for similar work. Knowing what the competition pays provides the information for salary policy decisions. Does the library want to set the pay levels higher than the competition in order to attract the best and retain them? Would the library prefer to offer lower base pay but greater opportunity for advancement, overtime, greater benefits, or job security? The external competitiveness policy decisions are aimed at hiring and retaining the best employees while also controlling personnel costs. Employers who place a high value on competitiveness will likely match or exceed job offers that their employees receive from others and may devote more time and resources to determining what competitors are paying. The library may also be in the position of having no nearby competitors. The market for librarians is quite different from the market for library staff. In addition, external competitiveness for an Association of Research Libraries member will differ for those librarians who may be able to move from one library to another, from one state to another. Library staff members are often unable to move in the same way but may find other positions within the larger organization.

Individual Contributions

Policies regarding individual contributions relate to pay for performance. An organization's decisions on whether to use performance appraisals to determine salary levels is an important one. Should all employees doing the same work receive the same pay, or should those individuals for whom supervisors can document superior performance receive higher pay? How is that determined, and how much of a differential is there? The organization's policy and the library's adherence to such a policy have a direct effect on the employee's motivation, attitudes, and work behaviors and thus on improving efficiency and achieving equity.

Compensation Administration

Although it is possible to design a system that pays attention to internal equity, external competitiveness, and employee contributions, the system will not achieve its objectives if it is not properly administered. Administration involves planning the elements of pay that should be included in the pay system, evaluating how the pay system is operating, communicating with employees, and judging whether the system is achieving its objectives. The library managers' responsibilities regarding the pay system are to guarantee that the library adheres to the overarching organization's pay policies and procedures. The following are among the kinds of questions library managers should ask:

- Is the library able to attract and keep skilled workers? If not, why not?
- Do library employees feel the system is fair?
- Have the managers communicated to the librarians and staff what factors go into setting their pay?
- Do librarians and staff agree that these factors are important?
- Do librarians and staff have a means by which to raise questions and voice concerns about salary issues?
- How does the competition pay its employees?
- Is the library in danger of losing its best employees to the competition?
- Is it better to have internal equity than external competitiveness?
- Is it preferable to reward star performers than to pay all persons doing similar work the same salary?
- Are the organization's pay policies understood?
- Have the managers made an effort to explain or bring in others to explain how the pay system works?
- Do the managers understand how the pay system works?

Managers need to have a thorough understanding of the organization's pay policies and the library's interpretation of those policies in order to communicate them and defend them to library employees.

This book will investigate how libraries can establish internal equity and the various forms of job analysis and job evaluation, examine pay-equity issues in libraries, and develop a philosophy for internal consistency in libraries. It will look at how salaries compare among libraries of various types and discuss ways that libraries can improve their retention of librarians and staff. Pay for performance, merit plans, incentive pay, and seniority-based increases, as well as forms of appraisal, will be examined. Lastly, the effective administration of the organization's and library's pay policy will be discussed, along with case studies dealing with pay issues. The overriding purpose of this book is to provide a complete compensation handbook for library managers and library personnel interested in how the pay structure and pay policies of organizations work and how they can be improved.

COMPENSATION DEFINED

Simply defined, employee compensation is everything an employed individual receives in return for work done. It covers all expenditures of valued resources by the organization for all employees—managers or professionals, blue- or white-collar workers, and full-time, part-time, or contract workers. Included in compensation are wages or hourly rates of pay, salaries covering a longer period of time than wages, and incentive or merit pay. Also included are the expanding number of fringe benefits, or indirect benefits, such as annual leave or vacation pay, employee discounts, unemployment insurance, stock options, and retirement benefits.

Library employees include librarians and other professional staff, library faculty in some university libraries, staff at various levels, and student employees. Contract and other salaried employees are exempt from the protections afforded by the Fair Labor Standards Act (FLSA) and are usually paid for a set number of days or are required to report absences for whatever reason, which are deducted from their allocation of hours. Employees covered by the FLSA are paid for hours worked and are required to report both hours worked and absences. In addition, unions and bargaining units represent various groups of employees, often negotiating salaries and benefits for their members.

Compensation usually accounts for a large share of any organization's expenses and in libraries is often at least 60 percent of the budget. Managing compensation is difficult not only because of the complexity involved but also because compensation is such an important issue for employees. A number of research studies have shown that employees consider salary to be one of the most important factors on the job and that perceived inadequate compensation is a major source of job dissatisfaction.

INFLUENCE OF FREE-MARKET ECONOMY ON SALARIES

Setting and maintaining salary policies would be far easier if central control and absolute standards existed that administrators could use to determine appropriate salaries and benefit packages. The key to understanding the current compensation decision-making process in most organizations, both public and private, is recognizing the impact of the free-market economy in the United States. This system relies on marketplace forces to determine demands, supplies, and labor prices.

With the exception of wage and price controls imposed during World War II and an attempt during the early years of the Vietnam conflict to establish wage guideposts that were intended to determine acceptable noninflationary wage increases, the United States has relied on the marketplace. Because of the lack of central control and standards, wage decisions are usually made and evaluated on a relative basis. Decision makers use the pay of some other group or individual to determine the pay of their employees, and employees use what others are paid as a basis for deciding whether their own pay is fair. For example, the federal government uses pay rates in private industry as a basis for establishing federal employee pay rates.

ORGANIZATIONAL COMPENSATION OBJECTIVES

Organizations of all types exist to provide something that is of value to a segment of society. Whether an organization is manufacturing automobiles or offering library services, it exists because there is a need for it. The goods or services produced by an organization are its task objectives. The organization is judged successful if it accomplishes its task objectives and considered effective if it accomplishes these objectives using a minimum of resources, often referred to as its productivity goal. To meet its productivity goal, an organization needs productive employees who believe they are compensated well enough to perform the required work. But it is essential that an organization not allow its labor costs to become excessive. Labor costs influence the costs of goods and services, which in turn affect profits. For obvious reasons, organizations are inclined to pay the lowest wages possible while still attracting and motivating employees. Public-employee salaries are influenced by salaries in the private sector and also by the additional pressures put on elected officials to hold down costs of government.

An organization's compensation program has three primary objectives in helping the organization to meet the productivity goal:

- Help the organization attract the most-qualified employees.
- Motivate employees to perform at a consistently high or at least satisfactory level.
- Encourage employees to improve their knowledge, skills, and abilities in order to perform their present jobs and new tasks efficiently and effectively.

Organizational maintenance is a second organizational goal. To continue or maintain its existence as functioning, successful entity, an organization must pay attention to how its compensation policies and practices affect the recruitment of new employees and the retention of current employees. If stress and friction caused by concerns about wages and salary are minimized and turnover is kept to an acceptable level, the organization is more likely to succeed in its productivity goal.

Library administrators and managers charged with human resources management responsibilities have a part in helping the organization efficiently use compensation in advancing both the productivity and maintenance goals of the organization. Understanding the interrelationship is the first step.

ORGANIZATIONAL COMPENSATION REFERENCE GROUPS

Decision makers and employees look to three different groups for guidance and information about compensation: 1) employees working in similar kinds of jobs in other organizations, 2) employees working in different jobs within the organization, and 3) employees working in the same job within the organization.

An organization must keep its compensation program in harmony with other organizations that are competing for the same type of employees. An organization that pays either much more or less than its competing organizations likely faces either excessive labor costs, unfilled vacancies, or excessive turnover. Determining the overall compensation position is a wage-level decision. If the organization decides to pay a wage level somewhat higher than that being paid by the competition, it does so in hopes of attracting the most-qualified workforce, a group of employees that has high morale, is motivated to perform well, is loyal to the organization, is less prone to unionization, and is less inclined to quit. The result of such a policy may be excessive personnel costs. Another alternative is to pay approximately the going rate and depend on various management practices to motivate employees to keep production high and costs low. The success of this second policy hinges on the effectiveness of managers. It is also the safest and probably the most prevalent policy in organizations of which libraries are a part. A third policy is to pay salaries below the going rate. Such a policy would likely result in low morale and high turnover if other alternatives are available nearby. The advantage for the organization would be lower labor costs.

A second important reference group is composed of employees in different jobs within the same organization. The differences in wages paid to employees in different types of jobs are called wage differentials. Wage differentials should be related to the nature and requirements of each kind of work. Jobs that require more education, are more hazardous, or require skills that are in short supply are considered to deserve higher pay than less-demanding jobs. This requires that the organization have a wage-structure system with job descriptions and a salary schedule that clearly define the differences in compensation for different jobs.

The third important reference group comprises other employees performing the same jobs within the organization. Most organizations do not pay everyone doing the same job the same amount. The organization's policies and practices need to make the rationale for this clear. For example, not all employees are likely to be able or inclined to do the same amount or quality of work, and the organization can argue that different levels of quantity or quality of work ought to be rewarded differently. In addition, others can argue that pay differentials between employees performing the same job ought to reflect the different lengths of service to the organization. The widespread use of merit, or pay-for-performance, and seniority systems requires that organizations make it clear how to differentiate between individuals and gain employees' acceptance of the resulting differences.

The use of the three reference groups for wage-policy decisions is important because even if the organization does not pay attention to them, employees will.

6

It is important that the library understand what these groups provide in the way of comparisons.

Organizations make three fundamental compensation decisions in developing their compensation policies:

- Wage-level decision. What should the organization pay its employees relative to what the competition pays?
- Wage-structure decision. What should the pay differentials be between different jobs in the organization?
- Individual wage determination. How much pay should each individual receive, based on performance or seniority or both?

These three decisions are most likely to be made in the order just given, with the last decision, the individual-wage decision, based on the first two.

COMPENSATION CONTROL

All organizations recognize the need to use their resources wisely. Because compensation is a major part of budgets, it follows that compensation expenditures must be controlled, which is a difficult task.

That organization members are inclined to put their own self-interests and that of their coworkers and those they supervise ahead of the organization's interests is the primary cause of compensation control problems. For example, a supervisor may seek large salary increases for subordinates even though they may not deserve those raises. Why? Perhaps the supervisor cannot say no to employees, is unable to differentiate between the performance levels of employees, believes that all employees are paid too little, or is simply unable or unwilling to make salary recommendations.

Pressures are continually placed on an organization to raise compensation expenditures. Such pressures may come from individuals who want more money for personal needs, from union leaders for political reasons, and from those who want to do a better job of recruiting and retaining employees. Many supervisors will admit that they would rather keep the low-performing employee than take a chance on a new employee or on not refilling the vacancy if the poor performer left.

On the other side are the pressures to hold the line or reduce compensation expenditures. The pressures of controlling costs to improve profits are constant in private industry. In the public sector, organizations are continually being asked to cut costs in response to taxpayer concerns. Legislators and state government officials regularly question public-institution officials about their growing compensation expenditures.

IMPORTANCE OF COMPENSATION
TO LIBRARIES AND EMPLOYEES

If organizations could simply regard the compensation paid to employees as just another factor of production, management of employees would be much easier.

However, unlike a standardized unit of resources an organization might purchase, the unit of labor is unpredictable. Each unit of labor is capable of differing levels of performance, varying over time. Because of these labor idiosyncrasies, an organization cannot be sure of the result if a particular compensation policy or practice is implemented.

The importance of wages and salaries to individuals in an organization is the subject of much study. Suffice it to say that pay is one of the most important job factors and is a central factor in inducing people to accept employment. What an individual earns and what other individuals earn by comparison is the subject of many discussions among employees. It can be a means for stimulating productivity, but dissatisfaction with pay can have the opposite effect and become a source of constant discussion and complaint in an organization.

HISTORICAL BACKGROUND

Modern wage and salary administration in the United States had its beginnings with Frederick Taylor's differential piece rate incentive system in the late nineteenth century. Civil service commissions began experimenting with job-evaluation systems as early as 1871, and Commonwealth Edison Corporation implemented the first job-evaluation plan in 1914. Large-scale implementation of job evaluations, however, did not take place until World War II. During that period, the National War Labor Board was established to help settle labor disputes and control wages under the wage and price ceilings enacted at that time. The board was largely responsible for industry's adoption of job-analysis and job-evaluation systems as wage-administration systems. It was also during that period that the U.S. Bureau of Labor Statistics, under the direction of the National War Labor Board, increased the frequency and comprehensiveness of its wage surveys, which were used by both the government and industry. These surveys continue to be used.

It is easy to forget that there was a time when an employee received a day's pay at the end of each day because there were no real guarantees that the laborer would be paid at all. During the Great Depression, the federal government stepped in to establish when employees were to be paid, where employees had to be paid, how much extra employees had to be paid for working especially long hours, how long employees could be made to work, and under what circumstances children could be employed. The Fair Labor Standards Act of 1938, which has been amended numerous times, controls minimum wages, overtime, equal pay, and the employment of minors. Chapter 11 provides a full discussion of the FLSA.

WAGES AND SALARIES

Wages and salaries are simply the payment received for performing work. Although wages and salaries are often used synonymously, they are slightly different in meaning. *Wages*, or hourly pay, refers to an hourly rate of pay and is the basis for pay used most often for production and maintenance employees or blue-collar workers. *Salary* refers to a weekly, monthly, or yearly rate of pay. Professional and management employees, as well as faculty, are usually salaried or earn a set salary for the week, month, or year.

Hourly wage-earning employees normally get paid only for the hours they work, whereas salaried employees earn a set salary even though the number of hours they work may vary from pay period to pay period. Salaried employees are normally classified as exempt employees—exempt from the provisions of the FLSA.

DEVELOPING A PAY STRUCTURE

The wage-level decisions that provide guidelines for the compensation manager in developing a pay structure are made at the highest levels of an organization. These policy decisions include guidelines regarding 1) minimum and maximum levels of pay, 2) the general relationships among levels of pay, and 3) the division of the total compensation dollar. The issues that must be determined include the following:

- The minimum and maximum levels of pay, taking into consideration the organization's ability to pay, government regulations regarding pay, union influences, and what the competition is paying.
- Whether the organization wishes to pay above market, at market, or below market.
- How the relationships among levels-of-pay decisions relate to the rates paid nonexempt and exempt employees, supervisors, and nonsupervisory personnel, and between professional, faculty, and clerical personnel.
- What portion of the compensation budget will go to base pay, to benefits, and to salary increases.
- The breakdown of increases for across-the-board, merit, pay-for-performance, and seniority programs.
- How annual increases are determined and how they are communicated.

The compensation manager needs the answers to the following questions before proceeding with the development of a pay structure:

- What is the lowest rate of pay that can be offered for a job that will allow the organization to hire the quality of employees needed?
- What is the rate of pay that must be offered to existing employees to ensure that they will stay with the organization?
- Does the organization wish to recognize seniority and merit in its base-pay schedule?
- Will more than one rate of pay be offered to employees performing identical or similar work?
- What is considered to be a significant difference in pay rates among jobs requiring varying levels of knowledge and skills?

LIBRARY COMPENSATION MANAGEMENT

Change is one of the least predictable but most reliable factors affecting libraries today. They brace themselves for change because they know it will occur, but they do not know what those changes will bring. Challenge, adaptation, and change have become part of a library's normal activities. Libraries today are confronted with the challenges of meeting changing patron needs and technology-driven innovations, improving the quality of service, and raising productivity with budgets that do not keep pace. At the same time, libraries are required to improve the quality of work life and to comply with laws, guidelines, and court decisions that govern the use of human resources. Because people are the key to meeting these challenges, the human resources management function is an increasingly more important part of every manager's job.

Compensation issues demand library managers' attention. Every manager is faced with questions and expressions of concern from employees about salaries. The library's organizational structure should provide managers with the support they need to address these questions.

ADMINISTRATIVE ORGANIZATION

In examining a library's administrative organization, this book focuses on the duties and responsibilities of the library directors and deans, department heads, and human resources officers as they relate to direct and indirect compensation issues.

Library Director, Dean, or Head Librarian

The library's director or dean is responsible for the library's programs, budget, and personnel. As the library's chief administrative officer, the director is responsible for formulating and administering personnel policies, including assignment of duties, service standards, and staff development, and for creating an environment conducive to maintaining high staff morale. The library director appoints new members of the staff, makes decisions on promotions and transfers, and approves salary adjustments in compliance with established policy. The director has the authority to dismiss staff members, subject to policy and is also the representative and spokesperson of the staff to the administration.

The director or dean is responsible for representing the administration to the library's staff in compensation matters. Working closely with other library managers and employees, the director must assure that the administration's policies and guidelines are followed. The director is also usually that last court of appeal within the library on salary matters. The director usually has the final decision on who will be hired and what they will be paid, as well as on all budgetary matters within the library. Although the library's human resources staff may represent the director in the central human resources offices, and others in the library play particular roles in compensation issues, it is the director who must present and defend the library's decisions to the administration.

Department Heads

To facilitate the functioning of the library, larger organizations are arranged into departments, each of which is responsible for a major type of operation or service. Responsibility regarding the work of each department rests with the head of the unit, who in turn delegates responsibilities and duties to others, making clear the correct line of supervision in each case. In all of their management and supervisory responsibilities, none is more challenging to managers than dealing with compensation-related issues. Hiring, classification, planning, directing, and everyday management are all impacted by compensation decisions. Department heads are charged with the appraisals of staff and the assignment of merit using agreed-upon guidelines.

Human Resources Director

The library's supervisors are on the front line in dealing with compensation and must have the support of administrators when (not if) their decisions are questioned. An important person in this process is the library's human resources director or officer. The library's human resources functions should be handled by a single individual. With a staff of more than 25, the library's director may delegate these duties to an assistant librarian or human resources officer. The Personnel Administration Section of the American Library Association's Library Administration Division recommends a full-time human resources officer for a library with a staff of more than 75 members. The human resources officer occupies a liaison position in the library, exercising no supervisory authority over other departments, but seeking to interpret personnel policies and adjusting personnel problems throughout the system.

Human resources personnel are usually responsible for

- recruitment;
- preliminary selection of candidates for employment;
- development, administration, and periodic audits of the classification system;
- development and administration of the performance appraisal system;
- development, administration, and periodic audits of the pay plan;
- orientation, development, and training programs;
- interpretation of personnel policies and regulations;
- employee counseling;
- investigation and adjustment of complaints, working conditions, and staff welfare; and
- maintenance of personnel records, including the employment record of each library staff member.

Of course, many libraries do not employ 25 staff members, in which case the personnel responsibilities typically fall to the library director. That individual can usually call on someone in the organization (college, city, county, school district, etc.) who is responsible for the organization's human resources, who knows the law, and who can assist in personnel matters.

In libraries large enough to employ human resources officers, those officers are responsible, together with the library's administration, for the following functions:

- Plan for human resource needs. Plan and forecast the organization's short- and long-range human resources requirements and analyze the library's staffing needs.
- Staff the organization's personnel needs. Recruit, screen, and advise hiring officers on procedures and legal requirements and maintain appropriate records.
- Appraise and compensate employee performance. Assure that performance appraisals are conducted by supervisors and managers. Assist with corrective or disciplinary actions and assure compliance with laws protecting employee rights. Assist with administering direct and indirect compensation.
- Improve employee skill level and the work environment. Assess, design, and implement employee training and development programs. Improve and work to assure a safe work environment.
- Establish and maintain effective working relationships. Recognize and respect employee rights, work with bargaining groups, address employee grievances, and maintain current awareness in human resources management.

Library human resources personnel can play several roles in an organization. The more roles human resources personnel play and the better they perform those functions, the more effective they will be in improving the library's productivity, enhancing the quality of work life, and complying with the laws and regulations relating to human resources. Potential roles include policy formulator, advisor, auditor, and innovator.

- Policy formulator role. Provide information to top management for planning. Information on employee concerns, the library's work environment, training and staff development needs, and the university's human resources activities is useful for the library's planning and decision-making processes.
- Advisor role. Assist library administrators, managers, and supervisors in the traditional personnel activities—screening, interviewing, hiring, training, evaluating, counseling, promoting, and firing. Provide advice on equal employment opportunity and safety and health standards.
- Auditor role. Assure fairness and consistency in hiring, training, and appraisals.
- Innovator role. Provide information to line managers and library administration about current techniques and approaches to human resources issues.

To allow the human resources director to perform these roles effectively, to participate in human resources policy formulation, and to have the authority necessary for fair and consistent policy implementation, this position should report to the top of the organizational hierarchy and be part of the library's decision-making group. The director of the library's human resources office is primarily responsible for human resources management, but the administrators, department heads, branch heads, line managers, and unit heads must also be involved in the day-to-day implementation of personnel functions. The cooperation between the human resources office and library managers is critical to effective human resources management.

Employees are increasingly taking a larger role in human resources management. For example, employees may be involved in peer appraisals and in developing their own performance standards and goals. It is not uncommon for employees to be involved in developing their own job descriptions, and they are always involved in job-classification studies. More and more employees are involved in quality circles, total quality improvement teams, and other teams that help them take an active role in daily operations.

The library human resources administrator has all of the responsibilities of being a manager and providing support to the administration and the library faculty and staff in all matters relating to human resources, including all aspects of hiring and any action involving personnel up to and including termination, whether voluntary or involuntary. It is therefore incumbent on human resources administrators to fully understand the law as it relates to labor. They need to be able to work well with the library administration, as well as with all of the managers and supervisors in the library. Human resources personnel must also be able to represent the library to the staff in the various university human resources offices, including legal counsel, employment, benefits, and equal opportunity program offices.

In addition to involvement in recruitment and hiring, human resources personnel assist with job analysis and evaluation, classification studies, market studies, performance appraisals, and merit processes. It is important that the human resources office not only work in support of the administration in carrying out its responsibilities but also serve to represent individual employees and supervisors in addressing working conditions issues and employment problems.

BIBLIOGRAPHY

Bach, Stephen, and Keith Sisson. *Personnel Management: A Comprehensive Guide to Theory and Practice*. Oxford and Malden, MA: Blackwell Business, 2000.

Baldwin, David A., Frances Wilkinson, and Daniel Barkley. *Effective Management of Student Employment: Organizing for Student Employment in Academic Libraries*. Englewood, CO: Libraries Unlimited, 2000.

Berger, Lance A., and Dorothy R. Berger. *The Compensation Handbook: A State-of-the-Art Guide to Compensation Strategy and Design*. New York: McGraw-Hill, 2000.

Donlin, Johanna. *Compensation Commissions*. Denver, CO: National Conference of State Legislatures, 1999.

Federal Employees News Digest. *Federal Workers' Compensation Guide: A Federal Employees News Digest*. Reston, VA: Federal Employees News Digest, 1999.

———. *Your Pay*. Reston, VA: Federal Employees News Digest, 2000.

Fisher, Cynthia D., Lyle F. Schoenfeldt, and James B. Shaw. *Human Resource Management*. Boston: Houghton Mifflin, 1999.

Henderson, Richard I. *Compensation Management in a Knowledge-Based World*. 7th ed. Upper Saddle River, NJ: Prentice-Hall, 1997.

Heneman, Robert L., Gerald E. Ledford Jr., and Maria T. Gresham. "The Changing Nature of Work and Its Effects on Compensation Design and Delivery." In S. Rynes and B. Gerhart (eds.), *Compensation in Organizations: Current Research and Practice*, 195–240. San Francisco: Jossey-Bass, 2000.

Irving (Texas) Human Resources Department. *Study of Total Compensation*. Irving, TX: Irving (Texas) Human Resources Department, 2000.

Kohler, Frederick, K. Kaufmann, and Robert Walker. *The Nonprofit Guide to Compensation Policies*. San Francisco: Management Center, 1999.

Meuter J., Fred. "Compensation: Some Guiding Principles." *Directors and Boards* 25, no. 3 (Spring 2001): 34–7.

Pennsylvania Bar Institute. *Creative Compensation Techniques: Options Are Not the Only Option*. Mechanicsburg, PA: Pennsylvania Bar Institute, 2001.

Ruhm, Christopher J., and Carey Borkoski. *Compensation in the Nonprofit Sector*. Cambridge, MA: National Bureau of Economic Research, 2000.

Sheehan, Michael F., Robert E. Lee, and Lisa Nuss. *Oregon's Prevailing Wage Law: Benefiting the Public, the Worker, and the Employer*. Portland, OR: Oregon and Southwest Washington Fair Contracting Foundation, 2000.

Wilson, Thomas B. "What's Hot and What's Not: Key Trends in Total Compensation." *Compensation and Benefits Management* 17, no. 2 (Spring 2001): 45–51.

Wright, John W. *The American Almanac of Jobs and Salaries*. New York: Avon Books, 2000.

2 DEVELOPING AN INTERNAL LIBRARY JOB STRUCTURE

In the business world, an executive knows something about everything, a technician knows everything about something—and the switchboard operator knows everything.

—HAROLD COFFIN

The structure of jobs in the organization determines the pay structure. Because of the many types of jobs and skill levels in a large library, there is a need for a pay structure that differentiates between work and skills of unequal worth. By the same token, the pay structure should reflect that certain jobs demand greater qualifications and skills for which differential pay is required. The relationships between jobs are determined through job analysis, job descriptions, and job evaluation, which lead to job structure, an ordering of jobs based on their content or relative value. This chapter examines how job analysis and evaluation lead to the development of a job structure, which in turn provides the basis for a salary structure.

JOB ANALYSIS

The basic tool in developing a job structure is job analysis, a method for finding out in an orderly way the duties, requirements, and skills of a job. Information is gathered about a job by any of three methods: sending a questionnaire to supervisors and employees, interviewing supervisors and employees and recording significant facts on a survey form, and observing the job as it is performed. Data collected during the analysis become the raw material for job evaluation. The more accurate the data, the better the evaluation. Specialists in human resources are often charged with job analysis in an organization.

The following major questions need to be answered before conducting job analysis: Why perform job analysis? What information should be collected? What method should be used? Who should be involved? Is job analysis useful?

- Why perform job analysis? For what purpose is the information collected? Often a job analysis is performed in response to concerns that a position may be misclassified, resulting in a pay issue. Pay decisions must be based on work-related logic and administered fairly. An individual has the right to question those decisions, and job analysis is sometimes the only way to justify a pay issue. Occasionally, job analyses are performed on groups of jobs that have changed to determine their appropriate levels.
- What information should be collected? The types of information collected can range from the job title to the frequency with which specific tasks are performed. The U.S. Department of Labor has a detailed handbook for analyzing jobs[1] which should be reviewed before any analyses are performed. The two types of data to be collected are 1) actual work performed and 2) worker traits and characteristics.
- What method should be used? The most common form for collecting data is the questionnaire followed by individual or group interviews. Using a standardized form, jobholders and supervisors describe the work. A follow-up interview is often scheduled to clarify some answers. The standardized form allows for easier compilation and analysis of data.
- Who should be involved? Staff in the human resources department typically analyze and collect the data. Usually, the jobholders and their supervisors are asked to provide the data.
- Is job analysis useful? There is always disagreement about usefulness and validity when judgment is involved. Data provided by the supervisors are, by their nature, subjective. The analyst can only evaluate what has been collected. Perhaps the most important aspect of the process is acceptance of the results by the jobholder and supervisor. If they do not have faith in the process or in the job analysts, jobholders and supervisors may believe the results are unfair.

With all of its faults, job analysis remains the only real method for collecting information and making judgments about the nature of specific jobs, which is essential to the development of a job structure.

JOB EVALUATION

Job evaluation is a method for systematically assigning jobs to wage or salary grades. Generally, managers speak of *jobs* as work done by employees paid by the hour and refer to *positions* as work done by salaried employees. The words are used interchangeably in everyday management; in this instance, positions and jobs are both covered by a job-evaluation system. At best, job evaluation is systematic, methodical, and consistent—employees do not give it a second thought. At worst, it can be an ineffectual way of ordering quasi-scientific information, and employees believe the system is unfair. Job evaluation is concerned with jobs, not individuals in jobs, and places a relative value on a grouping of tasks or duties of a job, regardless of the incumbent. Job evaluation is meant to take much of the guesswork out of building a job structure, with the hope that the result will be largely acceptable to both management and employees. Often there is general acceptance merely because there is presently no better alternative to job evaluation available. Although computerization offers improvement in the areas of data collection and analysis, some disenchantment still remains with a system that by its nature involves subjective judgments.

Although job evaluation helps determine the relationship among various jobs, it does not measure worth or value of a job to the library, nor does it assign degrees of importance or difficulty to jobs.

Job evaluation is performed in larger libraries by job-evaluation specialists who are often part of a human relations department. Because salary administration and job evaluation appear to be so similar, these duties are sometimes combined. There is, however, conflict between the two. Job evaluations determine job levels—internal relationships between jobs—and should not be concerned about individual rates of pay. The salary administrator, on the other hand, deals with job pay and is concerned with dollars and people. If possible, it is better to keep the two processes separate.

JOB-EVALUATION SYSTEMS

Virtually all government employers use some form of job evaluation. Small employers generally do not have a need for job-evaluation systems. Many corporations rely on what is referred to as market pricing, with salary grades determined by assigning jobs to ranges that provide for competitive pay opportunities. With this approach, internal equity is often not a consideration—the primary goal is to maintain competitive salaries.

Evaluation systems adopted beginning in the 1990s have generally relied on the conventional systems but use computers to improve the process. There are four principle methods to convert the job analysis into the job-evaluation system: ranking, classification, factor comparison, and point factor.

Ranking

The ranking method is one of the simplest to administer. Evaluators compare jobs with each other based on the overall worth of the job to the library. The "worth" of a job is usually based on judgments of skill, effort (physical and mental), responsibility (supervisory and fiscal), and working conditions.

Ranking has the following advantages:

- It is simple.
- Ranking is quite effective when there are relatively few jobs to be evaluated (less than 30).

17

Disadvantages include the following:

- It is difficult to administer as the number of jobs increases.
- Rank judgments are subjective.
- Because there is no standard used for comparison, new jobs have to be compared with the existing jobs to determine their appropriate rank. In essence, the ranking process has to be repeated each time a new job is added to the library.

One technique for ranking includes ordering, in which job titles are written on 3-by-5-inch index cards. The evaluator then places the titles in order by the relative importance to the library. Other techniques include weighting and paired comparison. After ranking, the evaluator should group the jobs to determine the appropriate salary levels.

Classification

In the classification method, jobs are classified into an existing grade structure, category structure, or hierarchy. Each level in the grade structure has a description and associated job titles. Each job is then assigned to the grade or category that provides the closest match to the job. The classification of a position is decided by comparing the whole job with the appropriate job-grade standard. To ensure equity in job grading and wage rates, a common set of job-grade standards and instructions is used. Because of differences in duties, skills and knowledge, and other aspects of trades and labor jobs, job-grade standards are developed mainly along occupational lines. The standards do not attempt to describe every work assignment of each position in the occupation covered. The standards identify and describe just those key characteristics of occupations that are significant for distinguishing different levels of work. They define these characteristics in such a way as to provide a basis for assigning the appropriate grade level to all positions in the occupation to which the standards apply.

Advantages of the classification method include the following:

- It is easy to use.
- The grade-category structure exists independently of the jobs. Therefore, new jobs can be classified more easily with this method than in the ranking method.

The following are among the disadvantages:

- Classification judgments are subjective.
- The standard used for comparison (the grade-category structure) may have built-in biases that would affect certain groups of employees (females or minorities).
- Some jobs may appear to fit within more than one grade or category. When the classification system is used, it is a good idea to define the grades so that they do not overlap one another. Overlaps in the descriptions and factors used to identify the grade could lead to problems when assigning jobs to the grades.
- All of the grade or categories must be examined for inherent biases against females and minorities.

Factor Comparison

In the factor-comparison method, a set of compensable factors are identified as determining the worth of jobs. Typically, the number of compensable factors is small (four or five). Examples of compensable factors are skill, responsibilities, effort, and working conditions.

Next, benchmark jobs are identified. Benchmark jobs should be selected as having certain characteristics, such as equitable pay (not overpaid or underpaid) and a range of the factors (for each factor, some jobs would be at the low end and others would be at the high end of the factor). The jobs are then priced, and the total pay for each job is divided to produce the pay for each factor.

Table 2.1 shows how the hourly rate of pay is divided for each of the factors. This process establishes the rate of pay for each factor for each benchmark job. Slight adjustments may need to be made to ensure equitable dollar weighting of the factors.

The other jobs in the library are then compared with the benchmark jobs, and rates of pay for each factor are summed to determine the rates of pay for each of the other jobs.

The factor-comparison method has the following advantages:

- The value of the job is expressed in monetary terms.
- The method can be applied to a wide range of jobs.
- It can be applied to newly created jobs.

Disadvantages include the following:

- The pay for each factor is based on subjective judgments.
- The standard used for determining the pay for each factor may have built-in biases that would affect females or minorities.

When using the factor-comparison method, it is a good idea to use a few well-identifiable factors. Evaluators should also examine the factor dollar weights for inherent biases against females and minorities.

Table 2.1. **Illustration of Breakdown of Factors in Hourly Rates of Pay for Various Job Categories**

		Factor			
Job	*Hourly Rate*	*Pay for Skill*	*Pay for Effort*	*Pay for Responsibility*	*Pay for Working Conditions*
Secretary	$9.00	$4.50	$2.00	$2.00	$0.50
Administrative Assistant	$11.00	$5.50	$2.50	$2.50	$0.50
Supervisor	$15.00	$6.00	$3.50	$4.00	$1.50
Manager	$21.00	$9.00	$3.50	$7.00	$1.50

Point-Factor Method

The point-factor method is an extension of the factor-comparison method and is used by most large libraries. A set of compensable factors are identified as determining the worth of jobs. Typically, the compensable factors include the major categories of skill, responsibilities, effort, and working conditions. These factors can then be further defined:

Skill
- experience
- education
- ability

Responsibilities
- fiscal
- supervisory

Effort
- Mental
- Physical

Working Conditions
- location
- hazards
- extremes in environment

Once identified, each factor is then divided into levels or degrees, which are then assigned points. Each job is rated using the job-evaluation instrument, the points for each factor are summed to form a total point score for the job, and jobs are then grouped by total point scores and assigned to wage or salary grades so that similarly rated jobs are placed in the same wage or salary grade.

Advantages of the point-factor method include the following:

- The value of the job is expressed in monetary terms.
- The method can be applied to a wide range of jobs.
- It can be applied to newly created jobs.
- It is the most widely used job-evaluation system in large organizations

The following are disadvantages:

- The pay for each factor is based on subjective judgments.
- The standard used for determining the pay for each factor may have built-in biases that would affect females or minorities.

As with the factor-comparison method, it is best to use a few easily identifiable factors for the point-factor method. In addition, the evaluator should examine the factor dollar weights for inherent biases against females and minorities.

How the Job-Evaluation Methods Compare

The information in table 2.2 shows how each of the four basic methods of job evaluation compare for different features. If your library is small, a straight ranking system may well suffice. In a larger library, a more analytical system is probably called for.

SAMPLE POINT-FACTOR SYSTEM

A point-factor system for evaluating salaried positions identifies a set of factors that are present in varying degrees in most of the jobs under review and provides a

Table 2.2. Comparison of the Four Basic Methods of Job Evaluation

Feature	Ranking	Classification	Factor Comparison	Point Factor
Job compared to scale	X	X		
Job compared to job			X	X
Useful for large groups of jobs			X	X
Useful for exempt, managerial, professional jobs	X	X		X
Useful for nonexempt clerical, technical, maintenance jobs			X	X
Time consuming (more than four hours per job)			X	X
Higher cost per job			X	X

scale of point values for each factor. It then provides a series of statements that define each degree of point values for each factor. For any job, the "amount" of each factor present can be stated in terms of points. The point value of a job is the sum of the points from all the factors.

The following basic evaluation plan has four points: knowledge, initiative, complexity, and supervision.

Knowledge

Level 1. Elementary knowledge: simple arithmetic, reading, punctuation	10 points
Level 2. English grammar, typing, laboratory and clerical procedures, departmental systems	20 points
Level 3. Library-wide systems, applied technologies	30 points
Level 4. Nonprofessional skills	40 points
Level 5. Professional skills	50 points
Level 6. Advanced professional skills	60 points

Initiative

Level 1. Follows detailed instructions or procedures in repetitive situations	10 points
Level 2. Follows detailed instructions in varied situations	20 points
Level 3. Selects established methods of doing specific tasks to achieve specified end results	30 points
Level 4. Develops methods for achieving specified end results	40 points
Level 5. Determines end results to be achieved in own job or in jobs being supervised	50 points
Level 6. Determines policies	60 points

Complexity

Level 1. Performs essentially the same functions daily	10 points
Level 2. Performs a variety of functions that are repeated weekly or monthly	20 points
Level 3. Performs a variety of nonrepetitive functions	30 points
Level 4. Integrates related functions	40 points
Level 5. Integrates conflicting functions	50 points

Supervision

Zero points are assigned if employee does not supervise.

Level 1. Acts as a lead person for a small group	10 points
Level 2. Supervises 1–10 persons	20 points
Level 3. Supervises 11–30 persons	30 points
Level 4. Supervises 31–100 persons	40 points
Level 5. Supervises 101–500 persons	50 points
Level 6. Supervises more than 500 persons	60 points

Using this simple job-evaluation form, the evaluator could assign various kinds of jobs and end up with point values for each, as in the following cases.

Circulation Aide: Counter worker charges and discharges books

Knowledge	Level 3	30 points
Initiative	Level 1	20 points
Complexity	Level 1	10 points
Supervision		0 points
Total		60 points

Reference Aide: Information desk with professional backup

Knowledge	Level 4	40 points
Initiative	Level 2	20 points
Complexity	Level 2	20 points
Supervision	Level 0	0 points
Total		80 points

Cataloger: Original cataloging without revision

Knowledge	Level 5	50 points
Initiative	Level 3	30 points
Complexity	Level 2	20 points
Supervision	Level 1	10 points
Total		110 points

Head, Interlibrary Loan: Directs the work of six staff members

Knowledge	Level 5	50 points
Initiative	Level 5	50 points
Complexity	Level 4	40 points
Supervision	Level 2	20 points
Total		160 points

Branch Library Director: Library has 14 staff

Knowledge	Level 6	60 points
Initiative	Level 6	60 points
Complexity	Level 5	50 points
Supervision	Level 3	30 points
Total		200 points

By matching each job to the appropriate levels of each factor, the evaluator can determine the total point value for these five positions. In each case, the job, not the person performing that job, has been examined, and levels are assigned in terms of average, not ideal requirements. A ranking of these five positions would show the following:

Circulation aide	60 points
Reference aide	80 points
Cataloger	110 points
Head, interlibrary loan	160 points
Director, branch library	200 points

This creates a top-to-bottom listing that has space between the positions, something that simple ranking does not do. For a larger library, an evaluator could develop a job structure as shown in table 2.3.

Table 2.4 illustrates the generic titles assigned to each grade, including librarians, who may well be faculty and not covered by the staff descriptions and titles. Chapter 9 discusses how librarian salaries relate to staff salaries and equity issues.

Once point values have been determined for all library titles, one can construct a salary structure. One can assign minimum yearly salaries to grades using the following formula, where the variable is established from the agreed-upon minimum salary of the lowest grade:

$$\text{Variable} \times 12 \times \text{Point Value} = \text{Salary}$$

Here is a sample assignment for formulating minimum salaries.

Grade	Variable	Variable × 12	Points	Salary
1	20	240	60	$14,400
2	20	240	70	$16,800
3	20	240	80	$19,200
4	20	240	90	$21,600
5	20	240	100	$24,000
6	20	240	110	$26,400
7	20	240	120	$28,800
8	20	240	130	$31,200
9	20	240	140	$33,600
10	20	240	150	$36,000

(continues on page 27)

Table 2.3. Sample Job Structure for a Large Library, Using a Point-Factor System

Grade	Points	Sample Positions	Library Titles					
			Reference Titles	Circulation Titles	Acquisitions Titles	Catalog Titles	Administrative Titles
1	60	Circulation Aide 1		Circulation Aide 1	Acquisitions Aide 1	Cataloging Aide	Receptionist
2	70			Shelver			
3	80	Reference Aide 1	Reference Aide 1	Circulation Aide 2	Acquisitions Assistant 1	Cataloging Assistant	
4	90		Reference Aide 2			Cataloger, 050	Accounting Specialist
5	100		Reference Aide 3	Circulation Specialist 1	Acquisitions Assistant 2	Cataloger 090	
6	110	Cataloger, Original	Reference Specialist	Circulation Specialist 2	Acquisitions Specialist	Cataloger, Original	Accountant
7	120		Lead Reference Assistant	Lead Circulation Assistant			
8	130		Supervisor, Reference	Supervisor, Circulation		Supervisor, Catalog	Chief Accountant

9	140						
10	150						
11	160	Head, Inter-library Loan	Head, Inter-library Loan	Head, Circulation	Head, Acquisitions	Team Leader, Catalog	Personnel Specialist
12	170						
13	180		Head, Reference	Head, Access	Head, Collections	Head, Catalog	Head, Administration
14	190						
15	200	Director, Branch Library	Director, Branch Library	Director, Branch Library	Director, Branch Library	Director, Branch Library	
16	210						
17	220						
18	230						

Table 2.4. Sample Job Structure Averaged by Grade

Grade	Title	Reference Titles	Circulation Titles	Acquisitions Titles	Catalog Titles
1	Library Clerk		Circulation Aide 1	Acquisitions Aide 1	Cataloging Aide
2	Library Technical Assistant I		Shelver		
3	Library Technical Assistant II	Reference Aide 1	Circulation Aide 2	Acquisitions Assistant 1	Cataloging Assistant
4	Library Information Specialist I	Reference Aide 2			Cataloger, 050
5	Library Information Specialist II	Reference Aide 3	Circulation Specialist 1	Acquisitions Assistant 2	Cataloger 090
6	Library Information Specialist III	Reference Specialist	Circulation Specialist 2	Acquisitions Specialist	Cataloger, Original
7	Library Information Specialist IV	Lead Reference Assistant	Lead Circulation Assistant		
8	Manager, Library Operations	Supervisor, Reference	Supervisor, Circulation		Supervisor Catalog
9	Librarian				
10	Librarian				
11	Program Manager/ Librarian	Head, Interlibrary Loan	Head, Circulation	Head, Acquisitions	Team Leader, Catalog
12	Librarian				
13	Program Director/ Librarian	Head, Reference	Head, Access	Head, Collections	Head, Catalog
14	Librarian				
15	Librarian	Director, Branch Library			
16	Librarian				
17	Librarian				
18	Librarian				

(*continued from page 23*)

Grade	Variable	Variable × 12	Points	Salary
11	20	240	160	$38,400
12	20	240	170	$40,800
13	20	240	180	$43,200
14	20	240	190	$45,600
15	20	240	200	$48,000
16	20	240	210	$50,400
17	20	240	220	$52,800
18	20	240	230	$55,200

The five sample positions would have the following minimum yearly salaries:

Circulation aide	60 points—$14,400
Reference aide	80 points—$19,200
Cataloger	110 points—$26,400
Head, interlibrary loan	160 points—$38,400
Director, branch library	200 points—$48,000

The final step is to establish a schedule with minimum, median or midpoint, and maximum yearly salaries, as shown in this example:

Grade	Minimum	Median	Maximum
1	$14,400	$15,600	$16,799
2	$16,800	$18,000	$19,199
3	$19,200	$20,400	$21,599
4	$21,600	$22,800	$23,999
5	$24,000	$25,200	$26,399
6	$26,400	$27,600	$28,799
7	$28,800	$30,000	$31,199
8	$31,200	$32,400	$33,599
9	$33,600	$34,800	$35,999
10	$36,000	$37,200	$38,399
11	$38,400	$39,600	$40,799
12	$40,800	$42,000	$43,199
13	$43,200	$44,400	$45,599
14	$45,600	$46,800	$47,999
15	$48,000	$49,200	$50,399
16	$50,400	$51,600	$52,799
17	$52,800	$54,000	$55,199
18	$55,200	$56,400	$57,600

Grades are now established through the point-factor system for each position in a hierarchical listing. And salaries that are relatively reasonable have been established. The lowest graded positions are paid higher hourly wages than minimum wage, and the higher positions appear to be relatively comparable to market. It is important to do a market analysis to affirm that this is true.

Unlike the positions shown in the tables given in this chapter, librarian positions are often not included, especially if the librarians hold faculty appointments. Those salaries are usually determined through a combination of starting salary (based on market and negotiations), annual increases, merit increases, promotions, and the timing of each of those increases.

Evaluators should be aware of one final aspect of the point-factor system. Employees are normally informed of their grades and salary ranges. In a point-factor system, the employee's grade is determined by the number of points. But it is not a good idea to disclose job points to employees. Once employees know their job points, they naturally want to know how those points were assigned, and the library may soon be filled with amateur job evaluators. Once employees and supervisors know what aspects of a job yield the most points, jobs suddenly change to reflect those types of activities. Job evaluation is a skill that requires not only training in the system but also experience in its use on many jobs. If employees and supervisors have concerns about how a job is point factored, it may be that the problem is one of placement. The salary may not be too low for the job's demands; it may be too low for the employee's abilities. A promotion to a higher-level position may be in order.

PROBLEMS WITH JOB-EVALUATION SYSTEMS

To be competitive, libraries must be more dynamic, more flexible, more innovative, and more cost effective. Libraries are being managed with fewer levels of management and different types of supervisory relationships, often transferring responsibility to groups or teams. Instead of having specific job duties, individuals are being asked to have areas of responsibility, team memberships, and group tasks. Job evaluation, however, is based on a job, one that is stable and relatively unchanging, and on supervision based on the number of employees supervised. The issue becomes further complicated when these duties are translated to job descriptions and evaluated for the purpose of establishing pay. If jobs are continually changing, how can they be assigned grades and salaries?

Another issue is that libraries set salary ranges by evaluating jobs and assign raises by evaluating people. People have market value; jobs do not. Jobs do not quit; people do. Jobs are not either great or average performers; people are. The most important compensation issues relate to what individuals are worth, not what jobs are worth.

Finally, a system that rewards only supervision is problematic in an academic environment. In order to advance in most classification systems, an employee needs to become a manager. Many great specialists, and even more great workers, have become awful supervisors and are transformed from useful and effective individuals into persons who dislike their work, do not perform well, and are extremely unhappy at work.

To best use a system like that examined here, it may behoove you to recommend the following changes to your job-evaluation specialists in order to recognize expertise as being equal to supervision.

Supervision, Expertise

Level 0. Does not supervise, or does not have a specialization	0 points
Level 1. Acts as a lead person for a small group, or uses education or training in providing leadership to group	10 points
Level 2. Supervises 1–10 persons, or uses subject background, interest, and training for collection development, reference, or cataloging specialization	20 points
Level 3. Supervises 11–30 persons, or has advanced degree and performs specialized reference, cataloging, or selection liaison work	30 points
Level 4. Supervises 31–100 persons, or uses advanced degree and training to provide instruction to students or colleagues in a structured environment	40 points
Level 5. Supervises 101–500 persons, or uses advanced degree and training to serve library as collection development coordinator or reference specialist	50 points
Level 6. Supervises more than 500 persons, or performs collection development officer duties	60 points

CLASSIFICATION METHODS FOR LIBRARIANS

It is not difficult to rank some of the various job titles for librarians in some libraries. For example, one could assume that the order librarian, senior librarian, department head, assistant director or dean, associate director or dean, and director or dean provides a logical hierarchical arrangement of library positions. The titles of lecturer, instructor, assistant professor, associate professor, and professor form a straightforward hierarchical arrangement of faculty librarian ranks. But what about children's librarian, science librarian, archivist, history librarian, and reference librarian? Are they all equal? Is one more valuable than another? The market will dictate starting salaries for all these positions. Future salaries will be determined by advancement in rank and levels of responsibility. In essence, most classification issues in libraries relate to staff and how to structure rewarding, challenging positions with appropriate grades for the most-talented staff members.

THE SYSTEM IN PRACTICE

In practice, when a question about an individual's classification is raised, the manager will typically consult with the library's human resources specialists. Often the complaints concern individuals who feel they are underclassified. They may have been assigned, or have assumed, higher-level duties without changing jobs. As noted previously, many times their jobs have not changed but the workers have higher-level skills than the job requires. Often the problems are related not to the job but to how the manager or employee views the job.

When an individual employee has concerns about the job's classification, that issue can be brought to a committee of peers in some libraries. Their role is to review these complaints and to examine similar positions to ensure that there is internal equity. These committees are not trained in job evaluation but can be effectively used to point out areas of concern to the administration. For example, jobs in many areas are drastically affected by integrated automated systems. It is essential that these jobs be evaluated to determine how these jobs have changed and to see whether grade changes are warranted. A second (separate) committee of peers can be effectively used to address salary concerns brought to the group by individuals. This will be discussed in chapter 9.

SUMMARY

Information provided in this chapter can help the reader understand how a salary schedule evolves from a ranked listing of staff positions based on predetermined job factors. Job analysis involves gathering data from employees in order to place their jobs in the graduated structure of positions. The point-factor method can be used to rank jobs with similar types of duties even if the work being performed is quite different. Persons with duties as different as landscapers, library technicians, computer specialists, and cafeteria workers can all be assigned to grades using this process. Recall that pay-equity advocates use the job-evaluation system to identify sex-segregated positions and to compare the market value of individuals performing similar-level duties. This information is analyzed to determine if persons in male-dominated positions are paid more than persons in female-dominated positions. Job evaluation is a useful process, but its users have to be aware of the problems associated with it. (As an aid to the reader, the appendix to this chapter includes a group of library-specific job descriptions in use at the University of New Mexico General Library.)

APPENDIX

The following library-specific job descriptions are used at the University of New Mexico General Library.

JOB DESCRIPTION:

Library Aide
FLSA: Nonexempt
Grade: 4

> *The following statements are intended to describe the general nature and level of work being performed. They are not intended to be construed as an exhaustive list of all responsibilities, duties, and skills required of personnel so classified.*

Summary:
Under direct supervision, prepares books and other library materials for circulation; produces spine labels, enters data into automated system, and performs miscellaneous clerical duties.

Duties and Responsibilities:
- Checks in and checks out library materials.
- Renews and verifies the circulation status of library materials.
- Produces spine labels for library materials.
- Enters call numbers or other specific numerical data into the library's automated system.
- Types memoranda, letters, and other documents, and performs related clerical duties.
- May provide coverage at the circulation desk.
- May lead, guide, and train staff and student employees, interns, or volunteers performing related work; may participate in the recruitment of volunteers, as appropriate to the area of operation.
- Performs miscellaneous job-related duties as assigned.

Minimum Education and Experience:
High school diploma or equivalent. Six months to one year experience directly related to the duties and responsibilities specified.

Licenses or Certifications Required:
In addition to the following, all new employees are required to attend new employee orientation.
- Basic annual safety training

Knowledge, Skills, and Abilities Required:
Knowledge of library cataloging rules and procedures. Knowledge of library check-in and check-out procedures. Skill in the use of automated library systems. Clerical, word processing, and office skills.

Distinguishing Characteristics:
Position requires 1) routine filing of library information, 2) routine data entry into automated library system, and 3) routine typing.

Working Conditions:
Work is normally performed in a typical interior office work environment.

Physical Effort:
Considerable physical activity. Requires heavy physical work; heavy lifting, pushing, or pulling required of objects up to 50 pounds. Physical work is a primary part (more than 70 percent) of job.

Environmental Conditions:
No or very limited exposure to physical risk.

Revised Date: 6/1/00

JOB DESCRIPTION:

Library Technical Assistant
FLSA: Nonexempt
Grade: 6

> *The following statements are intended to describe the general nature and level of work being performed. They are not intended to be construed as an exhaustive list of all responsibilities, duties, and skills required of personnel so classified.*

Summary:

Under direct supervision, performs defined routine technical or clerical procedures, customer information services, or both, within a library specialist unit, such as circulation, bindery operations, bibliographic services, technical services, or cataloging.

Duties and Responsibilities:

- Responds to individual requests for information from library clients; refers clients to appropriate information source; and answers routine operational and procedural questions.
- Provides technical assistance to specialist staff in the processing or maintenance of library documents and materials.
- Uses automated online library systems to perform basic library activities or processes; verifies and enters data or statistics.
- Provides periodical statistical data and assists with report preparation for the unit, as appropriate.
- Maintains inventories of equipment and supplies for the unit; assists the unit in the processing of administrative and financial transactions.
- Covers for the circulation desk on an as-needed basis.
- May assign duties to and monitor the activities of students performing routine library duties and services.
- Performs miscellaneous job-related duties as assigned.

Minimum Education and Experience:

High school diploma or equivalent. Six months to one year experience directly related to the duties and responsibilities specified.

Licenses or Certifications Required:

In addition to the following, all new employees are required to attend new employee orientation.

- Basic annual safety training

Knowledge, Skills, and Abilities Required:

Ability to interpret and refer informational requests. Knowledge of library principles, practices, and terminology. Knowledge of procedures and standards for the processing or maintenance of library materials. Word processing, data-entry skills, or both. Ability to understand and follow specific instructions and procedures. Ability to process computer data and to format and generate reports. Ability to complete moderately complex administrative paperwork. Knowledge of basic office practices, procedures, and equipment. Knowledge of customer-service standards and procedures.

Distinguishing Characteristics:
Position requires 1) customer service and interaction with library clients, 2) use of automated library systems to enter or verify data, 3) use of computerized software to provide data and reports, and 4) routine fiscal or administrative support in financial or inventory areas.

Working Conditions:
Work is normally performed in a typical interior office work environment.

Physical Effort:
Considerable physical activity. Requires heavy physical work; heavy lifting, pushing, or pulling required of objects up to 50 pounds. Physical work is a primary part (more than 70 percent) of job.

Environmental Conditions:
No or very limited exposure to physical risk.

Revised Date: 6/1/00

JOB DESCRIPTION:

Library Information Specialist I
FLSA: Nonexempt
Grade: 7

> *The following statements are intended to describe the general nature and level of work being performed. They are not intended to be construed as an exhaustive list of all responsibilities, duties, and skills required of personnel so classified.*

Summary:
Under direct supervision, performs defined tasks and services making up a component of a library operational unit. Provides technical support and assistance in the performance of routine library duties in one or more particular library specializations, such as circulation, bibliographic services, or technical services.

Duties and Responsibilities:
- Provides guidance and assistance to patrons regarding general and specific information about the library and library resources.
- With minimal supervision, performs or oversees routine tasks, using automated database systems, to include materials check-in, circulation, searching, ordering of materials, or copy cataloging.
- Resolves routine operational problems and provides first-level troubleshooting of relevant library systems.
- Assists higher-level staff and librarians with basic reference services; staffs public service desks, providing customer service and assistance.

- Carries out and communicates policies pertaining to unit services, operations, and activities.
- Assists with collection maintenance activities and projects as appropriate.
- May lead, guide, and train student employees, set work schedules, and ensure compliance with established procedures for a specific activity within a library unit.
- Performs miscellaneous job-related duties as assigned.

Minimum Education and Experience:
High school diploma or equivalent. One to three years experience directly related to the duties and responsibilities specified.

Licenses or Certifications Required:
In addition to the following, all new employees are required to attend new employee orientation.
- Basic annual safety training

Knowledge, Skills, and Abilities Required:
Knowledge of customer-service standards and procedures. Ability to communicate technical information to nontechnical personnel. Knowledge of library principles, practices, and terminology. Skill in the use of relevant automated database systems. Skill in the use of library resources. Ability to analyze and solve problems. Ability to communicate effectively, both orally and in writing.

Distinguishing Characteristics:
Position requires 1) resolving operational problems and providing first-level troubleshooting of relevant library systems; 2) routine tasks using database systems; plus a combination of the following characteristics, based on the library department. Please see your library administration for specific department characteristics: 3) routine circulation, routing, and searches for missing books or visual resources; 4) routine processing and maintenance of the reserve material collection; 5) material preparation, checking invoices; 5) routine liaison with public regarding gifts, physical processing and handling of gifts and exchange material; 6) routine receiving of library materials; 7) routine bibliographic searching on OCLC or online catalog; 8) create or modify records for online catalog; 9) basic copy cataloging of AACR2 U.S. National Library records excluding compound surnames, series, and uniform title headings, with revision; 10) visual resources maintenance and database records maintenance; 11) processing collection inventories; 12) serials loose-leaf filing; and 13) providing assistance to patrons regarding routine general and specific information about library resources.

Working Conditions:
Work is normally performed in a typical interior office work environment.

Physical Effort:
Considerable physical activity. Requires heavy physical work; heavy lifting, pushing, or pulling required of objects up to 50 pounds. Physical work is a primary part (more than 70 percent) of job.

Environmental Conditions:
No or very limited exposure to physical risk.

Revised Date: 2/21/00

JOB DESCRIPTION:

Library Information Specialist II
FLSA: Nonexempt
Grade: 8

> *The following statements are intended to describe the general nature and level of work being performed. They are not intended to be construed as an exhaustive list of all responsibilities, duties, and skills required of personnel so classified.*

Summary:
Under general supervision, performs an integrated range of tasks and processes associated with a small library specialty unit or shift operation. Coordinates and prioritizes work, and monitors daily operations. Provides technical support and assistance in the performance and coordination of routine and complex library duties in a particular specialization.

Duties and Responsibilities:
- Provides guidance and assistance to patrons regarding general and specific information about the library and library resources.
- With minimal supervision, performs or oversees routine to moderately complex database tasks, using automated database systems, to include materials check-in, circulation, searching, ordering of materials, or copy cataloging.
- Provides assistance to higher-level staff and librarians with reference services, using proficiency in specialized indexes, reference sources, and online databases; may staff reference desk with backup assistance.
- Performs specialized library tasks, including copy cataloging without review or original cataloging with review, processing of nontraditional materials (such as manuscripts and archival materials) without review, and handling of routine and complex invoices and orders, using specialized databases.
- Implements and communicates policies pertaining to services, operations, and activities; resolves complex departmental problems, and develops and implements operational procedures.
- Initiates and assists with collection maintenance activities and projects.
- Trains lower-graded staff or student employees.
- Performs miscellaneous job-related duties as assigned.

Minimum Education and Experience:
Bachelor's degree in a related administrative, business, liberal arts, or social sciences discipline. One to three years experience directly related to the duties and responsibilities specified.

Licenses or Certifications Required:

In addition to the following, all new employees are required to attend new employee orientation.

- Basic annual safety training

Knowledge, Skills, and Abilities Required:

Knowledge of customer-service standards and procedures. Ability to communicate technical information to nontechnical personnel. Knowledge of library principles, practices, and terminology. Skill in the use of relevant automated library systems. Skill in the use of specialized library indexes and reference sources. Skill in the use of library resources. Ability to perform a variety of specialized library tasks. Skill in the use of specialized library resources. Ability to analyze and solve problems. Ability to communicate effectively, both orally and in writing. Ability to provide training to staff or student employees.

Distinguishing Characteristics:

Position requires 1) provision of guidance and problem resolution to lower-level staff on moderately complex problems; plus a combination of the following characteristics, based on the library department. Please see your library administration for specific department characteristics: 2) moderately complex bibliographic searching on OCLC or online catalog and electronic resources; 3) with minimal supervision, performing or overseeing routine to moderately complex database tasks, using automated database systems; 4) creation and maintenance of local bibliographic or visual resources records; 5) liaison with selectors, vendors, and publishers regarding orders and payments and checking invoices; 6) processing orders and payments, resolving problems with invoices and orders; 7) proficiency in use of specialized indexes, references sources, and online databases to assist higher-level client base and librarians with reference services; 8) staffing reference desk with backup assistance to provide general to moderately complex reference services and tools to assist patrons; 9) moderately complex copy cataloging of AACR2 U.S. National Library records including compound surnames, series, and uniform title headings, without review; 10) processing nontraditional materials (such as manuscripts or archival materials or audio visual) without review; 11) preparing reference materials; 12) contact with other libraries and consortia on moderately complex matters involving loan of material, verification of citations, and lending policy; 13) ordering and payment for materials electronically using publishers online systems; 14) planning and organizing collection maintenance of activities and projects; and 15) providing backup assistance to day- and night-time team leaders.

Working Conditions:

Work is normally performed in a typical interior office work environment.

Physical Effort:

Considerable physical activity. Requires heavy physical work; heavy lifting, pushing, or pulling required of objects up to 50 pounds. Physical work is a primary part (more than 70 percent) of job.

Environmental Conditions:
No or very limited exposure to physical risk.

Revised Date: 2/21/00

JOB DESCRIPTION:

Library Information Specialist III
FLSA: Exempt
Grade: 10

> *The following statements are intended to describe the general nature and level of work being performed. They are not intended to be construed as an exhaustive list of all responsibilities, duties, and skills required of personnel so classified.*

Summary:
Under indirect supervision, performs complex and specialized tasks requiring advanced skills in a particular library specialization, such as circulation, bibliographic services, education, cataloging, media services, or library systems management. Oversees the total operations of a specialty unit, participating in the development of policy and procedures. Plans, implements, and evaluates services, and establishes service standards.

Duties and Responsibilities:
- Oversees, coordinates, or performs the integrated activities of the unit; plans, organizes, and implements the provision of services within area of specialty.
- Supervises and trains lower-graded specialist staff, student employees, volunteers, and interns, as appropriate.
- Reviews, evaluates, and initiates services to library clients, to include students, faculty, staff, and the general public.
- Implements and maintains service quality and productivity standards for the unit.
- Participates in planning and policy setting for the services and operations of the unit; implements, communicates, and monitors policy and procedures relevant to the unit.
- May provide liaison services and consultation for faculty in a particular subject area.
- Maintains professional knowledge base and skills through continued education or research.
- Performs miscellaneous job-related duties as assigned.

Minimum Education and Experience:
Bachelor's degree in a related administrative, business, liberal arts, or social sciences discipline. Three to five years experience directly related to the duties and responsibilities specified.

Licenses or Certifications Required:

In addition to the following, all new employees are required to attend new employee orientation.

- Basic annual safety training

Knowledge, Skills, and Abilities Required:

Ability to plan, organize, and oversee the operations of an integrated library-service activity. Ability to foster a cooperative work environment. Ability to supervise and train assigned staff including organizing, prioritizing, and scheduling work assignments. Skill in the use of automated library systems. Ability to provide technical advice and information to faculty in area of expertise. Ability to make evaluative judgments. Knowledge of library acquisitions practices and budget availability. Ability to coordinate quality-assurance programs in area of specialty. Ability to plan and implement operational policies and procedures in area of expertise. Knowledge of customer-service standards and procedures. Ability to analyze and solve problems.

Distinguishing Characteristics:

Position requires 1) overseeing, coordinating, or performing the integrated activities of the library unit; planning, organizing, and implementing the provision of services within area of library specialization; 2) providing leadership or supervision of staff or student employees, including training, assigning, and monitoring of work, and evaluation; 3) participation in planning and policy setting for the services and operations of the library unit; implementing, communicating, and monitoring policies and procedures relevant to the library unit; 4) implementing and maintaining service quality and productivity standards for the unit; 5) providing high-level technical advice and complex specialized information in the area of library expertise; plus a combination of the following characteristics, based on the library department. Please see your library administration for specific department characteristics: 6) analyzing and resolving complex problems with overdue materials and lost-book bills, making evaluative judgments regarding fines and invoice charges; 7) researching and resolving complex problems with library patron records requiring a high-level of knowledge of customer-service standards and procedures; 8) resolving complex problems with library invoices, orders and claims, prepayments, and reconciliation prepayments and monitoring specialized library funds; 9) oversight of integrity of complex databases, requiring a high level of skill in the use of automated library systems; 10) developing and providing training sessions to reference personnel on specific reference tools; 11) creating user guides and bibliographies for print and electronic reference sources and services; 12) performing complex copy cataloging of Pre-AACR2 and AACR2 member records, performing original cataloging; cataloging book or nonprint or visual resources or electronic formats; creating and contributing national bibliographic records, without review; 13) reviewing or creating name/series authority headings; 14) reviewing and maintaining standards of bibliographic records input and department downloads; 15) creating multi-institutional web-links of archival and other specialized library collections without review; 16) developing and providing library instruction or training sessions to classes, groups, staff, or individual patrons; and 17) sole staffing of a reference desk, providing complex reference services and high-level technical advice to patrons using subject-based print and electronic resources.

Working Conditions:
Work is normally performed in a typical interior office work environment.

Physical Effort:
Considerable physical activity. Requires heavy physical work; heavy lifting, pushing, or pulling required of objects up to 50 pounds. Physical work is a primary part (more than 70 percent) of job.

Environmental Conditions:
No or very limited exposure to physical risk.

Revised Date: 2/21/00

JOB DESCRIPTION:

Manager, Library Operations
FLSA: Exempt
Grade: 11

> *The following statements are intended to describe the general nature and level of work being performed. They are not intended to be construed as an exhaustive list of all responsibilities, duties, and skills required of personnel so classified.*

Summary:
Under limited supervision, provides operational management of a small, self-contained library unit, or branch library operation, to include planning and organizing workflow, initiating and implementing operating policies and procedures, personnel and budget management, and record maintenance; assists in long-term needs assessment and goal planning.

Duties and Responsibilities:
- Oversees all facets of the daily operations of the organizational unit, ensuring compliance with university, state, and federal laws, policies, and regulations.
- Plans and implements projects; develops and establishes deadlines, goals, objectives, workflow, and operational procedures; establishes, interprets, and enforces policy.
- Oversees the supervision of assigned personnel, which includes work allocation, training, and problem resolution; evaluates performance and makes recommendations for personnel actions; motivates employees to achieve peak productivity and performance.
- Develops and implements systems to maintain records on employees, equipment inventories, and compliance activities.
- Assists with the development and management of annual operating budget(s).

- Develops or assists with the development and implementation of policies and procedures consistent with those of the organization to ensure efficient and safe operation of the department.
- Participates as a member of the management team that coordinates the goals, decisions, and projects involving all library departments, branches, and centers.
- May perform complex and specialized reference or information-service activities in a specific operating unit or area of subject expertise.
- May oversee, coordinate, and perform 050 (Cataloging in Publication) copy cataloging and 090 (OCLC member) copy cataloging without revision; may perform original cataloging in a specialized field of knowledge without revision.
- May review, evaluate, and select library materials in specific areas of expertise for library collection development, and may serve as a liaison to teaching faculty in assigned departments.
- Maintains professional knowledge and skills through continued education or research.
- Performs miscellaneous job-related duties as assigned.

Minimum Education and Experience:
Bachelor's degree in a related administrative, business, liberal arts, or social sciences discipline. Three to five years experience directly related to the duties and responsibilities specified.

Licenses or Certifications Required:
In addition to the following, all new employees are required to attend new employee orientation.

- Defensive driving course required to operate state vehicles
- Supervisor's safety training
- Basic annual safety training

Knowledge, Skills, and Abilities Required:
Ability to supervise and train assigned staff, including organizing, prioritizing, and scheduling work assignments. Skill in organizing resources and establishing priorities. Skill in the use of computers, preferably in a PC, Windows-based operating environment. Ability to develop and maintain record-keeping systems and procedures. Ability to develop, plan, and implement short- and long-range goals. Ability to interpret, adapt, and apply guidelines and procedures. Knowledge of all facets of library operations. Ability to assess objectives and operational requirements and to develop and implement suitable operational policies and procedures. Employee development and performance management skills. Knowledge of faculty or staff hiring procedures. Ability to foster a cooperative work environment. Skill in examining and reengineering operations and procedures, formulating policy, and developing and implementing new strategies and procedures. Ability to communicate effectively, both orally and in writing.

Distinguishing Characteristics:

Position requires 1) technical and administrative management of a separately administered library operation; 2) supervision of specialist and support staff to include work allocation, training, problem resolution, performance management, and productivity; 3) assisting with development and management of systems and annual operating and fiscal budgets; 4) development and implementation of policies and procedures; and 5) operational and administrative decision making regarding departments, branches, and centers, as a member of the overall management team.

Working Conditions:

Work is normally performed in a typical interior office work environment.

Physical Effort:

Light physical effort. Requires handling of average-weight objects up to 10 pounds or some standing or walking. Effort applies to no more than two hours per day.

Environmental Conditions:

No or very limited exposure to physical risk.

Revised Date: 6/1/00

JOB DESCRIPTION:

Archivist
FLSA: Exempt
Grade: 12

> *The following statements are intended to describe the general nature and level of work being performed. They are not intended to be construed as an exhaustive list of all responsibilities, duties, and skills required of personnel so classified.*

Summary:

Under indirect supervision, plans, organizes, maintains, and preserves a specified print or nonprint archival collection. Appraises or edits archival records and historically valuable materials of the institution. Participates in research activities based on archival materials. Develops policy and procedure and directly manages the acquisition, disposition, and safekeeping of archival materials.

Duties and Responsibilities:

- Plans and develops archival collections, including participation in the establishment and implementation of policies and standards for the archive.
- Analyzes and evaluates print or nonprint materials to appraise value to posterity; coordinates the acquisition, cataloging, maintenance, and preservation of valuable material and the disposition of worthless material.
- Prepares descriptions and reference aids for use of archives, such as lists, indexes, guides, bibliographies, abstracts, and microfilmed copies; cross-indexes materials as required.
- Develops and implements procedures for the acquisition, processing, and preservation of archival materials.

- Advises and assists researchers in the application of archival materials in research activities; interprets requirements and supplies and consults on archival information.
- Requests or recommends pertinent materials available in libraries, private collections, or other sources for inclusion into archives.
- Performs miscellaneous job-related duties as assigned.

Minimum Education and Experience:
Bachelor's degree in a related administrative, business, liberal arts, or social sciences discipline. Three to five years experience directly related to the duties and responsibilities specified.

Licenses or Certifications Required:
In addition to the following, all new employees are required to attend new employee orientation.

- Basic annual safety training

Knowledge, Skills, and Abilities Required:
Ability to assess objectives and operational requirements and to develop and implement suitable operational policies and procedures. Knowledge of archival concepts, methodology, and techniques. Skill in organizing resources and establishing priorities. Knowledge of the historical contexts governing archival operations. Ability to make evaluative judgments. Ability to develop and maintain indexes, bibliographies, and other reference guides and materials. Skill in the use of personal computers and related software applications. Ability to create, compose, and edit written materials. Ability to interpret client informational needs and to determine appropriate alternative solutions. Ability to communicate technical information to nontechnical personnel. Knowledge of available sources of archival materials.

Distinguishing Characteristics:
Position requires 1) knowledge of archival concepts, methodology and techniques; 2) following and maintaining established procedures for archival collection; 3) performing research, identification, and evaluation and appraisal of potential archived collections; 4) use of detailed knowledge of collections to prepare descriptions and finding aids; 5) developing and implementing procedures for the acquisition, processing, and preservation of archival materials; and 6) performing outreach in the solicitation of donors and acquisition of collections.

Working Conditions:
Work is normally performed in a typical interior office work environment.

Physical Effort:
Moderate physical activity. Requires handling of average-weight objects up to 25 pounds or standing or walking for more than four hours per day.

Environmental Conditions:
No or very limited exposure to physical risk.

Revised Date: 6/1/00

NOTE

1. U.S. Department of Labor, *Revised Handbook for Analyzing Jobs* (Washington, DC: U.S. Department of Labor, 1991).

BIBLIOGRAPHY

Allen, Steven G. "Technology and the Wage Structure." *Journal of Labor Economics* 19, no. 2 (April 2001): 440–84.

Arnault, E. Jane. "An Experimental Study of Job Evaluation and Comparable Worth." *Industrial and Labor Relations Review* 54, no. 4 (July 2001): 806–15.

Chen, Shih-Neng, Peter F. Orazem, and J. Peter Mattila. "Measurement Error in Job Evaluation and the Gender Wage Gap." *Economic Inquiry* 37, no. 2 (1999): 181–94.

Figart, Deborah M. "Equal Pay for Equal Work: The Role of Job Evaluation in an Evolving Social Norm." *Journal of Economic Issues* 34, no. 1 (2000): 1–19.

Hay Group. *Study to Assess the Compensation and Skills of Medical Library Professionals vs. Information Technology Professionals*. Chicago: Medical Library Association, 2000.

Kanin-Lovers, Jill, and Sandra O'Neil. "The Choices in Job Evaluation Systems." *Journal of Compensation and Benefits* 6, no. 1 (July/August 1990): 52–6.

Lofstrom, Asa. "Can Job Evaluation Improve Women's Wages?" *Applied Economics* 31, no. 9 (1999): 1053–60.

McNabb, Robert, and Keith Whitfield. "Job Evaluation and High Performance Work Practices: Compatible or Conflictual?" *Journal of Management Studies* 38, no. 2 (2001): 293–312.

Mosley, Shelley. "How to Survive a Classification Study." *Library Journal* 123, no. 17 (October 15, 1998): 48–50.

Ohio University, University Human Resources. *Classification and Compensation Plans: Resolution 2001–1781*. Athens, OH: Ohio University, University Human Resources, 2001.

Riggs, Susan. "Comparing Apples and Oranges: Job Evaluations." *Worklife Report* 8, no. 1 (1991): 7–9.

Rutt, Sheila M., and Dennis Doverspike. "Salary and Organizational Level Effects on Job Evaluation Ratings." *Human Resources Abstracts* 35, no. 1 (2000).

U.S. Department of Labor. *Revised Handbook for Analyzing Jobs*. Washington, DC: U.S. Department of Labor, 1991.

Williams, Caitlin P. "The End of the Job as We Know It." *Training and Development* 53, no. 1 (January 1999): 52–5.

3 DEVELOPING A LIBRARY PAY STRUCTURE

Maybe they call it take-home pay because there is no other place you can afford to go with it.

—FRANKLIN P. JONES

SALARY RANGES AND GRADES

Job levels determined through job evaluation are a reflection of the internal relationships among jobs. Those relationships must be reflected in the salary structure—the higher the evaluation of a job, the higher the salary. Salary ranges usually have a minimum, a midpoint, and a maximum salary. Ranges are assigned to each grade. Whereas ranges represent the vertical dimension of the salary structure, grades represent the horizontal dimension. Each grade contains jobs with a range of points assigned in a point-factor process. For example, a grade 4 may contain jobs with point values from 375 to 390.

Grouping jobs in grades allows an organization to communicate the relative status of positions and assign salary ranges to each. Some organizations have as many as 30 grades; others have as few as 10. It is more satisfactory for employees if they can move between jobs with slightly different salaries than to be in a system that makes movement difficult. On the other hand, large jumps from grade to grade mean that there will be fewer instances of overlap where people in widely different grades are earning the same salary and where a promotion is significant. Although grades offer the advantage of grouping like jobs together, they have the disadvantage of separating "close" jobs. For example, a job with 391 points may be a grade 5 whereas the one with 390 points is a grade 4. If the holder of the 390-point job learns that it is "high in its grade," efforts may be made to move it up a notch.

JOB- OR SKILL-BASED PAY

The distribution of financial and status rewards in organizations is based on the types of jobs people do. The standard practice in organizations, to set the salary level by evaluating the job rather than the person, is based on the assumption that the job's worth can be determined and that the person doing the job is worth only as much to the organization as what the job is worth. Determining the worth of the job through job evaluation allows the organization to compare its jobs with other employers' jobs. It is less clear, however, that a person's worth can be equated to the worth of their job.

An alternative to job-based pay is to pay people based on their skills and competencies. This does not necessarily result in pay rates dramatically different than job-based pay, but it can lead to some employees being paid more. Or the reverse may also be true. Some employees do not have all the skills they need for the job for which they are being paid. Instead of moving up the hierarchy, people are rewarded for increasing their skills and developing themselves. The pros and cons of job-based pay and skills-based pay approaches follow.

Job-Based Pay

Job-based pay is based on the job-evaluation system discussed in the previous chapter. Frequently, organizations use a point-factor system, which begins with a carefully written job description and which assigns points to determine the classification or grade of the position. The most important reason that many large organizations employ the job evaluation is that it facilitates comparisons to what other units within the organization, as well as other organizations, are paying for similar work.

The more widely used job-evaluation systems, such as the Hay system, make available extensive market data from other large organizations that allow comparisons to related organizations by size and geographical location. This type of data is extremely important for market comparisons that permit an organization to attract and retain employees and effectively manage labor costs.

Internal equity is also very important. An organization that uses a job-based pay system makes both movement from one part of the organization to another and movement from a lower-level job to a higher-level job possible, therefore leading to a pay increase. An organization that uses more than one pay system may find that advancement does not always translate to a pay increase.

Managing labor costs is an important aspect of a job-based pay system. Job evaluation can ensure that no division or unit is out of line in terms of pay rates. Some of the commercially available job-evaluation systems that have been in use for a while are relatively easy-to-use approaches to determining pay rates. They have the appearance, at least, of objectivity. Senior managers like the idea that people are paid the same regardless of where they work in the organization, lessening conflicts over salaries.

Disadvantages of Job-Evaluation–Based Pay

Specific criticisms of job evaluation rest on the argument that it is more than a way to pay employees; it is an approach to management. Among the criticisms of job evaluation and job-based pay are the following:

• It promotes a bureaucratic management style. Basic to a bureaucratic approach to management is the job description, which carefully prescribes activities to perform and how the person will be held accountable. It emphasizes control and what the organization dictates. This management style was seen as the best approach when job evaluation was originally developed in the early twentieth century.

• The job description implicitly specifies what the employee should not do. This fits well with the bureaucratic management style but is incongruent with the orientation that an individual should jump in and do what is right for the situation rather than what is called for by the job description. Sometimes employees refuse to perform tasks not in their job descriptions because their pay is so closely related to that description.

• The job description is difficult to change. When job descriptions change, the employees often feel that pay increases are needed. They believe what the organization has implied through the job-evaluation system: that the employees are worth what they do. If they are asked to do more things, they obviously should have their job reevaluated and upgraded. Organizations such as libraries, which are undergoing constant change, find that job descriptions are difficult to alter as quickly as needed.

• It reinforces hierarchy. Job-evaluation points are typically assigned to factors concerned with the level of responsibility and the number of reporting relationships. As a result, job-evaluation scores make clear who has the most responsible job and spell out the hierarchy of positions. In knowledge and high-technology work, there is a need for a system that recognizes people for their expertise and ideas, not for the "value" of the job they hold.

• It depersonalizes people. Job evaluation is based on the principle that people are worth what they do, which tends to depersonalize employees. It deemphasizes paying people for their skills and their performance and rewards employees for outgrowing their jobs and getting promoted.

• It focuses on internal pay relationships. Employees can look at the organization's job structure and see how their job should compare in terms of pay. The natural tendency is to find a job that is relatively highly paid and use it as a benchmark. This leads inevitably to higher and higher pay levels.

• It works against strategic pay. An organization may believe that it can be most competitive in the market by having specific units or divisions pay more, something not allowed in job-based systems. For example, if a library believes that it cannot hire and retain automation personnel without reclassifying certain positions, they cannot be competitive. Paying a computer person more than a collections person is inevitable, but does the job-evaluation system permit it?

• It discourages organizational change. Because of the work required to create a job description and do a job evaluation, organizational change and reorganization become major workload issues. If the job-evaluation approach is used, a reassignment of responsibilities means that some people get more pay than others. This sets up a competition for higher-level duties and can lead to resistance to needed changes.

• It encourages point inflation. Individuals become quite adept at getting their jobs evaluated highly. They realize that creatively written job descriptions and added job duties can lead to pay increases. Some employees may spend an inordinate amount of time and effort on rewriting job descriptions to take advantage of the point-factor system. Adding responsibilities and subordinates translates to higher salaries. In effect, then, the point-factor system that is designed to control costs can lead to higher costs.

• It can reward dishonesty. Over time, writing inflated job descriptions to beat the job-evaluation system can become common in an organization. Both employees and their supervisors become involved in an effort to increase employee pay by upgrading jobs. Efforts to beat the system may result in

- the organization paying everyone too much,
- inflated operating costs for performing job audits,
- creation of a culture in which providing misinformation to the human resources department is acceptable, or
- the library having an adversarial relationship with the compensation unit.

• It fails to encourage skill development. The job-evaluation system emphasizes level of responsibility and reporting relationships and does not reinforce the technical excellence that is needed in high-technology and knowledge work. Persons who operate as integrators and effective problem solvers are not helped by a system that rewards supervision. As organizations become flatter, there are fewer opportunities for moving up the hierarchy, raising further questions about a system that rewards upward mobility. In fact, a system that encourages a participative management style and teamwork produces large numbers of employees in dead-end jobs.

• It rewards the wrong behavior and makes promotion too important. Sometimes job level dictates other nonpay benefits such as parking spaces, who gets included in meetings, or who is informed about what. This makes getting more points and being promoted to a higher level important. It is a use for the job-evaluation system that was really not originally intended. These decisions are subject to manipulation and error, which can lead employees in a job-based pay system to spend too much time worrying about what their next job will be.

Despite its problems, job evaluation is still the best approach to determining pay structure if high levels of internal equity and centralized control of salary costs are desirable. An alternative is skill-based or knowledge-based pay.

Skill-Based Pay

In contrast to job-based pay, skill-based or knowledge-based pay is focused on people and on what the market pays. A skill-based system can help an organization actively manage the skill-acquisition process by directly motivating individuals to learn specific skills. In a job-based system, overpayment is possible when employees are still learning their jobs, and underpayment is likely in the case of an experienced individual who has worked in a number of different jobs or has developed great skill in an important area. Individuals are typically paid for taking a new job before they learn that job. In a skill-based pay system, individuals are rewarded for mastering job skills.

The design of a skill-based job first requires the identification of those tasks and skills that need to be performed. Next, tests or measures must be developed to determine whether an individual has learned those skills. Those skills then need to be "priced" for pay rates to be determined. The number and kind of skills each individual can learn is determined. Individuals are typically paid only for those skills that they currently can and are willing to perform.

In traditional compensation systems, the assumption is that if an employee holds a job, that employee is skilled at all of the tasks. There is often no assessment of skill levels as in the skill-based plan, which includes formal processes to certify competency. In the skill-based pay system, pay-rate changes occur only when additional skills are acquired, meaning that an employee who changes jobs may not necessarily change pay rates. This provides greater flexibility to managers.

Seniority in the skill-based compensation system is important only in the sense that it takes time to acquire new skills, unlike a traditional system in which time in grade usually means pay increases. Advancement opportunities are enhanced in the skill-based system because employees who acquire additional skills can be more valuable to the organization. The emphasis in the skill-based compensation system is on the individual who can perform various skills rather than on the employee's job title and grade.

Skill-based pay is more often found in flat organizations with only two tiers separating the lowest-level employee from the top manager. There is usually a team-based approach, and employees tend to be empowered in a skill-based organization. Hierarchical and authoritarian management styles are not conducive to this pay system.

Skill-based systems are sometimes recommended only for the lowest-level jobs and for small, newly established organizations that do not have to contend with changing an ingrained traditional system. Private-sector companies are experimenting with skill-based pay for some white-collar jobs such as tellers, loan officers, and insurance agents. In the public sector, skill-based pay can be effective in operations such as highway maintenance and warehousing operations.

Experiences with skill-based compensation systems in the private sector can provide lessons for public-sector organizations considering their implementation. Among those considerations are the following:

- Skill-based pay must be consistent with the prevailing managerial style and organizational structure.
- Skill-based pay must have commitment from all levels of the organization.
- Skill-based pay must be used with a view toward long-term, not short-term, success.
- Skill-based pay must be used within a culture of participation and employee empowerment.
- Skill-based pay must be carefully planned prior to implementation and be tailored to the organization; it is not a one-size-fits-all plan.
- Skill-based pay can raise administrative and training costs and average pay rates.
- Skill-based pay can result in lower overall labor costs due to more flexible staffing.

The skill-based pay system, in use for more than 20 years, has the potential of aligning what organizations want (productivity, flexibility, and improved service) with what employees want (more money) while facilitating team-based flat organization with multiskilled employees.

Although skill-based pay is most effectively used in production settings, it can also be applied to knowledge work. The development of a skill-based pay system for managerial and professional employees can take several forms:

- Managers and higher-level professionals can be paid for learning skills that are horizontal. For example, a personnel manager can learn accounting.
- Managers can also learn skills that are lower or higher—downwardly vertical or upwardly vertical skills.
- Finally, managers can learn skills useful for performing their jobs in greater depth. This is especially relevant in high-technology fields.

The greatest advantage of the skill-based system is flexibility. When individuals can perform multiple tasks, the organization gains flexibility, allowing it to respond more quickly to change. Multiskilled employees have a greater understanding of the big picture. Employees tend to gain a greater sense of commitment when they have a broader view, which enhances participative management and teamwork. Employees with multiple skills also tend to be more self-managing. They see and can do what needs done. Self-management in turn encourages individuals to do a high-quality job and to be concerned about results.

The disadvantages of skill-based systems are the high costs of training, both in terms of dollars and time away from the job. Skill assessment is also a critical feature of skill-based pay and must be done well. In addition, comparing jobs to the market is difficult because finding comparable positions to the multiskilled individual positions is harder.

The basis of skill-based pay is that individuals are paid for the number, kind, and depth of skills that they develop and use. These skills may be horizontal, in-depth, or vertical skills. Skill-based pay is well suited to a matrix organization or a participative management setting in which the work is highly interdependent and/or is rapidly changing.

COMPONENTS OF PAY STRUCTURE

A conventional pay structure contains a series of overlapping grades and ranges. All salary management decisions are typically made within the framework of the pay structure. Each job is assigned to a grade based on its relative value, and each grade has an assigned range of salaries from a minimum to a maximum. In most salary programs, the minimum salary is generally treated as the appropriate salary for a new employee who meets the minimum requirements of the position. As employees gain experience or improve their skills, their salaries are increased, and over time they advance through the range.

Relationship Between Job Structure and Pay Structure

The last chapter addressed how jobs are assigned to grades. The grades in turn become the basis for a job structure, grouping jobs with similar level tasks and du-ties together regardless of the similarity of the whole jobs themselves. A land-scaper and a clerk-typist may be the same grade even though the descriptions of the two jobs are dissimilar. Now that the jobs have been ordered on the basis of total points (point factor), classes (classification), or ranks (ranking), the organi-zation is ready to convert the job structure to a wage or salary structure. This process is usually referred to as pricing the structure.

Public- and Private-Sector Pay

Typically, private-sector salary programs are based on merit-pay principles, es-pecially in white-collar occupations, and public-sector programs are based pri-marily on time in position. Private-sector salary structures are usually based on a range of 50 percent from the minimum to the maximum, whereas public-sector structures tend to be smaller, 30 to 40 percent. Corporation salary schedules have midpoint salaries that are regularly adjusted to competitive pay levels based on salary surveys. By contrast, public-sector structures are usually adjusted through across-the-board increases and are not tied to market salaries. Adjustments to the midpoint salaries are made but not usually because of competitive market salaries.

DECISIONS RELATING TO PAY STRUCTURE

Decisions that guide the development of a library's pay structure are made at the highest levels of the organization. Such policy decisions include guidelines con-cerning the following:

- the minimum and maximum levels of pay
- the general relationships among levels of pay
- the division of the total compensation budget
- the extent to which compensation policies are communicated
- whether compensation policy is open or secret

Typically, the organization's senior management establishes the salary structure and makes recommendations on guidelines and specific annual increase packages to the board, which determines policy. The following questions relating to policies have to be answered in developing these guidelines:

- What is the lowest rate that can be offered for a job that will entice the quality of employees the library wants?
- What is the rate of pay that must be offered to incumbents to ensure that they stay with the library?
- Should seniority be recognized through the base-pay schedule?
- Should meritorious performance be recognized through the base-pay schedule?
- Should there be more than one rate of pay for employees performing either identical or similar work?
- What is considered to be a sufficient difference in base rates of pay among jobs requiring varying levels of knowledge, skills, responsibilities, and duties?
- Should dangerous working conditions be recognized within the base-pay schedule?
- Should there be a difference in changes in base-pay progression opportunities among jobs of varying worth?
- Is there opportunity to progress to higher-level jobs?
- How does promotion affect base pay?
- Should incumbents be allowed to earn pay higher than established maximums or lower than established minimums?
- How will the pay structure accommodate across-the-board, cost-of-living, or other adjustments not related to seniority, performance, or job changes?

A CONVENTIONAL SALARY STRUCTURE

Salary structures tend to be very similar because they follow accepted practice and replicate each other. In designing the structure, an organization makes decisions on the number of grades, the range spread from minimum to maximum, and the percentage differences between ranges. This will determine the overlap from one range to the next. The overlap means that some portion of a range covers the same salaries as the ranges above and below. The range progression, or the salary change between grades, is normally expressed as a percentage and is usually between 5 and 10 percent. If the progression is at the lower end, 5 percent, for example, there will be more grades. If the range progression is 10 percent, there will be fewer grades and probably fewer upward reclassifications. The conventional salary structure was developed in the early 1940s and has seen little in the way of innovation. A more recent alternative concept is broad-banding.

BROAD-BANDING

Instead of having 5 or 10 percent range progressions as with the traditional salary structure, broad-banding combines four or five salary ranges yielding range spreads from 30 to 50 percent. The result is 3 or 4 grades instead of 15 or 20. Organizations faced with reevaluating jobs because they are reorganizing, downsizing, or simply trying to respond to change find that the larger ranges reduce the need to constantly change job grades. They also lessen the possibility that a person's job will be downgraded. New programs can be staffed through transfers to same-grade positions in a broad-banded structure more readily than under a system with many grades. Banding places less emphasis on job-content changes and is more flexible. It also reduces hierarchy and allows for a number of positions within the band to be considered more equal, improving relations among team members. This approach appears to solve many of the problems of the traditional salary structure.

MINIMUMS AND MAXIMUMS

In establishing minimum and maximum levels of pay, the organization must first review the minimum standards prescribed by the federal government though regulations set under the 1938 FLSA, as amended. Some states set even higher minimum wages. When this is the case, the state law prevails. Collective-bargaining organizations may have minimum wages set through negotiations. Another major consideration is the local labor market. Minimum-wage rates must be set high enough to attract qualified applicants and retain good employees. A primary reason for conducting pay surveys is to establish a reasonable minimum salary for various grades. Establishing the maximum salary for each grade is more subjective but should take into account the ability to pay, competitive salaries, and the organization's ability to attract and retain individuals with specific knowledge and skills.

NUMBER OF PAY GRADES

There is no optimum number of pay grades. They range from as few as 4 to as many as 60. If there are few pay grades, the number of jobs in each grade will be relatively large, as will the dollar increments between the grades. If there are many pay grades, the number of jobs in each grade will be relatively small, as will the increments between grades. The principal considerations in determining the number of pay grades is the size of the library, the number of job clusters, and pay increase policies. Current practice is to try to reduce the number of pay grades to between 10 and 16 grades. Often the first 10 grades are for nonexempt employees, and the highest 6 or 8 grades for exempt. The difference between midpoints for clerical and hourly employees is typically 5 to 7 percent, and 8 to 10 percent for professional and managerial employees.

Figure 3.1 and table 3.1 present in different forms a sample salary schedule for a system with 14 grades. Note the minimum, midpoint, and maximum salaries. Note also the overlap between the grades. The sample salary schedule is divided roughly into fourths, or quarters. For each grade is a minimum, midpoint, and maximum salary. The midpoint is not the average of minimum and maximum but a point that is set through the use of market surveys. In addition, there are salaries listed for the top of the first quarter and the top of the third quarter. Employees may refer to the schedule to determine where their salaries lie within their grades. It is possible for an individual to move up through the grade as well as to move to another grade.

COMPA-RATIO

In building a salary schedule, it is critical that the organization make midpoint salaries competitive. The midpoint salary is the top of the second quarter of a salary range and is normally set by market salary surveys. One measure of the midpoint's validity is the compa-ratio, which compares actual salaries being paid to employees with those paid to employees of other organizations for the same work. Compa-ratio, or salary index, is a comparative ratio or index used in norming operations in building and maintaining pay structures. Compa-ratio equals average

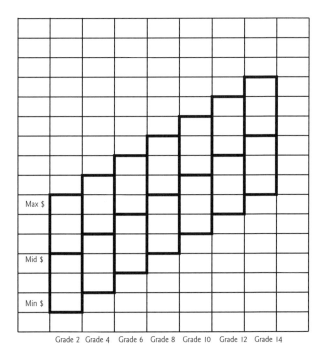

Figure 3.1 Sample Salary Schedule with 14 Grades

Table 3.1. Sample Salary Schedule with 14 Grades

Grade	Method	Minimum Pay	Pay Top of 1st Quarter	Midpoint Pay (Top of 2nd Quarter)	Pay Top of 3rd Quarter	Maximum Pay
1	Annually	$12,480.00	$13,728.00	$14,830.00	$16,349.00	$17,846.00
	Monthly	$1,040.00	$1,144.00	$1,235.83	$1,362.42	$1,487.17
	Hourly	$6.00	$6.60	$7.13	$7.86	$8.58
2	Annually	$12,950.00	$14,643.00	$16,307.00	$17,534.00	$18,762.00
	Monthly	$1,079.17	$1,220.25	$1,358.92	$1,461.17	$1,563.50
	Hourly	$6.23	$7.04	$7.84	$8.43	$9.02
3	Annually	$13,885.00	$15,912.00	$17,930.00	$19,822.00	$21,715.00
	Monthly	$1,157.08	$1,326.00	$1,494.17	$1,651.83	$1,809.58
	Hourly	$6.68	$7.65	$8.62	$9.53	$10.44
4	Annually	$15,206.00	$17,472.00	$19,739.00	$21,861.00	$23,961.00
	Monthly	$1,267.17	$1,456.00	$1,644.92	$1,821.75	$1,996.75
	Hourly	$7.31	$8.40	$9.49	$10.51	$11.52
5	Annually	$16,650.00	$19,178.00	$21,715.00	$24,086.00	$26,436.00
	Monthly	$1,387.50	$1,598.17	$1,809.58	$2,007.17	$2,203.00
	Hourly	$8.00	$9.22	$10.44	$11.58	$12.71
6	Annually	$18,230.00	$21,278.00	$24,336.00	$27,040.00	$29,723.00
	Monthly	$1,519.17	$1,773.17	$2,028.00	$2,253.33	$2,476.92
	Hourly	$8.76	$10.23	$11.70	$13.00	$14.29
7	Annually	$19,957.00	$23,379.00	$26,790.00	$29,806.00	$32,802.00
	Monthly	$1,663.08	$1,948.25	$2,232.50	$2,483.83	$2,733.50
	Hourly	$9.59	$11.24	$12.88	$14.33	$15.77

(continued)

Table 3.1. Sample Salary Schedule with 14 Grades (continued)

Grade	Method	Minimum Pay	Pay Top of 1st Quarter	Midpoint Pay (Top of 2nd Quarter)	Pay Top of 3rd Quarter	Maximum Pay
8	Annually	$21,846.00	$25,646.00	$29,453.00	$32,822.00	$36,192.00
	Monthly	$1,820.50	$2,137.17	$2,454.42	$2,735.17	$3,016.00
	Hourly	$10.50	$12.33	$14.16	$15.78	$17.40
9	Annually	$23,912.00	$28,163.00	$32,406.00	$36,171.00	$39,936.00
	Monthly	$1,992.67	$2,346.92	$2,700.50	$3,014.25	$3,328.00
	Hourly	$11.50	$13.54	$15.58	$17.39	$19.20
10	Annually	$26,173.00	$30,909.00	$35,651.00	$39,874.00	$44,075.00
	Monthly	$2,181.08	$2,575.75	$2,970.92	$3,322.83	$3,672.92
	Hourly	$12.58	$14.86	$17.14	$19.17	$21.19
11	Annually	$28,644.00	$34,299.00	$39,957.00	$44,762.00	$49,566.00
	Monthly	$2,387.00	$2,858.25	$3,329.75	$3,730.17	$4,130.50
	Hourly	$13.77	$16.49	$19.21	$21.52	$23.83
12	Annually	$31,347.00	$37,648.00	$43,950.00	$49,317.00	$54,683.00
	Monthly	$2,612.25	$3,137.33	$3,662.50	$4,109.75	$4,556.92
	Hourly	$15.07	$18.10	$21.13	$23.71	$26.29
13	Annually	$34,301.00	$41,330.00	$48,360.00	$54,350.00	$60,341.00
	Monthly	$2,858.42	$3,444.17	$4,030.00	$4,529.17	$5,028.42
	Hourly	$16.49	$19.87	$23.25	$26.13	$29.01
14	Annually	$40,941.00	$49,483.00	$58,032.00	$65,354.00	$72,654.00
	Monthly	$3,411.75	$4,123.58	$4,836.00	$5,446.17	$6,054.50
	Hourly	$19.68	$23.79	$27.90	$31.42	$34.93

pay rates actually paid divided by the range midpoint. It is the expression of the relationship between actual salaries paid in the marketplace and the midpoint salaries. For example, a compa-ratio of .948 would mean that the weighted average salary of every employee in a specific grade indicates that the employer is paying salaries a little below the midpoint for other workers in that level of work. The midpoint that is exactly the midpoint market salary would have a compa-ratio of 1.00.

The compa-ratio is sensitive to the general overrating or underrating of employees in an organization in that their merit increases affect overall averages. A manager who decides to reward all of the employees that report to him can skew the compa-ratio for all other grade 12 employees. The result could be not only inequitable compensation for grade 12 employees reporting to managers who are not attempting to beat the performance appraisal system but also a higher compa-ratio, making it difficult for other grade 12s to raise their salaries.

A natural movement in the compa-ratio occurs at the higher grades if senior employees are raised up through the grades via promotions or reclassifications. These employees may well have salaries higher than the midpoint, whereas employees who are beginning their careers are more likely to be nearer the minimum salaries for their grades. The compa-ratio is nothing more than an indicator of how the library's employees compare with other organizations.

FORCES AFFECTING SALARY STRUCTURE

Once a structure is established, the library has only just begun to address salary issues. Outside labor forces at work will cause the library to adjust the salary schedule to market salaries to allow it to continue to recruit and retain good employees. There are internal forces as well. It is common for duties and tasks to change, causing an upward creep in job classifications. Supervisors need to be in tune with such changes, which are usually not envisioned when the jobs are originally classified. In some instances, single jobs will need reevaluation. In other cases, whole classes of jobs need to be studied. Requests for these reevaluations are normally initiated by the supervisor or incumbent. In addition, some employees and supervisors will attempt to defeat a job-classification system in order to obtain raises for their charges and themselves. Even without those problems, major reorganizations will require a systematic reevaluation of jobs in some areas, if not throughout the whole library. If the job and wage structures are not flexible enough to meet changing needs, supervisors and employees will begin to question their validity.

CONVENTIONAL STRUCTURE OR BROAD-BANDING?

Both public- and private-sector employers are justifiably reluctant to change their salary structures. Continued reliance on the traditional structure provides stability and gives employees a sense of where they stand in the hierarchy. It is important to recognize that the pay structure is nothing more than a framework to facilitate decision making. The pay structure is normally taken for granted until there is a decision to change it or its validity is challenged. The introduction of a new salary structure is normally associated with reorganization or other attempts to change an organization. The following questions need to be answered before changing from a traditional to a broad-band approach:

- How many organizational layers need to be accommodated by grade distinctions?
- Is there a desire to downplay hierarchy?
- Is it important to treat all occupational groups the same, or would it be useful to have a traditional structure for lower grades and broad bands for upper grades?
- Has the library made a commitment to teams?
- How will annual increases be handled relative to merit, across the board, team performance, or the market?
- What is the appropriate role of human resources in the development and management of salary structure?

CHECKING UP

There are a number of ways of evaluating how well your pay system is working. One way is a form of ratio analysis. To each pay grade, apply the following formula:

$$T / (N \times M)$$

Where: T = total salary of all employees in the grade
 N = number of employees in the grade
 M = midpoint salary

If there is a spread of 50 percent between minimum and maximum salaries, the possible results of this calculation are .80 to 1.20. A ratio of .80 means that everyone is earning only the minimum salary for the grade, which could be explained if all of the employees in the grade are new employees who start at the minimum salary either because a new unit was established or because of high turnover. High turnover can be a sign of problems, and it would be useful to know what percentage of each group leaves each year and even more useful to look behind the numbers to find out why turnover is so high. A ratio of 1.20 means that everyone's salary is compressed near the top. This may signal an outstanding group of employees who have earned highest merit. A ratio of around 1.00 indicates that the group's average salary is near midpoint.

INDIVIDUAL WAGE DETERMINATION

The amount of an individual's paycheck is related partly to what employees in other organizations are being paid for the same work and partly to the perceived worth of the individual's tasks and responsibilities relative to other kinds of work performed within the library. It is also related to the individual's performance as compared to the performance of others. In addition, other forces are at work:

- How consistent are the performance evaluations of various employees by various supervisors?
- How are those evaluations reviewed for fairness and equity?
- Are certain supervisors intent on getting more money for staff, unable to honestly assess performance, or unwilling to go to bat for their employees?
- Have the supervisors been adequately trained in evaluating the work of others?

The actual pools of funds available for across-the-board, merit, and equity pay each year also affect salaries. The individual who has a terrific year when the library is giving only cost-of-living raises will not benefit from even the best merit system. In addition, an organizational salary equity adjustment may bring everyone, regardless of salary history, up to the salary of the star performer. Is this equity?

These kinds of salary adjustments are seen in libraries that attempt to bring the salaries of librarians doing similar work up to a regional, peer, or national average. The data available often relate to position—that is, reference librarian, branch director, cataloger, and so on—and to years of experience. With such adjustments, librarians who have faculty status and who have worked for promotion have often seen those promotion bonuses wiped out in an attempt to achieve equitable salaries.

The most important compensation decisions within an organization are those that differentiate among the amounts of pay received by individuals who are performing the same work. The problems of relating compensation to performance differences among individuals are complicated by several facets of performance to which the compensation system should be responsive. These facets can be shown in terms of time—past, current, and future performance.

Past Performance

Long-term, loyal employees are often rewarded because the organization feels that their faithful service and past performance warrant a raise, even if their current performance does not. Seniority is often a factor in determining individual wage rates. In some organizations, a payment for continuing membership in the organization, rather than payment for past performance, is built into the salary schedule. Automatic increase provisions that provide for raises at specific intervals have little to do with performance. If a person is still on the job, that increase is awarded. There is also a general feeling by management that employees who are no longer productive but are a few years from retirement deserve to be treated well, if not out of sentiment, then out of a sense that the supervisors want the same kind of treatment when they near retirement. Retirement benefits are often tied directly to either the highest salary over a period of time or the last salary. One could argue that it is better to be humane than to strictly enforce a cold unfeeling policy.

Current Performance

Current performance is the most universally accepted concept in wage and salary administration. Although it is difficult to assess what might happen if performance differences are not reflected in pay received, human nature is such that inadequately rewarded superior performers are likely to reduce their efforts—"Why should I work hard if we all get paid the same?" The adoption of pay-for-performance appraisal systems is aimed at incorporating a reward system for superior performance and identifying those individuals who deserve higher pay. A good performance appraisal system should do three things:

- It should give employees a reliable means of knowing how well they are doing.
- It should serve as a basis for improvement, identifying weaknesses to be corrected and training that might be useful.
- It should provide information with which to make pay decisions and future job assignments.

Unfortunately, there are many ways a perfectly good performance appraisal system can produce the wrong results, including the following:

- The judgment by a supervisor is often subjective, based on impressions, not facts.
- Even supervisors who strive to make sound, factually based judgments often act without a thorough understanding of the job.
- Ratings done by different persons often are inconsistent.
- A results-based rating system can penalize a person who makes a significant contribution of a kind that is not easily measured.
- Challenges to appraisal systems often reveal inadequate data to support those decisions.

Appraisal is not just a system; it is a human process. And most systems evaluate quantity and not quality. Chapter 5 describes various performance appraisal systems designed to reward employee effort.

Future Performance

Future performance is less often rewarded than current or past performance. In some organizations, new employees who are still learning their jobs may receive automatic increases in an effort to retain them and as an expression of belief in their potential. Individuals who are ready for promotion but for whom there are presently no higher-level positions available sometimes receive automatic increases. In both instances, employees are being rewarded for their potential contributions and are being paid in part to stay with the library until their potential can be realized. In some cases, an individual may be given a relatively high starting salary as recognition of potential contributions. But care must be taken in such cases that instant inequities do not result from the hiring process.

PROGRESSING THROUGH A SALARY RANGE

There are a number of ways individuals move through salary ranges for each grade or job class. For example, union agreements often specify that a single job rate should be paid to everyone on a particular job. Such an approach is often a reflection of the feeling that performance judgments by managers are frequently unreliable and inaccurate, that managers can exercise too much control over union members when they determine salaries, and that union members performing the same work should receive the same pay for the sake of cohesiveness.

The approach that contains the weakest relationship between individual wage decisions and individual performance is automatic progression through the range. Here, all employees are awarded specific pay increases at preestablished time intervals throughout their tenure on the job. The use of automatic progression assumes that there is little variability in the performance of a job or that the performance cannot be accurately measured.

PROBLEMS AND RISKS OF SALARY MANAGEMENT

There are three general rules for the administration and control of salaries:

1. There shall be a set of rules setting forth exactly how individual salaries are to be determined and how increases are to be awarded.
2. All salaries and changes to salaries shall conform to those rules.
3. And the unwritten rule: People will make ad hoc exceptions to the first two rules.

The problems inherent in the third rule include exceptions at hiring, red-circle salaries, below-minimum salaries, salary concentration, and range overlap.

Exceptions at Hiring

Exceptions at hiring occur in situations whereby a hiring officer hires an individual, for whatever reason, at a salary at or above that paid to incumbents performing the same work. This move is a major cause of dissatisfaction among workers. There are times when it is necessary to pay a higher starting salary to get someone hired, but the supervisor must be prepared for the fallout. Does the supervisor attempt to withhold future raises in order to appease the others or attempt get equity increases for the incumbents? Best to follow rules 1 and 2—have a set of guidelines and follow them.

Red-Circle Salaries

Red-circle salaries are those salaries that for one reason or another are above the maximum of the range. Employees in this category typically have higher salaries for one of four reasons:

- The employee was transferred downward from a higher-graded position.
- The employee has a higher salary because of a former evaluation system or salary schedule.
- The employee was a superstar and is no longer.
- The employee received raises in order to keep from leaving for a better job elsewhere.

The obvious solution to red-circle salaries is to promote the employee to a grade with a range that the salary will fit. Some organizations will attempt to hold increases until the maximum is raised or until others catch up, but this often creates serious morale problems.

Below-Minimum Salaries

Employees may have below-minimum salaries because of rule number 3—making ad hoc exceptions to the rule. For example, an individual is an obvious choice to replace a retiring official. The problem is that the person does not really meet the minimum requirements for experience, and awarding a person the minimum salary would result in a huge percentage increase, which goes against everyone's best judgment. The result is that the individual is offered a large increase but a salary below minimum. Again, rule number 3 should be avoided at all costs.

Concentration

Concentration refers to a situation in which there is low turnover and employees tend to be concentrated at the top of the salary range. These may be employees who are still far from retirement but who have accumulated years of service. These employees may also perform effectively dead-end jobs with few opportunities for promotion and little competitive demand, so they cannot easily get other jobs. A group of employees may be concentrated at the top of the range because the best employees have resigned or been promoted, leaving only those employees who do not or can not leave. Poor people movement leads to salary problems.

Range Overlap

Range overlap can be a problem when the salary ranges permit the kind of situation in which an employee who is above midpoint in one grade is given a promotion to the next higher grade. Because of the overlap, the new salary may exceed the midpoint of the next grade. This situation leaves little room for salary increases in the new position. In addition, the new person may well be earning a higher salary than many of the people already in that grade, causing morale problems. Less overlap of the grade helps prevent this problem.

Figure 3.2 shows a high degree of overlap and low midpoint differentials for twelve grades, which indicates small differences in the value of jobs in the adjoining grades. Figure 3.3 shows fewer grades and ranges that result in wider midpoint differentials and less overlap between adjacent grades. A situation as shown in figure 3.3 would allow a manager to reinforce a promotion or movement into a new range with a greater amount of dollars. The differential should be large enough to encourage employees to seek or accept a promotion or to undertake the training required for a promotion.

As the discussion in this chapter shows, the establishment of a pay structure is extremely important for an organization. Many problems can stem from a poorly

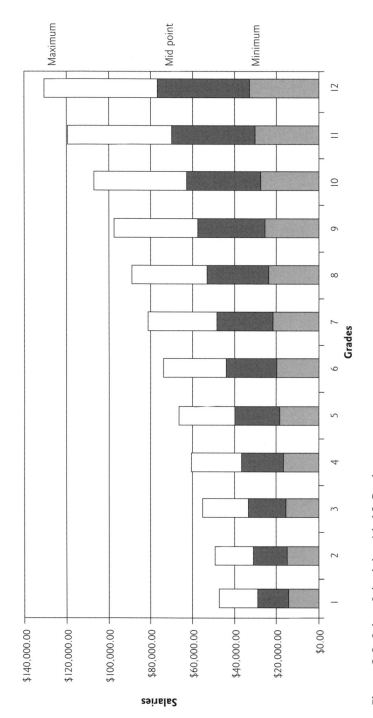

Figure 3.2 Salary Schedule with 12 Grades

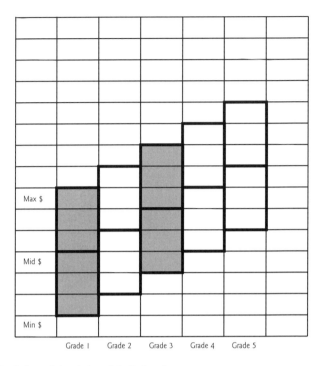

Figure 3.3 Salary Schedule with 5 Grades

designed structure and others can be resolved by a good structure. Chapter 9 addresses specific pay issues and problems.

BIBLIOGRAPHY

Clugston, Michael, Jon P. Howell, and Peter W. Dorfman. "Dispositional Influences on Pay Preferences." *Journal of Business and Psychology* 15, no. 2 (Winter 2000): 311–21.

Eagle, Joan M. "Wage and Hour Traps for the Unwary." *Journal of Property Management* 64, no. 2 (March/April 1999): 94–6.

Gustafson, Bobette M. "Skill-Based Pay Improves PFS Staff Recruitment, Retention, and Performance." *Healthcare Financial Management* 54, no. 1 (January 2000): 62–4.

Guthrie, James P. "Alternative Pay Practices and Employee Turnover: An Organization Economics Perspective." *Group and Organization Management* 25, no. 4 (December 2000): 419–40.

Hadley, Ernest C., and Eleanor J. Laws. *Federal Sector Workers' Compensation.* Arlington, VA: Dewey Publications, 1999.

Hamermesh, Daniel S. *12 Million Salaried Workers Are Missing.* Cambridge, MA: National Bureau of Economic Research, 2000.

Heneman, Robert L. "The Changing Nature of Pay Systems and the Need for New Midrange Theories of Pay." *Human Resource Management Review* 10, no. 3 (Fall 2000): 245–8.

Hickman, E. Stewart. "Pay the Person, Not the Job." *Training and Development* 54, no. 10 (October 2000): 52–8.

Hines, James R., Hilary Williamson Hoynes, and Alan B. Krueger. *Another Look at Whether a Rising Tide Lifts All Boats*. Cambridge, MA: National Bureau of Economic Research, 2001.

Lee, Cynthia, Kenneth S. Law, and Philip Bobko. "The Importance of Justice Perceptions on Pay Effectiveness: A Two Year Study of a Skill-Based Pay Plan." *Journal of Management* 25, no. 6 (1999): 851–74.

Liccione, William J. "Evaluate the Strategic Value of Jobs." *HR Focus* 72, no. 4 (April 1995): 10.

Littlefield, David. "Wages Must Reward Skills and Innovation: IPD Compensation Forum Conference." *People Management* 2 (February 8, 1996): 13.

Mannering, Ward. "Give Pay Decisions a Human Face." *Government Executive* 33, no. 12 (September 2001): 78–80.

Mericle, Kenneth, and Kim Dong-One. "From Job-Based Pay to Skill-Based Pay in Unionized Establishments." *Industrial Relations (Quebec)* 54, no. 3 (Summer 1999): 549–81.

Murray, Brian. "Skill-Based Pay and Skill Seeking." *Human Resource Management Review* 10, no. 3 (Fall 2000): 271–88.

Neumark, David. *Living Wages Protection for or Protection from Low-Wage Workers?* Cambridge, MA: National Bureau of Economic Research, 2001.

Parker, Gary. "Establishing Remuneration Practices Across Culturally Diverse Environments." *Compensation and Benefits Management* 17, no. 2 (Spring 2001): 23–8.

"Public and Private Sector Pay: Unfair Comparison?" *Worklife Report* 12, no. 4 (2000): 3–5.

Risher, Howard W. *New Strategies for Public Pay: Rethinking Government Compensation Programs*. San Francisco: Jossey-Bass, 1997.

Ruhm, Christopher J., and Carey Borkoski. *Compensation in the Nonprofit Sector*. Cambridge, MA: National Bureau of Economic Research, 2000.

Thompson, James R., and Charles W. LeHew. "Skill-Based Pay as an Organizational Innovation." *Review of Public Personnel Administration* 20, no. 1 (Winter 2000): 20–41.

U.S. Department of Labor, Employment Standards Administration. *Resource Book: Training for Federal Employing Agency Compensation Specialists*. Washington, DC: U.S. Department of Labor, Employment Standards Administration, 2000.

Watson Wyatt Data Services. *The ECS Report on Information Technology Personnel Compensation*. Rochelle Park, NJ: Watson Wyatt Data Services, 1999.

4 PAY FOR PERFORMANCE

When a fellow says it ain't the money but the principle of the thing, it's the money.

—ABE MARTIN

The many different ways of paying for performance can be divided into two general types. The first provides merit-pay increases based on individual performance. The second provides a one-time payment or bonus for accomplishing a particular objective or reaching a particular performance level—variable pay.

DETERMINING INDIVIDUAL PAY

Pay for performance sounds as though it would be a viable policy for improving employee performance in organizations. Some studies have shown that employees who believe pay is dependent on performance actually perform at a higher level. Nonetheless, three key problems exist in translating this philosophy into practice. First, employees must value pay. Although pay can at least indirectly satisfy individual needs, it should not be assumed that pay is the motivator capable of solving all organizational motivation problems. Pay alone will not lead to high performance. Second, other detractors to pay as a motivator must be removed. An organization must develop sound human resources systems (e.g., selection, planning, performance appraisal, and training) that complement the wage and salary system. Third, employees must believe that pay is tied to performance. Salary increases must be allocated to merit so that differences in performances translate into differences in salary increases. Supervisors must be trained to discriminate among subordinates in performance and to provide feedback to employees about performance. Supervisors must provide a supportive environment in which performance is considered a team effort. All of these practices must be adhered to consistently over time.

Many organizations are more concerned with doing the wrong things right than with searching for the right pay practices. Their pay systems are driven more by history and what other organizations do than by a strategic analysis of organizational needs. On the other hand, effective pay programs can

- motivate employees to perform more effectively,
- create a culture in which people care about the organization and its success,
- provide the fringe benefits that individuals want in a cost-effective manner,
- attract and retain the kind of talent that an organization needs in order to be effective, and
- encourage people to develop their skills and abilities in areas that best aid the organization.

Why not pay excellent performers more than everyone else? Since Frederick W. Taylor made individual pay for performance an important part of scientific management in the early 1900s, pay for performance has been a basic principle in management. Given its popularity, it must be effective, right? In many cases, it is not. It does little to motivate performance and does little to retain the right employees. It is often the source of employee dissatisfaction. Two reasons that pay for performance does not work well are problems with performance appraisal and the annuity nature of pay for performance. Both problems will be discussed in detail in this and the next chapter.

PERFORMANCE-BASED PAY SYSTEMS

Pay for performance covers a broad spectrum of compensation systems that can be grouped under two general categories: merit-pay plans and variable-pay plans. Although the primary focus of this chapter is on merit pay, it will help to first review variable pay.

Variable pay can be divided into individual and group incentive plans. In the most common individual incentive plans—piece rate and sales on commission— payouts are separate from the base salary. Although the pay amounts can be large, individual incentive plans carry the risk to the individual of no payout if performance thresholds are not met. Group incentive plans base compensation decisions on unit or system performance rather than individual performance. Profit-sharing plans or equity plans link payouts to the overall fortunes of the company. Group incentive payouts can be large but may also be zero. As with the individual plans, payouts are separate from any base pay.

All pay-for-performance plans are designed to deliver pay increases to employees based at least in part on some measure of performance. Potential benefits of pay-for-performance plans include the following:

- Performance-based pay plans support the organization's personnel philosophy by helping to communicate organization goals to the employees. If financial goals are paramount, then a plan tied to the achievement of financial goals helps reinforce their importance to employees.
- Performance-based pay plans can support a certain level of performance that is consistent with the organization's goals. An organization that agrees to payouts for 80 percent achievement of financial goals sends a different message than if goals have to be completely met (100 percent). Employees who receive no increase if a performance standard is not met will pay attention to the performance standards.
- Performance-based pay plans can help ensure consistency in the distribution of pay increases. Under a plan that pays all employees when a goal is met, payouts are made only when the goal is met. When individuals know what performance standards are, pay increases go consistently only to persons who meet those goals.
- Performance-based pay plans can positively influence individuals to achieve goals that will be rewarded. To the extent that these goals contribute to organizational effectiveness, one can conclude that pay for performance influences individual and organizational effectiveness.

PAY FOR PERFORMANCE IN PRACTICE

As an example from the private sector, MetLife has implemented a pay-for-performance plan that rates employees on a 1- to 5-point scale based on the following competency models of core behaviors—one for leaders and managers, another for individual employees:[1]

Core Behaviors of a Leader or Manager

- Champions change. Proactively leads and embraces change with innovation, courage, and resiliency. Questions the existing ways of getting things done and endeavors to improve quality and efficiency.
- Inspires a shared vision. Creates a compelling mission and purpose for the organization and energizes people to work toward shared goals.
- Promotes key values. Consistently demonstrates MetLife values. Emphasizes that people count and that the company promotes winning from within.
- Communicates effectively. Shares information and encourages candid and open dialogue. Ensures that people share information and have access to the information they need to meet their business objectives.
- Develops talent for the future. Identifies critical skills needed to get results. Creates a work environment that attracts and retains top talent.
- Focuses on customers. Works to exceed expectations of customers externally and internally. Takes immediate action to resolve customers' problems.
- Produces results. Directs action toward achieving goals that are critical to MetLife's success. Sets clear performance expectations that are aligned to

business priorities. Ensures that rewards—financial and nonfinancial—are linked to performance.

- Uses sound business judgment. Applies knowledge of the business and the industry, and common sense, to make the best decisions.
- Builds relationships. Excels at building partnerships and fostering teamwork. Works collaboratively within and across organizational boundaries to achieve common goals.

Core Behaviors of an Individual Employee

- Adapts to and implements change. Embraces change with innovation, courage, and resiliency.
- Promotes key values. Consistently demonstrates company values. Conducts business endeavors with truth, sincerity, and fairness.
- Communicates effectively. Shares information and engages in candid and open dialogue.
- Focuses on customers. Works to exceed customers' expectations.
- Produces results. Directs action toward achieving goals that are critical to the company's success.
- Completes work without close supervision.
- Manages own performance effectively. Organizes time and priorities to achieve business results.
- Uses sound business judgment. Applies knowledge of the business and the industry, and common sense, to make the best decisions.
- Builds relationships and works collaboratively. Excels at building partnerships and working as part of a team.
- Demonstrates technical and functional expertise.

MERIT PAY DEFINED

Merit pay is one of many forms of compensation provided by an organization for services rendered by its employees. It concerns compensation decisions rather than other personnel decisions such as staffing and training. Merit pay should not be confused with merit system, a term used in the public sector to describe hiring and promotion systems and not compensation decisions. Merit pay is a form of incentive pay, whereby pay is allocated based on performance. Merit pay is defined as individual pay increases based on the rated performance of individual employees during a specific time period. Although the salary increase under a merit plan is based on previous performance, it is also intended to motivate the recipient to continue to that level of performance in the future.

HISTORY OF MERIT PAY

Although the term *merit pay* is relatively new, the philosophy of linking pay to performance dates back to the Protestant Reformation of the sixteenth and seventeenth centuries. Hard work was viewed as self-sacrifice in the service of God—

hard work equaled economic success equaled willingness to serve God. Modern merit-pay plans began to appear around the early twentieth century. Many urban U.S. school districts had merit plans in the 1920s, and their use increased dramatically after World War II. Today, at least 80 percent of U.S. organizations have some type of merit-pay plan.

Merit-pay plans are important as evidenced by their frequent use by organizations in both the public and private sectors. The existence of a merit-pay plan sends the message to employees that the organization will reward good performance instead of distributing raises based on equality, need, or seniority. Merit-pay plans are generally considered by employees and employers to be successful.

VARIATIONS AMONG MERIT-PAY PLANS

There are a number of differences between the types of pay plans. It is important to keep in mind that no one type of merit-pay plan will work for all organizations.

- Standards used to assess performance differ among plans. Some organizations include seniority and market adjustments.
- Forms of payment. A salary increase is typically in the form of payment, although some organizations pay in the form of benefits.
- Method used to calculate increases. A merit increase could be calculated as an absolute dollar amount or as a percentage increase in salary.
- Permanency of the increase. Typically, the salary increase is added to the base salary and carried over as part of the base for future evaluation periods. Lump-sum payments could be used if the increase is not intended to be permanent.

MEASURES OF PERFORMANCE FOR MERIT PAY

Most people assume that the performance appraisal is used to establish a rating used in allocating merit pay, but other, relatively controversial measures are sometimes used. They include promotions, seniority, and market.

It is common for employees to receive pay increases in conjunction with upward promotions. What is less clear is why employees receive those increases. Are the pay increases awarded because of the acquisition of new skills, an increase in job responsibilities, good performance in previous jobs, or a combination of the three? Especially problematic is when a person is promoted and awarded merit simultaneously. One might assume that one reason employees are promoted is that they are meritorious in their present jobs, but organizations need to take care that promotional and merit increases be clearly delineated in order to avoid confusion.

Seniority is sometimes considered in merit-pay decisions. If seniority is used, organizations may find it difficult to contain compensation costs. On the other hand, such a measure may serve as an incentive for less-senior employees to remain with the organization in the expectation of higher pay increases later.

Sometimes organizations use worth in the outside market in merit decisions. For example, scientists or professors whose research is valued by outside organizations create an externally determined merit. The market therefore can be used to determine the merit increase required. If shortages are the cause of higher market value, the actual performance of the employee is not the determining factor, which is arguably unfair. Market adjustments could be justified if they are provided only to good performers.

FULL COST OF MERIT ADDED TO THE BASE

The traditional approach to awarding merit pay increases is to add those increases to the base salary. Employees tend to view the small difference between the amount given to strong performers and average performers (exceeds expectations and meets expectations) as being too little money to motivate them to work for the higher rating. In truth, the cost of the difference over the working career of an employee can be quite significant. For example, take two employees, Employee A and Employee B, who both earn $40,000 annually. Employee A earns an "exceeds expectations" rating and receives a 4 percent merit increase. Employee B earns a "meets expectations" and receives a 2 percent increase.

As illustrated in table 4.1, Employee A received 4 percent in the first year and no additional increases, earning an additional $32,000 over a 20-year career if that initial amount was not compounded, whereas Employee B received 2 percent in the first year and earned an additional $16,000 over the 20 years. In the second illustration, Employee A receives a 4 percent raise and Employee B receives a 2 percent raise each year for the 20 twenty years. With that raise compounded, Employee A would earn an additional $47,645 and Employee B an additional $19,438 (see table 4.2). Although the difference in raises might seem insignificant in the first year, the change in the size of the merit amounts grows dramatically over a 20-year career.

FEDERAL STUDY ON PERFORMANCE APPRAISAL FOR MERIT PAY

The Committee on Performance Appraisal for Merit Pay, which was established late in 1989 at the request of the federal Office of Personnel Management, analyzed research on the assessment of job performance and on the effectiveness of performance-based pay systems. Its report was published in 1991 by the National Academy of Sciences.[2]

Among the committee's findings were the following:

• Performance-appraisal ratings can influence many personnel decisions, and thus care in the development and use of performance appraisal systems is warranted. Further refinements in the technology of performance appraisals (e.g., extensive new job analysis, modifications of existing rating scales, or rater training programs) are unlikely to provide substantially more valid and accurate appraisal than those currently in force, particularly for managerial and professional jobs. There is also no evidence to indicate that one particular appraisal format is clearly superior to all others.

Table 4.1. Value to Employees Receiving 4% or 2% Merit Increase in Year One Only

	Employee A: 4% in Year 1 (Assumes No Compounding)					Employee B: 2% in Year 1 (Assumes No Compounding)			
Year	Salary	Annual Base Pay Amount	Cumulative Amount	% of Original Base Pay	Year	Salary	Annual Base Pay Amount	Cumulative Amount	% of Original Base Pay
1	$40,000	$1,600	$1,600	4.0%	1	$40,000	$800	$800	2.0%
2	$41,600	$1,600	$3,200	8.0%	2	$40,800	$800	$1,600	4.0%
3	$43,200	$1,600	$4,800	12.0%	3	$41,600	$800	$2,400	6.0%
4	$44,800	$1,600	$6,400	16.0%	4	$42,400	$800	$3,200	8.0%
5	$46,400	$1,600	$8,000	20.0%	5	$43,200	$800	$4,000	10.0%
6	$48,000	$1,600	$9,600	24.0%	6	$44,000	$800	$4,800	12.0%
7	$49,600	$1,600	$11,200	28.0%	7	$44,800	$800	$5,600	14.0%
8	$51,200	$1,600	$12,800	32.0%	8	$45,600	$800	$6,400	16.0%
9	$52,800	$1,600	$14,400	36.0%	9	$46,400	$800	$7,200	18.0%
10	$54,400	$1,600	$16,000	40.0%	10	$47,200	$800	$8,000	20.0%
11	$56,000	$1,600	$17,600	44.0%	11	$48,000	$800	$8,800	22.0%
12	$57,600	$1,600	$19,200	48.0%	12	$48,800	$800	$9,600	24.0%
13	$59,200	$1,600	$20,800	52.0%	13	$49,600	$800	$10,400	26.0%
14	$60,800	$1,600	$22,400	56.0%	14	$50,400	$800	$11,200	28.0%
15	$62,400	$1,600	$24,000	60.0%	15	$51,200	$800	$12,000	30.0%
16	$64,000	$1,600	$25,600	64.0%	16	$52,000	$800	$12,800	32.0%
17	$65,600	$1,600	$27,200	68.0%	17	$52,800	$800	$13,600	34.0%
18	$67,200	$1,600	$28,800	72.0%	18	$53,600	$800	$14,400	36.0%
19	$68,800	$1,600	$30,400	76.0%	19	$54,400	$800	$15,200	38.0%
20	$70,400	$1,600	$32,000	80.0%	20	$55,200	$800	$16,000	40.0%

Table 4.2. Value to Employees Receiving 4% or 2% Merit Increase in Year 1 and Each Year for 20 Years

	Employee A: 4% Each Year					Employee B: 2% Each Year			
Year	Salary	Annual Base Pay Amount	Cumulative Amount	% of Original Base Pay	Year	Salary	Annual Base Pay Amount	Cumulative Amount	% of Original Base Pay
1	$40,000	$1,600	$1,600	4.0%	1	$40,000	$800	$800	2.0%
2	$41,600	$1,664	$3,264	8.2%	2	$40,800	$816	$1,616	4.0%
3	$43,264	$1,731	$4,995	12.5%	3	$41,616	$832	$2,448	6.1%
4	$44,995	$1,800	$6,794	17.0%	4	$42,448	$849	$3,297	8.2%
5	$46,794	$1,872	$8,666	21.7%	5	$43,297	$866	$4,163	10.4%
6	$48,666	$1,947	$10,613	26.5%	6	$44,163	$883	$5,046	12.6%
7	$50,613	$2,025	$12,637	31.6%	7	$45,046	$901	$5,947	14.9%
8	$52,637	$2,105	$14,743	36.9%	8	$45,947	$919	$6,866	17.2%
9	$54,743	$2,190	$16,932	42.3%	9	$46,866	$937	$7,804	19.5%
10	$56,932	$2,277	$19,210	48.0%	10	$47,804	$956	$8,760	21.9%
11	$59,210	$2,368	$21,578	53.9%	11	$48,760	$975	$9,735	24.3%
12	$61,578	$2,463	$24,041	60.1%	12	$49,735	$995	$10,730	26.8%
13	$64,041	$2,562	$26,603	66.5%	13	$50,730	$1,015	$11,744	29.4%
14	$66,603	$2,664	$29,267	73.2%	14	$51,744	$1,035	$12,779	31.9%
15	$69,267	$2,771	$32,038	80.1%	15	$52,779	$1,056	$13,835	34.6%
16	$72,038	$2,882	$34,919	87.3%	16	$53,835	$1,077	$14,911	37.3%
17	$74,919	$2,997	$37,916	94.8%	17	$54,911	$1,098	$16,010	40.0%
18	$77,916	$3,117	$41,033	102.6%	18	$56,010	$1,120	$17,130	42.8%
19	$81,033	$3,241	$44,274	110.7%	19	$57,130	$1,143	$18,272	45.7%
20	$84,274	$3,371	$47,645	119.1%	20	$58,272	$1,165	$19,438	48.6%

- Where performance appraisal is viewed as most successful in the private sector, it is firmly embedded in the context of management and personnel systems that provide incentives for managers to use performance appraisal as the organization intends. These incentives include managerial flexibility or discretion in rewarding top performers and in dismissing those who continually perform below standards. The size of the merit pay offered allows managers to distribute pay that differentiates outstanding performer from good and poor performers and thus provides them with incentives to differentiate. Managers are also assessed on the results of their performance-appraisal activities.
- In order for any pay-for-performance plan to be effective it must

  - define and communicate performance goals that employees understand and view as doable,
  - consistently link pay and performance, and
  - provide payouts that employees see as meaningful.

- It is important to view performance appraisal and merit pay as embedded in broader pay, personnel, management, and organizational contexts.

When it came to purpose, the committee found that the performance-appraisal system has two goals: 1) to create a measure that accurately assesses the level of a person's performance in a job, and 2) to create an evaluation system that will advance one or more of the functions of promoting communication, clarifying organizational goals, informing pay-based decisions, and motivating employees.[3]

The committee also found the following:[4]

- Organizations cannot use job analysis and the specification of performance standards to replace managerial judgment.
- The evidence supports the premise that supervisors are capable of forming reasonably reliable estimates of their employees' overall performance levels.
- When using appraisal instruments based on well-chosen and clearly defined performance dimensions, supervisors can make valid evaluations of employee performance.
- A wide variety of rating scale types and formats of evaluations exists. Research suggests that they have relatively little impact on the quality of the evaluation as long as the items chosen for evaluation are clearly defined.
- The reliability of ratings drops if there are fewer than three or more than nine rating categories. There is little to be gained from having more than five response categories.
- Some evidence shows that performance appraisal can motivate employees when the employees trust and perceive the supervisor to be knowledgeable.
- Evidence supports the assumption that the intended use of performance ratings influences results. The most consistent finding is that ratings used to make decisions on pay and promotion are more lenient than ratings used for research purposes or for feedback.

PROBLEMS WITH MERIT-PAY SYSTEMS

An effective merit-pay system must have credible, comprehensive measurements for performance. Without them, it is impossible to relate pay to performance. In most organizations, performance appraisal is not done well. As a result, they have no good measures of individual performance. Sometimes, managers simply do not have the skills to appraise performance; in other cases, the system itself is defective.

In the absence of effective measurements for performance, organizations tend to rely on the managers' subjective judgments, which are often seen by subordinates as unfair, invalid, and discriminatory. Because employees do not trust these judgments, when pay is based on them, there is a definite perception that pay is not based on performance. Many employees in this situation have reason to believe that merit pay is a myth, one that managers are forced to perpetuate. Instead of motivating employees to perform more effectively, the merit system has the opposite effect and creates distrust in management and the organization. For a merit system to affect retention, the best employees must consistently get the largest raises, and this can happen only if there are valid performance measures and a useful performance appraisal system. Too often, the appraisal system is the weakest link.

PROBLEMS IN RELATING PAY TO PERFORMANCE

Pay practices and policies can work against relating pay to performance if the library does not have the money to fund these raises. The typical pay increases often allow for only small changes in total pay. This is particularly true in years of low inflation. The difference between raises given to poor performers and those given to good performers can end up being so small that their impact is minimal and the message is, "why bother?" In order for some to receive a large increase, others may receive zero or close-to-zero percentage increases. Merit pay further compounds the problem because merit payments often become part of the base salary, thereby creating an annuity that, for as long as the person stays with the organization, pays for past performance, a situation that can be especially acute in high inflation years.

Relating pay to performance is made more difficult by salary schedules that include a top rate the organization can pay. Good performers may well "top out," or reach the top of the range of their grade and henceforth be unable to receive any merit increases they have earned. The combined effect of raises given in low and high inflation years and the annuity effect of past performance increases nearly always creates a situation in which the best performers are likely to be paid the same as low performers who have simply been around for a long time and performed adequately. The latter have worked their way to the top because of the compounding effect of annual merit increases.

Poor and average performers rarely quit because of their treatment by merit-pay systems. On the other hand, the best performers are likely to look for other jobs. One response by managers is to find ways to frequently promote the best performers. Another approach is to attempt to give a higher increase to high-performing employees who are below average salary. The problem is that high-performing employees who have higher-than-average salaries may then be given low increases, especially if those raises are based on percentages. What could be less motivating than that? It simply says that performance does not count. The simple fact is that the annuity effect of merit pay means that there is no way to have both total compensation and changes in compensation reflect current performance.

POORLY MANAGED MERIT-PAY SYSTEMS

There are a number of ways in which poorly run merit-pay systems can actually negatively affect the relationship between performance and pay. Managers often fail to recommend widely different pay increases when widely different performance levels are present. Some are simply unwilling to explain their decisions to those they supervise. Often their rationale relates to the reality that not enough raise money is available to give both cost-of-living increases that everyone should receive and large merit increases to those who deserve them. Faced with informing employees of their low raises, managers also sometimes disown their own pay decisions: "I fought hard for you to get a good raise but lost out," or "My hands are tied by the administration." The message conveyed to the employee is that there is no relationship between performance and pay.

Newer forms of organizations have complex structures that entail matrix or network structures and teams. These structures make tying pay to performance even more difficult because of their multiple reporting relationships and interdependent activities, which makes judging individual performance more difficult.

Even though pay for performance is a desirable goal, more and more organizations distribute pay increases that are aimed at helping individuals keep from losing real income. The future of pay for performance would appear to be bleak. However, there are positive trends as well.

POSITIVE ASPECTS OF PAY FOR PERFORMANCE

More than ever, organizations need the performance motivation that can be generated when pay is successfully tied to performance. Organizations are becoming more flat, reducing the number of promotion opportunities. People are more likely to stay in their jobs for longer periods of time and need the motivation of pay.

There is a continuing belief in the United States that pay should be related to performance, even though there may be distrust in how that pay is distributed. In response to matrices and teams, organizations have encouraged employee participation in measuring performance and determining rewards. Peers often have better information, and when they are motivated to participate in appraisal, they can often make better judgments than the supervisor can do alone.

SUGGESTIONS FOR IMPLEMENTING MERIT PAY

The following suggestions are offered to libraries considering implementing a merit-pay plan.

- Use a bonus system. A merit-based bonus approach can produce a true pay-for-performance system. Rather than adjusting an individual's base pay for a good year, which is then compounded for the remainder of that person's career, consider a bonus system that rewards current performance. For a bonus system to work, it is also important that the base pay be adjusted annually to reflect the market. Often working against this in the public sector are state laws that prohibit a bonus system.

- Pay attention to the process. In addition to a good system of bonuses and base rates, the library will need to openly communicate its pay policies and decision processes. Attention must be given to describing the system and explaining how decisions are made. Employees must be able to see the relationship between performance and pay.

- Take performance appraisal seriously. All employees must be trained in how the performance-appraisal process works. All employees must be given an appraisal. No supervisor will be permitted to refuse. Performance measures must be mutually agreed upon, results jointly reviewed, and pay actions discussed. If these practices are not acceptable or possible, pay increases should not be based on performance appraisals.

- Focus on factors that affect the pay system. For example, jobs must be well defined and job descriptions up-to-date. An organization with poorly designed jobs or unclear assignment of responsibility will find it difficult to measure employee performance or assign merit values.

- Include group and team performance in the evaluation. One option is to award separate amounts of money for team performance and for individual performance. Another is to evaluate first the team and then the individuals in the team. Another possibility is to make team contributions part of the individual assessment process.

- Consider special awards. Normal merit budgets do not often permit the recognition of major performance accomplishments, but it might be possible to set aside money for separate, Nobel prize–type awards. Even small awards can be made important to employees.

- Develop an appeals process that is fair and perceived by employees as fair. Consider appointing a panel of peers to review appeals with the understanding that their recommendations are advisory to the decision maker. It is incumbent on the ultimate decision maker that panel recommendations be carefully considered and judiciously implemented.

- Adhere to rules for procedural justice. The effectiveness of a merit-pay plan depends on the perceived fairness of the procedures as well as the amounts allocated to increases. Rules that foster perceptions of fairness include consistent allocations, suppression of bias, accurate and correctable decisions, representation by the recipient, and ethical treatment.

- Consider pay secrecy. An open system is not necessarily better than a closed system. Under an open merit-pay plan, satisfaction may be greater but likely to produce smaller differences in the performance ratings and therefore smaller merit increase differences between the high and low performers.

- Be aware of laws and regulations. Merit-pay decisions must be made in compliance with laws and regulations as well as organizational policy. Major laws and regulations that relate to merit pay include Title VII of the 1964 Civil Rights Act, the Equal Pay Act, the Age Discrimination in Employment Act, the National Labor Relations Act, and the Merit Pay Reform Act.

PAY SECRECY

Pay systems can range from being "open" to being "closed." Under an open system, nearly all information relating to pay levels and increases is known to employees. An example of an open system are land grant universities. Employee salaries must be made public, and therefore all employees can easily find out the salaries of other employees. At the other extreme are organizations with closed pay systems in which pay information is kept totally confidential. In some organizations, only the employee is given information on pay level and salary increases. Although not an option for universities, some organizations use a partially closed system. Here, the individual employees are informed about their merit increases and also told the range of increases granted to others, but not the actual amounts. This allows the employees to view their own positions without knowing all of the other employees' pay levels and increases.

It is becoming more and more difficult to administer merit-pay systems as organizations become more complex and the workforce more demanding. There is no right answer for all organizations. If done well, however, pay for performance can be effective.

NOTES

1. Janet Wiscombe, "Can Pay for Performance Really Work?" *Workforce* 80, no. 8 (August 2001): 28–33.
2. George T. Milkovich and Alexandra K. Wigdor, eds., *Pay for Performance: Evaluating Performance Appraisals and Merit Pay* (Washington, DC: National Academy Press, 1991).
3. Ibid., p. 2.
4. Ibid., pp. 2–3.

BIBLIOGRAPHY

Abosch, Kenan S. "Variable Pay: Do We Have the Basics in Place?" *Compensation and Benefits Review* 30, no. 4 (July/August 1998): 12–22.

Aggarwal, Raj, and Andrew Samwick. *Performance Incentives Within Firms: The Effect of Managerial Responsibility.* Cambridge, MA: National Bureau of Economic Research, 1999.

Budman, Matthew. "Is There Merit in Merit Pay?" *Across the Board* 34 (June 1997): 33–6.

Cooke, Martha. "Humiliation as Motivator?" *Meetings and Conventions* 36, no. 8 (July 2001): 26–8.

Eskew, Don, and Robert L. Heneman. "A Survey of Merit Pay Plan Effectiveness: End of the Line for Merit Pay or Hope for Improvement?" *Human Resource Planning* 19, no. 2 (1996): 12–19.

Estes, Barbara. "Critical Elements in Developing an Effective Reward Strategy." *Employment Relations Today* 28, no. 1 (Spring 2001): 43–54.

Francese, Heather, and Elliot Susseles. "Pay-for-Performance in the Public Sector." *Journal of Compensation and Benefits* 16, no. 6 (November/December 2000): 32–6.

Gleason, Barbara. "Pay for Performance." *Educational Leadership* 57, no. 5 (February 2000): 82–3.

Heneman, Robert L., and Courtney Von Hippel. "Balancing Group and Individual Rewards: Rewarding Individual Contributions to the Team." *Compensation and Benefits Review* 27 (July/August 1995): 63.

Hollensbe, Elaine C. "Group Pay-for-Performance Plans: The Role of Spontaneous Goal Setting." *Academy of Management Review* 25, no. 4 (October 2000): 864–73.

Kamm, Robert H. "Compensation: Pay for Performance or Investment?" *Compensation and Benefits Management* 17, no. 2 (Spring 2001): 68–71.

Lavelle, Louis. "Undermining Pay for Performance Executives." *Business Week* no. 3715 (January 15, 2001): 70–2.

Lazear, Edward P. *Output-Based Pay: Incentives or Sorting?* Cambridge, MA: National Bureau of Economic Research, 1999.

McCollum, Sandra. "How Merit Pay Improves Education." *Educational Leadership* 58, no. 5 (February 2001): 21–4.

Milkovich, George T., and Alexandra K. Wigdor, eds. *Pay for Performance: Evaluating Performance Appraisals and Merit Pay.* Washington, DC: National Academy Press, 1991.

"Pay for Performance." *CMA Management* 74, no. 9 (November 2000): 8–10.

Schwartz, Andrew E. *Performance Management.* Hauppauge, NY: Barron's Educational Series, 1999.

Stajkovic, Alexander D., and Fred Luthans. "Differential Effects of Incentive Motivators on Work Performance." *Academy of Management Journal* 44, no. 3 (June 2001): 580–91.

Szypko, Mark A. "Variable Pay: Funding Design and Metrics." *HR Focus* 76, no. 8 (August 1999): S1–S2.

Thornburg, Linda. "Variable Compensation Software: An Emerging Market." *HR Magazine* 46, no. 5 (May 2001): 109–13.

Tulgan, Bruce. "Real Pay for Performance." *Journal of Business Strategy* 22, no. 3 (May/June 2001): 19–23.

U.S. Senate Committee on Governmental Affairs, Subcommittee on Oversight of Government Management, Restructuring, and the District Of Columbia. *The Effectiveness of Federal Employee Incentive Programs: Hearing Before the Oversight of Government Management, Restructuring, and the District of Colum-*

bia Subcommittee of the Committee on Governmental Affairs. 106th Cong., 2nd sess., May 2, 2000.

Wiscombe, Janet. "Can Pay for Performance Really Work?" *Workforce* 80, no. 8 (August 2001): 28–33.

Zingheim, Patricia K., and Jay R. Schuster. *Pay People Right! Breakthrough Reward Strategies to Create Great Companies.* San Francisco: Jossey-Bass, 2000.

5 PERFORMANCE APPRAISALS AND PAY

Recognition for a job well done is high on the list of motivating influences for all people; more important in many instances than compensation itself.

—JOHN M. WILSON

The appraisal of performance is both inevitable and universal. In the absence of a formal performance-appraisal system, people will judge the work performance of others, including subordinates, informally and arbitrarily. This inclination to judge others can create serious motivational, ethical, and legal problems, and without a well-thought-out appraisal system, there is little chance that the judgments made will be accurate or fair, let alone legally defensible. At its best, the performance-review process encourages employees to put forth their best effort and work to achieve both personal and organizational goals. At its worst, employees are made to feel unimportant, abused, and unappreciated for the job they have done. Tensions mount; feelings are hurt; goodwill is lost. Few issues stir up more controversy in the workplace than performance appraisals. What is written in an evaluation can have a huge impact on employee-supervisor and personal relationships. The result can be resentment and serious morale problems leading to workplace disruption and decline in productivity, which can potentially spread among coworkers.

Nonetheless, organizations must have a process by which rewards can be distributed fairly to those most deserving. Employees have a greater acceptance of the performance-appraisal process when the process is directly linked to rewards. When a performance appraisal is conducted properly, both supervisors and subordinates see the experience as beneficial and positive. It provides an opportunity to focus on work activities and goals, to identify and correct existing problems, and to encourage better performance in the future.

EFFECTS OF PERFORMANCE APPRAISAL

A performance appraisal provides employees with recognition—either positive or negative—for their efforts. The power of recognition should not be underestimated; some evidence suggests that human beings prefer negative recognition to no recognition at all. An appraisal program that tells employees that the organization is interested in their performance and development can have a strong positive influence on an individual's sense of worth, commitment, and belonging. In some organizations, absenteeism and turnover rates have been greatly reduced when more attention was given to performance appraisals.

APPRAISAL PROCESS

The performance-appraisal process is a structured interaction between an employee and supervisor that usually takes the form of an annual or semi-annual interview. During the interview, the work performance of the subordinate is examined and discussed, with the goal of identifying weaknesses and strengths, as well as opportunities for improvement, skill development, and career advancement. The most significant benefit of a performance appraisal is that it offers the opportunity for a supervisor and employee to have a one-on-one discussion of important work issues that might not otherwise be addressed. For some employees, the appraisal interview may be the only time they get to have exclusive, uninterrupted access to their supervisor. The value of this scheduled interaction between a supervisor and employee is that it gives the employee an opportunity to have a discussion focused on performance issues in a way that just is not possible during the ordinary course of the workday. Rarely do employees have an opportunity during day-to-day interactions to tell their supervisors how they could do better.

Performance appraisals also offer an opportunity for a supervisor and employee to recognize and agree on individual training and development needs. Performance appraisals can make the need for training more pressing and relevant by clearly linking it to performance outcomes and future career aspirations. For the organization as a whole, consolidated appraisal data can form a picture of the overall demand for training.

MEASURING PERFORMANCE: PERFORMANCE APPRAISAL FORMATS

In calling on supervisors to sort out how well individuals have performed and what their pay should be, an organization hopes that supervisors can disentangle the effects of ambiguous job descriptions, job changes, and their own likes and dislikes to make accurate and valid judgments. This hope is rarely realized, however, as supervisors and managers bring their own biases and concerns to the task.

The situation is made more difficult by the fact that most people think they are performing well. About 80 percent of employees believe they are above average in performance. As a result, many employees end up disappointed and in conflict with their supervisors over their performance ratings.

Despite the problems, it is possible to create performance-appraisal systems that work. There are six types of appraisal formats that fall into two general categories. In one category are all of the formats that involve ranking to compare employees to each other. These include straight ranking, alternate ranking, paired comparison, and forced distribution The second group includes formats that compare performance data against standards, including behaviorally anchored rating scales (BARS) and the management-by-objectives (MBO) appraisal process. MBO appears to have the most potential for evaluation of professional staff in libraries. Its biggest drawback is the difficulty in tying merit assignments to the evaluations.

Ranking

Ranking is the simplest and least costly form of evaluation for small groups of employees performing the same work. The key is "performing the same work." Seldom in libraries are there groups of employees performing the same work. The following are the most common ranking systems:

- Straight ranking. Employees are compared against each other in terms of the overall value of their performance to the organization. The highest performer is identified, and successive individuals are ordered by level of overall performance.
- Alternate ranking. The top and bottom performances in the group are identified and removed from the list. From the remaining list, the top and bottom performers are selected. This is continued until all employees are ranked.
- Paired comparison. Each employee is compared (paired) with every other employee. One's overall ranking depends on the number of times an employee is ranked higher in performance than the other employee in each pair.
- Forced distribution. This system requires the appraiser to allocate a certain percentage of work group members to certain categories such as superior (5 percent), above average (15 percent), average (60 percent), below average (15 percent), and unacceptable (5 percent) performances.

Although cost effective and relatively easy to administer, ranking methods for appraising are unusable with diverse work groups like those in libraries. They do nothing for employee development and are not useful for determining merit. They may be effective in production settings.

Standard Rating Scales

In standard rating scales, performance standards are developed and defined for the appraiser. For each performance standard, there is a measurement scale that the appraiser uses to assign a number to the performance level. Standard rating scales are inexpensive and easy to use. They provide point values that can be used for merit, but those points may not be easily defended if contested.

Behaviorally Anchored Rating Scales BARS are a variant of the standard rating scales in which the various scale levels are anchored with behavioral descriptions directly applicable to jobs being evaluated. These descriptions identify a complete range of behaviors relative to a performance dimension of a single job or group of jobs. Each behavior, from the most negative to the most acceptable, provides intervals for the assignment of specific numbers of points for each. This assessment format is costly and time consuming to develop and requires skilled personnel, but when done well, it yields useful information for employee development, merit decisions, and employee feedback.

Management by Objectives MBO is both a planning and an appraisal process. Organizational goals are identified and distributed to supervisors and staff. The employee and supervisor write individual work objectives or goals that support organizational goals in a participatory process. Once goals have been mutually determined, they become the standards against which employee performance is evaluated. In the review session, both the employee and the supervisor assess actual goal accomplishment. This process affords both parties an excellent opportunity to discuss the employee's work behavior and development. The supervisor has a role as teacher, leader, and counselor and is not viewed as a judge. If done correctly, the process is basically a self-appraisal by the employee. However, it is not easily used for merit decisions because of the difficulty of comparing objectives among employees. It is expensive to develop and time consuming to use. The MBO approach appeals to well-motivated, self-starting responsible individuals like those found in libraries. It is not as effective for those employees who rely heavily on the supervisor for planning and control of their work. Overall, MBO is the best system to use in libraries with largely exempt staff and librarians.

APPRAISER ERRORS

Over the years, appraisers have been guilty of making the following rater errors:

- Halo effect. A rating of excellent in one quality influences the appraiser to give the employee a similar rating in other qualities, higher than deserved.
- Horn effect. A rating of unsatisfactory in one quality influences the appraiser to give the employee a similar rating in other qualities, lower than deserved.
- Central tendency. A rating of average or around the midpoint for all qualities.
- Strict rating. Rating the employee lower than would the average appraiser. The appraiser is overly harsh in rating employee qualities.
- Lenient rating. Rating the employee higher than would the average appraiser. The appraiser is overly generous in rating employee qualities.
- Bias about recent behavior. Rating the employee by recent behavior and failing to recognize the most commonly demonstrated behavior over the entire appraisal period.

Like all other employees, appraisers are subject to the same problems and forces that influence all human behavior. The appraisal process is often a stressful activity for supervisors, and they make errors for a number of reasons:

- Desire to be accepted. When one employee is evaluated by another, there is always the possibility that the rating could damage their relationship.
- Concern with job security. Supervisors know that their success depends on the cooperation, effort, and contributions of those they supervise and that disagreements over evaluations can affect the performance of the entire group.
- Concern with self-protection. An individual's response to an appraisal can be unpredictable, and an appraiser may have reason to believe that the employee who receives an unsatisfactory rating may retaliate.
- Affiliation with those who hold similar views. It is always easier to communicate and be with people who have similar views or similar qualities. Those who have similar views or qualities may well receive higher ratings from the supervisors.

CRITICISMS OF PERFORMANCE APPRAISALS

Performance appraisals regularly get negative reviews. In fact, some individuals claim that performance-appraisal systems are so fundamentally flawed as to be manipulative, abusive, autocratic, and counterproductive. If such labels are indeed accurate, one conclusion might be to eliminate the process altogether. A number of management gurus have come to this very conclusion and have called for abolishing performance appraisals. Such a reaction, however, seems far too strong and—from a legal perspective—problematic for employers. Because performance appraisals provide many important legal and other benefits, employers should consider improving appraisals rather than discarding the process.

A major criticism of appraisals is that they tend to discourage collaboration. Performance appraisals undeniably focus on individual achievements and therefore produce self-focus rather than a team focus. This is particularly problematic in organizations that embrace teamwork. But this problem can be fixed: If collaboration is essential, make it a criterion on which employees are evaluated. Appraisals that focus on—and reward—collaborative behavior will encourage teamwork. Conversely, appraisals that punish employees for working contrary to the team (e.g., withholding information) discourage anticollaborative behaviors.

Employers that do away with appraisals altogether, or that fail to focus on teamwork in the evaluation process, actually take on more legal risk if they later take adverse action against employees who do not display the desired teamwork skills. When employers do not clearly communicate the requirements for success (or how employees fail to meet those requirements), any subsequent discharges will lack adequate foundation. That leaves the door open for employees to claim that the adverse action was based on illegal discrimination.

Critics also contend that appraisals are inconsistent. Evaluators often apply the same criteria in different ways or give different weights to the same criteria.

However, a good performance-appraisal instrument increases the potential for consistency by ensuring that all similarly situated employees are evaluated on the same criteria. The abolition of appraisals increases the likelihood of inconsistency (and discrimination claims) by eliminating this common benchmark.

Appraisals, of course, should be more consistent. One way to improve consistency is to provide training for supervisors. In addition, where feasible, the library's human resources personnel or the director should review a draft of all supervisors' appraisals before they are finalized. This gives the administration an additional opportunity to focus on the consistent application of the appraisal's criteria. Employers also may wish to consider evaluating all their employees at the same time each year (as opposed to throughout the year on employees' anniversary dates). When evaluations are done at the same time, supervisors are more likely to apply the same criteria or factors consistently.

Another criticism is that the appraisal process has value only at the extreme ends of the performance scale, for those who are exceptionally able or exceptionally poor performers. Critics claim that it is impossible to quantify precisely degrees of difference between acceptable levels of performance. Even if the critics were correct and appraisal processes truly are this limited, they still would have tremendous value to employers because most employment decisions are made not in the middle but at the extremes. Performance appraisals can help justify promotional decisions for extremely good performers. They can be equally helpful, if not absolutely necessary, when deciding whom to lay off. The appraisal also has practical value in between the extremes. If sufficient detail is provided in the comments, the appraisal provides a map for middle-of-the-road employees by showing what they need to do to increase their standing within the organization or to avoid falling below expectations.

Critics who want appraisals abolished see them as too autocratic—the supervisor has all the power in a supervisor-dependent relationship. To address this charge, one of the criteria on which supervisors should be evaluated is how they evaluate their subordinates. Supervisors are less likely to abuse their power or abdicate this responsibility if they know that their professional growth hinges on how they manage and evaluate their subordinates.

In response to critics who contend that appraisals are too subjective, libraries should acknowledge that there is substantial subjectivity in appraisals, particularly at senior positions. They should then include safeguards to make sure this subjectivity is applied in a defensible way.

Another concern about appraisals is that they produce emotional anguish—that employees worry about the process and are devastated by the results. Employers should be humane with their appraisal processes and should minimize adverse emotional impact on employees. As a result, appraisals should be conducted on time, and criticism should be delivered in a constructive, nonpunitive way. The longer employees wait, the more anxious they become. Libraries should not avoid appraisals out of fear that some employees may not like what they hear. Although it may stimulate them to leave on their own initiative, employees who leave on their own are less likely to sue.

BENEFITS OF PERFORMANCE APPRAISALS

As flawed as they may be, performance appraisals still provide employers with important benefits. First, they provide a way to communicate deficiencies. The performance-appraisal process requires that supervisors take note of deficiencies in employee performance at least once a year. Without this process, supervisors may be reluctant to undertake this difficult task, and employees might never be told that their work is subpar. If underperforming workers are terminated without being given a chance to improve, they will perceive the discharge to be unfair. Unfairness is not unlawful, but it can motivate employees to take legal action. Even the most average lawyer can turn an unfair treatment claim into a discrimination or wrongful discharge claim by arguing that the employee was fired for belonging to a protected group (e.g., age) or for engaging in a protected activity (e.g., complaining about harassment).

Second, appraisals can ensure consistency. Discrimination complaints often allege that employees with similar performance levels were treated differently. However, a good performance-appraisal process increases the potential for consistency by ensuring that all employees are evaluated on the same criteria.

Third, appraisals provide a means for distinguishing among employees. Personnel decisions between similar candidates can be difficult to make and to justify. When deciding whom to promote, employers often must choose between individuals with similar skill sets, experience, and performance histories. A properly conducted performance appraisal that is consistently applied throughout the organization can help employers pinpoint the strongest (and weakest) employees. It also can help justify in court, if necessary, any positive or negative personnel actions taken.

Fourth, the process recognizes valued performers. Even in the best libraries, employees complain about a lack of appreciation and recognition. In a labor shortage, such feelings can quickly result in the loss of the best employees. The performance appraisal lets top performers know, in a concrete way, how much they are valued by the organization and is an important component of a comprehensive employee retention program.

Finally, performance appraisals can communicate a strategic vision. An important element of conducting a performance appraisal is establishing employee goals tied to the organization's broad strategic goals. For example, an organization that values diversity can reflect this by evaluating supervisory personnel on their sensitivity to and appreciation of diversity.

DISTINGUISHING BETWEEN MEETS AND EXCEEDS EXPECTATIONS

Distinguishing between employees who have had a good year or an exceptional year is difficult. One method of making that distinction is to use a "resume-building" exercise. First, ask employees to list what they are proudest of—work accomplishments, skills acquired, and so on. Tell them that you want them to brag. Besides being a good exercise for employees, it can also be a face saver for managers. It is too easy to overlook what employees consider to be major accomplishments.

To help make the distinction between a performer who meets expectations and one who exceeds them, consider asking yourself the question, "What has the person done in the past year that was so important that it should go on his or her resume?" Employees whose resumes could be updated fit into the "exceeds" group. If they do not, the employees are at "meets expectations." This strategy helps managers make tough decisions and provides a rationale to employees who question their grade. Employees in turn can ask themselves, "Am I doing things that force me to update my resume?"

CONDUCTING A SELF-DIRECTED 360 ASSESSMENT

Usually, the performance-appraisal process is completed by a single person—the supervisor. Inevitably, the feedback is a one-sided view of the employee's performance. By contrast, a standard 360 evaluation, or mutual rating, solicits feedback from colleagues above, below, and around an employee to provide observations of performance in several skills and behavioral categories, typically in a report with numeric ratings or compilation of quotes. Although this kind of 360 assessment exposes employees to a broader range of perceptions, the confidentiality of the feedback means that details are not included in the report. Without real-time explanations and clarifications, perceptions are often misunderstood or ignored.

A self-directed 360 assessment takes the benefits of the standard 360 approach a step further by providing a process for getting feedback face-to-face directly from people who work closely with an employee. Self-directed 360 gives an employee the opportunity to ask questions, listen, and get clarification on the feedback. The self-directed 360 is as likely to be set in motion by an employee as by the employer. It also personalizes the categories of feedback. The self-directed 360 seeks information on an employee's specific role and goals, as well as on the company's needs at the time of the assessment.

The self-directed 360 is full-circle evaluation involving self-evaluation and feedback from other people about one's performance in predetermined competencies and should involve the following seven steps.

Step 1: Commit to Hearing the Truth

Any assessment should ultimately be about feedback and learning. You can use the self-directed 360 to enrich an existing 360 process or as a way to get feedback if your organization does not use a 360 evaluation. Listening to an accounting of one's shortcomings is not fun, and recognizing the benefits requires not being defensive. By comparing a self-assessment with the observations of others (even when the observations are hastily delivered criticism, brutal honesty, or clumsy praise), you gain information for making the changes that will serve you well. Self-directed 360 feedback reflects your decisions and behaviors and provides a clear view of what you do most effectively and what you most need to change. It also lets you receive feedback directly from the sources rather than secondhand.

Step 2: Conduct the Self-Assessment

Planning a self-directed 360 requires identifying objectives and conducting a self-assessment. Ask what you want to learn and experience as a result of the assessment. Then link those objectives to your self-assessment and your sense of the areas in which you shine and in which you experience difficulty. It is natural to vacillate between being overly self-critical and denying unflattering feedback. High achievers tend to be too critical of themselves. They can expend tremendous energy perfecting areas that are already good enough. With denial, real development areas that an employee should focus on but does not enjoy may remain unimproved—thus short-changing the weakest areas that truly need attention. To begin a self-assessment, list areas that need development. Facing weaknesses head-on sends a message to the feedback providers that you are open to hearing and discussing criticism. Your matter-of-fact approach will give the members of your feedback circle the permission to speak freely, resulting in a significant yield of useful feedback. Next, list your strengths. That will help determine if your assessment is realistic or if you have veered into self-criticism or denial. The following list shows typical competency areas included in a self-directed 360. You will use the same items in the self-assessment and interviews with feedback providers:

- leadership
- customer focus
- results focus
- problem solving
- innovation
- vision and strategy
- risk taking
- time management
- organization
- courage and integrity
- peer collaboration
- communications
- teamwork
- empowerment
- delegation and prioritizing
- staffing
- coaching and development
- openness to learning

Choose relevant areas for your job from these competencies, and add job-specific items.

Step 3: Plan the Interviews

Planning the interviews with feedback providers involves identifying who will be in your feedback circle. With the self-assessment as your guide, you will also establish performance categories for the interviews. That involves reviewing the categories on which you rated your performance in your self-assessment and being prepared to ask your colleagues about their perceptions of your skills, competence, and performance in those areas. Next, identify the most helpful sources for feedback. Because the 360 takes its name from the idea that the full circle of people with whom you work supplies your feedback, be certain to include your manager, managers in other departments with whom you work closely, your peers in your unit, and other peers with whom you work. If you are a manager, include all of your direct reports and high potentials the next level down. It is suggested that you limit the 360 circle to 6 to 8 people if you are in an individual contributor role and to 15 to 20 people if you are a manager.

Step 4: Prepare for the Feedback

In step 4, you prepare yourself mentally and emotionally to receive feedback. Everyone handles this differently. You know when and why you become defensive, so you are in the best position to prepare yourself to listen openly. People who perform the self-assessment truthfully and candidly are typically better prepared when it comes to receiving feedback from others. And you are unlikely to be surprised by other people's feedback, whether affirming or critical, if your self-assessment has been thorough and honest. It is important that you can reassure your 360 circle of your ability to respond positively to honest feedback. If you request genuine feedback and then become argumentative, you are unlikely to receive the kind of feedback you need.

Step 5: Conduct the Interviews

Several dos and don'ts can help make the most of the 360 interviews:

• Do not argue points with the feedback providers. Feedback is perceptual. Because it is based on your colleagues' actual experiences with you and their interpretation of those experiences, there are no wrongs or rights. In the same situation, you can be perceived as a problem to one person and a solution to another. A colleague could view you as aggressive when you think you are straightforward and direct. Or someone could view you as argumentative whereas another person could see you as courageous. Differences in perspective, incongruities, and outright conflicts do not take away from feedback's usefulness. They just mean that you will have to study the feedback to discover underlying patterns and the changes you need to make. It is unlikely everyone will agree on the changes you should make.

• Do not justify your actions as a response to critical feedback. Justifications are dressed-up arguments, excuses, or explanations for why you did something that did not work. Their intent, conscious or not, is to get other people to agree with you once they hear your reasoning. That communicates that you are less interested in hearing and understanding their perspectives and more interested in expressing your own. Why you did something is irrelevant to your goal in the 360—to learn what people think of you, why they think of you that way, and how you can make the necessary changes to improve your performance.

• Do seek clarification about people's comments, but do not use trying to understand as a pretext to imply that the feedback makes no sense. Before asking a question, be certain that you are really curious and are seeking more information.

• Do ask for suggestions, advice, and assistance in working on the issues identified in the 360. For example, if a colleague observes that you do not "pull your weight" in meetings, ask him or her to suggest specific ways you could do that. And make sure you understand precisely what "pull your weight" means to that person. Ask for an example, something the person has observed. Once you understand, brainstorm together for ways to be more effective until you both agree on one.

• Do find something to genuinely appreciate about the feedback—such as taking the time to do the interview, someone's courage to be frank, or a particular comment. Such appreciation builds relationships and abates defensive feelings.

All of these suggested actions are also appropriate for any appraisal interaction with your supervisors.

Step 6: Analyze the Feedback

Next, analyze the feedback in the way that yields the richest possible information. Then create and act on your development plan. The feedback will likely contain mixed comments about your strengths and need for improvement. Review the feedback when you feel you can be open to it. As you review the feedback comments, place each one in one of three categories: strengths, areas needing improvement, and areas needing clarification. If a comment has both positive and negative aspects, place it into each appropriate category. Once you have placed the feedback in the appropriate categories, create a fourth category: trends. Look in the first three groupings to see whether comments from two or more members of your feedback circle are similar. If so, note them under trends. These are the areas you will want to really focus on because they are manifesting themselves in multiple relationships or multiple instances. In addition, look at the feedback in terms of the various relationships. For example, do you tend to meet deadlines with managers but not with your staff?

Step 7: Describe a Key Area You Plan to Change or Modify

The final step involves creating your development plan. The act of writing your intentions and seeing them in black and white makes them more real and the changes more likely to become a reality. In your development plan, repeat the following information as many times as necessary for the areas of improvement you intend to focus on: 1) optimal outcome, 2) specific steps you will take, 3) and support and other resources you will need.

Seeking genuine feedback signals a true openness to learning and improvement. Carefully examining and fully integrating that feedback speaks volumes. Seeking and using feedback, even when it is difficult to accept, says clearly that you are committed to achieving excellence and your greatest potential.

ADMINISTRATIVE SUPPORT FOR APPRAISALS

It is crucial that the library's top management believes in the value of performance appraisals and expresses their visible commitment to it. Top managers are powerful role models for other managers and employees. Where performance appraisal fails to work well, lack of support from the top levels of management is often cited as a major contributing factor.

There is a lingering suspicion among many supervisors that an employee's poor appraisal result tends to reflect badly upon them also, as the employee's supervisor. Many supervisors therefore perceive that it is in their own interest to make their subordinates "look good" on paper. When this problem exists, the cause may be an organizational culture that is intolerant of failure; supervisors may fear negative repercussions—both for themselves and their subordinate. Surveys have shown that not only do many managers admit to a little fudging; they actually defend it as a tactic necessary for effective management. For example, supervisors who have given an overly generous appraisal to a marginal performer might claim that their "legitimate" motive was the hope of encouraging a better performance. Supervisors who misrepresent to avoid the possibility of unpleasant confrontations, to hide employee difficulties from senior managers, or to punish or reward employees are not using appraisals effectively.

When properly executed, an appraisal instrument can become a powerful tool for establishing organizational culture and ensuring that employees understand and act on the organization's broad strategic goals.

BIBLIOGRAPHY

Alexander Hamilton Institute. *Effective Interviews for Every Situation: Hiring, Performance Appraisal, Discipline, Promotion, Problem-Solving, Termination.* Ramsey, NJ: Alexander Hamilton Institute, 1999.

Barsky, Noah P., and Christopher D. Flick. "Look at the Net! Performance Management Resources Are out There (and They're Free)!" *Strategic Finance Magazine* 81, no. 6 (December 1999): 26–9.

Dutton, Gail. "Making Reviews More Efficient and Fair." *Workforce* 80, no. 4 (April 2001): 76–81.

Falcone, Paul. "Rejuvenate Your Performance Evaluation Writing Skills." *HR Magazine* 44, no. 10 (October 1999): 126–32.

Flynn, Peter. "You Are Simply Average." *Across the Board* 38, no. 2 (March/April 2001): 51–5.

Grote, Dick. "Performance Appraisals: Solving Tough Challenges." *HR Magazine* 45, no. 7 (July 2000): 145–50.

———. "The Secrets of Performance Appraisal." *Across the Board* 37, no. 5 (May 2000): 14–20.

Joinson, Carla. "Making Sure Employees Measure Up." *HR Magazine* 46, no. 3 (March 2001): 36–41.

Kennedy, Marilyn Moats. "The Case Against Performance Appraisals." *Across the Board* 36, no. 1 (January 1999): 51–2.

Kikoski, John F. "Effective Communication in the Performance Appraisal Interview: Face-to-Face Communication for Public Managers in the Culturally Diverse Workplace." *Public Personnel Management* 28, no. 2 (Summer 1999): 301–22.

Lawler, Edward E. *Rewarding Excellence: Pay Strategies for the New Economy.* San Francisco: Jossey-Bass, 2000.

Lindo, David K. "Where's My Raise? Performance Appraisal Process." *Supervision* 60, no. 4 (April 1999): 6–8.

Lowery, Christopher M., and M. M. Petty. "Assessing the Merit of Merit Pay: Employee Reactions to Performance-Based Pay." *Human Resource Planning* 19, no. 1 (1996): 26–37.

Lubans, John. "I've Closed My Eyes to the Cold Hard Truth I'm Seeing: Making Performance Appraisal Work." *Library Administration and Management* 13, no. 2 (Spring 1999): 87–9.

Maloney, Donna L. "Meeting Performance Appraisal Head-On at Chicago Public Library." *Public Libraries* 40, no. 3 (May/June 2001): 178–80.

Marsden, David, Stephen French, and Katsuyuki Kubo. *Why Does Performance Pay De-Motivate? Financial Incentives Versus Performance Appraisal.* London: Centre for Economic Performance, 2000.

Martin, David C., Kathryn M. Bartol, and Patrick E. Kehoe. "The Legal Ramifications of Performance Appraisal: The Growing Significance." *Public Personnel Management* 29, no. 3 (Fall 2000): 379–406.

McMahon, Gerard V. *Performance Appraisal Skills: Best Practice for Managers.* Dublin, Ireland: Oak Tree Press, 1999.

Meade, Jim. "Visual 360: A Performance Appraisal System That's 'Fun'—From Mindsolve Technologies." *HR Magazine* 44, no. 7 (July 1999): 118.

Meyer, Gary. "Performance Reviews Made Easy, Paperless: Exxceed Performance-pro.Net Software and Online Service." *HR Magazine* 45, no. 10 (October 2000): 181–4.

Painter, Charles N. "Ten Steps for Improved Appraisals." *Supervision* 60, no. 6 (June 1999): 11–3.

Ramirez, Al. "How Merit Pay Undermines Education." *Educational Leadership* 58, no. 5 (February 2001): 16–20.

Rubenstein, Hymie. *Rewarding University Professors: A Performance-Based Approach.* Vancouver, British Columbia: Fraser Institute, 2000.

Scott, Pamela J., and Anne E. Kirby. "The SLA Competencies: Raising the Bar on Performance—Six Prototypes for Putting the Competencies into Action." *Library Journal* 124, no. 12 (July 1999): 46–8.

Segal, Jonathan A. "86 Your Appraisal Process?" *HR Magazine* 45, no. 10 (October 2000): 199–206.

Smith, Wanda J., K. Vernard Harrington, and Jeffery D. Houghton. "Predictors of Performance Appraisal Discomfort: A Preliminary Examination." *Public Personnel Management* 29, no. 1 (Spring 2000): 21–32.

Taylor, Paul J., and Jon L. Pierce. "Effects of Introducing a Performance Management System on Employees' Subsequent Attitudes and Effort." *Public Personnel Management* 28, no. 3 (Fall 1999): 423–52.

Todaro, Julie Beth. "How Am I Doing? Performance Evaluation for Teams." *Library Administration and Management* 14, no. 1 (Winter 2000): 31–4.

———. "The Beast Within: Personnel Management and Assessment, Including Web Sites." *Library Administration and Management* 13, no. 4 (Fall 1999): 192–5.

U.S. General Accounting Office. *Performance Appraisal System for Administrative, Professional, and Support Staff.* Washington, DC: U.S. General Accounting Office, 1999.

6 LIBRARY STAFF PAY STRATEGIES

*It is common sense to take a method and try it. If it fails, admit it frankly and
try another. But above all, try something.*

—FRANKLIN D. ROOSEVELT

For the purposes of this chapter and the next, the library's complement of staffing is
divided into faculty and staff. Chapter 7 will look at pay strategies for librarians
and library faculty. The discussions in this chapter focus on how pay is established
for full-time and part-time nonexempt and exempt staff. This group also typically
includes student employees who are part-time nonbenefit, nonexempt staff.
Nonexempt staff members are those persons who are protected by (not exempt
from) the provisions of the FLSA of 1938 and all of its subsequent amendments.
These are typically the lowest-level staff in the organization. The exempt staff
(not protected by the provisions of the FLSA) are usually the professional staff, or
the highest-level staff in the library. Issues of salary, appraisal, merit, and market
for staff are different from those of faculty librarians. All references in this chapter
are to staff.

INCREASING PROPORTION OF PROFESSIONAL STAFF

The complexity of technological developments in libraries has created the need for
the employment of more highly specialized personnel with advanced degrees. In
addition, there is a trend toward pushing professional level work to lower levels of
staff. The result is that activities that were once the main ingredients of librarian

positions—reference, cataloging, instruction, management—are becoming the staple of staff positions, resulting in higher-level classifications and ensuing higher-level salaries. The line between professionals, staff, and librarians has become quite blurred. In addition, there is greater emphasis on project teams, which make appraisals of personnel more difficult. One effect on pay techniques is that the systems designed to determine job levels are less capable of assigning wage levels. There has also been a shift in the preference of professionals for nonmonetary rewards, such as indirect compensation, that impacts the compensation plan.

REWARDS IN THE PUBLIC SECTOR

In the private sector, businesses are downsizing (or "rightsizing"), and in the public sector, legislative bodies are constantly debating ways to reduce the size of government. The challenge is to reduce waste and inefficiency and at the same time increase productivity. How do public-sector organizations reduce the number of people but also ensure that those who remain give their best? It cannot be accomplished by simply telling employees that they have to do more or else. The punitive "or else" might work for a while but in the long run will be counterproductive. Managers in the public sector have to find ways to be both more efficient and more productive.

Administrators may wish that employees would do things just for the good of the organization, but in reality, people mostly first do what they think is good for themselves. It is important, therefore, that managers create systems whereby people can do what is good for themselves and in doing so, also do what is good for the organization. To accomplish that, managers should answer the following questions:

- What behaviors do you want employees to exhibit? Do you want large quantities of work, or do you want good quality of work? Do you want good quality service to users, or do you want fast service? Do you want specialization or versatility?
- What do employees want from work? How many employees would work for the joy of it? Remember that people want many things from work, but primary among them is money.
- How can employees get what they want from work from doing what the organization wants them to do? In order to be effective, the organization must have a compensation system that is structured in a way that employees get what they want (money) for doing what the organization wants them to do (be productive, give good service, be versatile, etc.). To be effective, the compensation system has to meet both needs.

This chapter examines how employees are rewarded. It discusses skill-based pay, competency-based pay, gainsharing, performance management and its relationship to pay, and pay for performance. Chapter 5 dealt with performance appraisal in greater detail.

ON WHAT BASIS SHOULD RAISES BE GIVEN?

On what basis should raises be given to employees? One can begin with the assumption that organizations want to treat employees equitably and fairly. This means that the allocation of rewards should be based on a standard of fairness consistently applied across individuals within the same job and organization. Most employers can point to instances in which an employee in one department was judged differently than an employee doing the same work in another department, or to one supervisor who simply ignored the guidelines followed by all other supervisors. Ideally, one could rely on the library's top management as the ultimate authority in resolving these problems, but what if those individuals are also guilty of inconsistent or unfair treatment?

What is fair? One strategy for giving raises emphasizes equivalent treatment—all employees receive the same pay increase. A strong argument can be made that any effort to differentiate pay increases is going to be unfair. Raises could be allocated as across-the-board increases, with the magnitude determined by the organization or in conjunction with a union. Cost-of-living increases tied to changes in the consumer price index could be awarded, or increases could be based on seniority. Some combination of the three may also be used. None of these are tied to variances in individual performance.

A second strategy is to adopt a plan that differentiates pay increases based on individual performance. This approach assumes that workers are not interchangeable or equally efficient. With this approach, the worth of jobs becomes a function of the job's value (the pay grade) and the individual's performance of the job.

WHY IS ONE EMPLOYEE BETTER THAN ANOTHER?

What leads one person to do a better job than another? Part of the answer lies in three factors that influence performance:

- Job-skills match. This refers to the quality of the match between the job requirements and the individual's abilities. Skills that are exceptionally important for one job may be useless in another. Everyone is familiar with individuals who were outstanding workers who, when promoted to supervisors, were horrible.
- Motivation. Some employees are motivated to do their best; others may loaf at every opportunity.
- Unforeseen conditions. Even highly skilled employees who are motivated to perform sometimes encounter conditions beyond their control.

IMPROVING STAFF PERFORMANCE

On a superficial level, the idea of pay for performance is a viable policy to improve employee performance in organizations. Three key problems exist in translating this philosophy into everyday practice:

- Employees must value pay. Although pay can at least indirectly satisfy individual needs, it should not be assumed that pay is the primary motivator capable of solving all organizational motivation problems. Pay alone may not lead to high performance.
- If pay is a primary motivator, other detractors must be eliminated. This means that an organization must develop sound human resources systems such as recruitment, selection, planning, performance appraisal, and training to complement salary.
- Employees must believe that pay is actually tied to performance. There must be more than a policy statement to that effect; organizational practice must match the policy.

SUCCESSFUL PAY FOR PERFORMANCE

In order for pay for performance to be successful, an organization must pay attention to the following issues:

- A reasonable amount of funds must be allocated to merit so that performance differences translate into meaningful differences in pay increases.
- Supervisors must be trained to discriminate among employees' performance.
- Supervisors must be willing and able to provide feedback to employees about performance.
- Supervisors must have a supportive environment in which to make these decisions.
- These practices must be adhered to consistently over time.

SKILL-BASED PAY

Skill-based pay is primarily a private-sector compensation system. Each particular system is unique, with many variations on what is rewarded. In a typical skill-based plan, employees start out at an entry pay rate and learn a specific skill unit. Once that skill is certified as mastered, the pay rate is increased by a set amount. Employees perform that skill unit for a period of time before they are eligible to learn a new skill unit. As more skill units are mastered, the employees' pay increases until a predetermined maximum pay rate is reached. Employees are paid for the number of skill units they perform and not for the job title they have. It is often desirable that employees be able to perform several different functions and be multiskilled. Skill-based pay is described in greater detail in chapter 3.

COMPETENCY-BASED PAY

Competencies are generally understood to be similar to skills except that competencies are normally associated with all jobs, whereas skills tend to be focused on manual occupations. Competency is a concept applicable to every job and every employee. A competent employee is generally considered a good performer. Competency-based pay is a relatively new concept and one that has been implemented in very few organizations. Many of its strengths and weaknesses are not fully known.

The intent in developing a competency-based pay system is to define what successful workers are expected to be able to do at each level on the career ladder. The underlying philosophy of a competency-based pay system is that employees' value depends on what they can do, based on individual competencies. The more an employee can do, the more the organization can expect and the greater the individual's value. The intent of the pay system is to ensure that the most competent employee on a career ladder has the highest salary, the second has the second-highest salary, and so on. Future salary increases are dependent on enhanced competency; those who do not continue to grow are passed over for increases or promotions.

Competency-based pay gives new emphasis to the importance of being a competent worker. The discussions related to identifying and designing competencies help everyone understand what it takes to be a successful employee. Involving employees in developing these competencies and career ladders helps them accept the results. The profiles that result from these discussions are available to all employees and define the competencies expected of workers at each level. With traditional performance appraisal, the supervisor is expected to help employees identify and understand their strengths and weaknesses. Most employees know where their weaknesses lie, however. The emphasis of performance appraisal in a competency-based pay system shifts to helping employees develop plans to improve because workers can identify their own strengths and weaknesses. The profile makes it possible for employees to manage their own career prospects and gives them the basis on which to plan their own personal development actions.

PLANNING A COMPETENCY-BASED PAY SYSTEM

One approach in planning a competency-based pay system is to use a career ladder as a framework. Generally, employees go through four stages in their careers. Employees who are viewed, for one reason or another, as less-than-solid performers tend to get stuck in one of the stages. By defining the competencies expected at each stage, employees can begin to assess their prospects for moving up the ladder. The expectations will be essentially the same across job families. The four stages are as follows:

1. The learning stage.
   - Assignments are typically an element of a larger project, detailed but routine in nature and performed under close supervision. Individuals typically work with a mentor who helps them to develop. As they learn, they are given more responsibility.
   - Sample competency: Completes assigned tasks involving detailed work that meets the expectations of a supervisor or mentor.
2. The independent-contributor stage.
   - Individuals have their own projects or areas of responsibility, work on their own, and are accountable for results. They are expected to manage

their own time. They develop specialized competency in an area that becomes the base for career direction.
- Sample competency: Develops recognized ability to plan and carry out a project independently with little direction from a supervisor or mentor.

3. The mentor stage.
- The individuals' technical expertise is recognized, and they are expected to originate ideas and work through others, who perform the detailed work. Individuals may be appointed as managers or supervisors. They participate in a professional network of peers. They may influence projects outside of their immediate areas of responsibility.
- Sample competency: Provides the leadership and conceptual thinking needed to plan, develop support for, and complete a project involving subordinate personnel.

4. The visionary stage.
- Individuals lead the organization into new areas or ways of operating. Typical roles include entrepreneur, organizational leader, or recognized expert in a professional field. They may have established reputation in a professional field. They are expected to represent the organization in external professional meetings and may serve as leaders in professional groups.
- Sample competency: Recognized as a world-class professional in the field.

Career stages provide a framework for managers to discuss careers with employees and to facilitate the identification and definition of competencies. Aligning these stages with grades or bands can facilitate salary management in terms of both classification and pay-increase decisions.

One of the primary differences between skill-based pay and competency-based pay is that skill-based pay is typically associated with manual duties and that pay increases for newly acquired skills are normally cents per hour. An employee can gain many skills, even some that are not presently needed by the organization, adding to payroll costs. Competency-based pay is based on subjective assessments, not tests, and salaries are adjusted annually based on performance, not automatically.

Competency-based pay systems have potential for changing the focus from the supervisor controlling employee advancement to allowing employees to look at a career ladder and make advancement plans and decisions on their own. It changes the focus from the supervisor identifying employee weaknesses to allowing employees to identify their own and to work with their supervisors on improvement.

GROUP PAY PLANS

Group pay plans take on many names and forms, including gainsharing, profit sharing, team incentives, goal sharing, achievement sharing, winsharing, and results sharing. The defining characteristic of group pay-for-performance plans is that compensation varies as a function of performance achieved by a group of employees. A "group of employees" consists of any number of individuals engaged in interdependent work for interdependent rewards. In practice, groups under group pay plans vary from small to very large, with the latter often comprising multiple interdependent subgroups. As an example of a group pay plan, the following section explores gainsharing.

GAINSHARING

The ideal compensation strategy is one that energizes and engages employees, focusing them on bettering the bottom-line performance of the organization, and that links their pay at least in part directly to that performance. The strategy would bring a work group together as a team and encourage them to motivate and manage themselves, without the destructive competition of merit pay. The ideal compensation may just be something called productivity gainsharing, a strategy that rewards employees for the productivity of their work groups. Gainsharing literally shares the monetary results of the productivity increases with the employees who achieve them. Although gainsharing has been around in the private sector for many years under a number of names (e.g., Scanlon, Improshare), it has not been used widely in the public sector.

Gainsharing is a performance-contingent reward system that directly translates increases in employee productivity into financial rewards. Usually distributed equally among the employees involved, gainshares are a form of variable pay—compensation that is at risk and not normally treated as part of base pay. It is not the same as profit sharing, which is based on different factors and may not be tied directly to employee performance. It is not piece rate in that the productivity of the group, not individual workers, is measured.

In the private sector, gainsharing is relatively easy to implement because there are known costs, output, and productivity as part of the bottom line. It is more challenging in the public sector, where output and outcomes are unclear and where productivity increases sometimes are turned into smaller allocations and fewer employees. In the public sector, productivity can be rewarded with punishment because those increases may mean that the agency's budget or staffing levels will be reduced by the savings generated.

Implementation of Gainsharing

Gainsharing is in use in more that 2,000 private-sector companies and has been tried in the federal government with mixed success. These trials point to several factors critical to the success of gainsharing in the public sector:

- The elected and appointed officials must provide strong, visible support for the program.
- Internal stakeholders must support the effort.
- A singular focus on the organization's outputs and outcomes and on the customers who receive them is required—a bottom-line orientation.

- Gainsharing must be implemented in a way that complements the various other performance-management systems.
- Gainsharing requires a new approach to the way public-sector organizations work. Organizations must eliminate the possibility that successful cost-saving efforts will be met with reduced allocations.

How Gainsharing Works

Gainsharing works best in organizations with measurable outputs. The plan identifies these measures and establishes a baseline on which all future productivity is measured. Public-sector organizations often have difficulty identifying these measures because the emphasis is constantly on resource inputs (people, dollars) and throughput (process activities) but seldom on output or outcomes. The exercise of identifying the organization's outputs and outcomes is useful even if gainsharing is not being considered. In a typical gainsharing contract, agreed to by all parties beforehand, half of the realized savings reverts to the administration and half is shared among all of the employees involved.

Is gainsharing a viable option for public-sector organizations? If the goal is the ideal compensation strategy—one that energizes and engages employees, improves bottom-line performance, and links their pay directly to that performance—it is worth further investigation.

PERFORMANCE APPRAISAL

Public-sector organizations depend on the performance of their employees. In libraries, employees include those individuals who provide direct services to users as well as those who indirectly serve users. To assess how well employees perform their jobs, there must be a system in place for performance appraisal. Performance appraisal is a necessary evil in organizations but can be made to accomplish multiple objectives. Among those objectives are advising employees of work expectations, improving work performance, administering pay based on merit, making promotion decisions, and counseling employees.

Perhaps the most important development in performance appraisal in recent years is the shift from measuring a person's performance after the fact to focusing on the entire performance process while relegating appraisal to a minor role—performance management instead of performance appraisal.

PERFORMANCE MANAGEMENT

A performance-management system normally has three stages: 1) performance planning, 2) the performance period, and 3) the performance appraisal. During the planning stage, the focus is on joint development of performance definitions and goals based on the library's priorities. Given an established set of objectives for the upcoming evaluation year, the supervisor and employee agree on standards of performance. A typical system might have five levels of accomplishment:

- greatly exceeds standards
- exceeds standards
- meets standards fully
- meets standards marginally
- fails to meet standards (unsatisfactory)

Note that the levels of performance refer to standards and not to the "goodness" of the employee. The supervisor and employee agree to commit to performance goals for the year. Goals are subject to renegotiation during the year.

During the performance period, the supervisor works with the employee to accomplish agreed-upon goals. Positive feedback is given for good performance, and corrective feedback is given to address poor performance. During this period, the supervisor refers back to the performance goals and the performance standards. The system requires frequent communication and feedback so employees know at any given time how they are doing with regard to the performance plan. The topic of conversation becomes goals and standards, not character flaws.

If the first two stages are done well, the performance appraisal is anticlimactic. The supervisor and the employee know precisely what the appraisal should say, and the emphasis is placed on planning for the next year. There does need to be a final assessment to be used in merit, but more often than not, there is little disagreement on what that merit value should be.

The next step is to assign a dollar value to the performance appraisal final assessment. Using a scale of one to five, for example, one can assign "greatly exceeds standards" a five, "exceeds standards" a four, and so on. Adding all of the merit points and dividing that total into the dollars available should yield a dollar per point value that can be awarded. If done openly and aboveboard, there should be little discussion when merit dollars are distributed.

SAMPLE PERFORMANCE-MANAGEMENT POLICY

The following is a sample policy for university library staff performance appraisal based on a performance-management model.

Introduction

The library is committed to providing all staff with meaningful performance appraisals. Performance appraisals are designed to determine how well employees achieve their established goals and perform job duties. Supervisors and managers are responsible for establishing departmental goals that contribute to the university's education, research, and public-service mission. They are also responsible for working with each employee in the department to establish individual employee goals and duties that contribute to both the department's goals and the library's mission. The library is committed to providing the resources necessary to review and recognize employees based on achievement and performance on a regular and ongoing basis.

Purpose

Performance appraisal and recognition is a clearly defined and ongoing process that contributes to positive communication, mutual respect, improved performance, individual growth, and career development. This ongoing process involves frequent communication between employees and supervisors about goals and duties, performance standards, and expectations. It seeks to provide greater accountability and effectiveness and to foster a culture of quality performance and continuous improvement with a focus on internal and external customer service. Performance appraisal also includes feedback from direct reports, peers, or customers that is intended to help employees improve and develop their performance. The performance-appraisal program is designed so that employees

- are aware of what is expected of them,
- receive timely feedback about their performance,
- receive opportunities for education, training, and career development, and
- receive recognition in a fair manner.

An employee's performance will be reviewed in a fair and reasonable manner. The performance appraisal may be used as the basis for personnel decisions, including such things as career development, salary increases, and disciplinary action, if appropriate. Any performance-based disciplinary actions will be taken in accordance with the performance-management policy, unless such actions are specifically covered by a collective bargaining agreement.

Responsibility

Employees and supervisors will work together to develop individual employee goals and identify the duties that will be the basis of the employee's performance appraisal. They should also agree on training and development opportunities necessary for high-quality performance and excellent customer service. Supervisors, having dual roles of supervisor and employee, must fulfill both sets of responsibilities.

All staff and faculty who supervise one or more employees will be reviewed on their performance of the following supervisory responsibilities and the timeliness and quality of the performance appraisals conducted for each of their employees. Supervisors are responsible for

- completing training on performance appraisal and recognition,
- establishing organizational goals,
- seeking input from employees and working with employees to develop individual employee goals and identifying duties and relevant job competencies,
- providing employees with clear expectations, consistent measures, and achievable standards of performance,
- supporting and providing resources for employees to meet performance standards,
- engaging in ongoing performance appraisal that includes regular feedback on established goals/duties as well as an annual written performance appraisal,

- identifying performance deficiencies and providing assistance and support for correction,
- initiating and coordinating a multi-rater feedback process for affected employees,
- assisting employees in identifying and participating in career development and training programs, and
- recognizing outstanding performance on a regular and ongoing basis.

All employees, including those covered by a collective bargaining agreement, are responsible for

- providing input to their supervisor in the development of individual goals that contribute to departmental goals and the library's mission,
- meeting expectations and achieving performance standards,
- providing their supervisor with a self-assessment of accomplishments with respect to goals and duties, job competencies, and university values,
- discussing concerns or questions about any part of their job description or performance appraisal with their supervisor,
- participating in the multi-rater feedback process when requested, and
- identifying and participating in career development and training opportunities.

Training is critical to a quality performance-appraisal and recognition program. Individuals responsible for reviewing employee performance will complete training on how to implement the performance appraisal and recognition program. Additional programs are available to train, support, and guide supervisors and employees setting goals, giving effective feedback, and writing performance standards.

Overview of the Performance-Appraisal Process

The library's performance-appraisal process begins with the supervisor meeting with the employee to set goals, performance standards, and expectations for the upcoming year. The supervisor will provide the employee with regular feedback about performance throughout the year and complete a written performance appraisal at least annually. The supervisor and employee will meet to discuss the performance appraisal. The employee will be given reasonable advance notice of the date of the written performance appraisal. The supervisor will ask the employee to complete and submit a self-assessment prior to the performance appraisal.

The performance-appraisal form is both a planning tool and a performance-appraisal instrument. At the beginning of the appraisal period, the supervisor defines the goals, duties, and job competencies on which the employee will be reviewed during the upcoming appraisal period and places them on the performance-appraisal form. The supervisor will give a copy of the form to the employee to assist the employee in striving for excellence during the appraisal period.

Each supervisor will complete a written performance appraisal at the end of an employee's probation or trial period and thereafter at the end of each appraisal period. The appraisal period is January 1–December 31. The written performance appraisal will be completed by March 31 of the following year. Each dean or director will verify that all performance appraisals are completed by March 31 of each year.

There are four summary rating categories (from highest to lowest):

- E—performance exceeds expectations
- M—performance meets expectations
- I—performance needs improvement
- U—performance is unsatisfactory

Setting Goals, Performance Standards, and Expectations

It is critical that each employee understands the goals and duties, competencies, performance standards, and expectations on which he or she will be reviewed. Therefore, the first step of the performance appraisal process is for the supervisor to clearly define and communicate to the employee goals and duties, standards, and expectations at the beginning of the appraisal period. These standards and expectations are the basis of the ratings on the written performance appraisal.

The supervisor will meet with each employee to discuss and agree on the employee's goals and duties that will be the basis for the employee's performance appraisal. This discussion will also address how the employee's goals and duties contribute to departmental goals and the library's mission. The next step is to establish the standards and expectations that will be used at the end of the appraisal period to determine how well the employee achieved his or her goals or performed his or her duties. To be useful, these standards and expectations should be specific, measurable, attainable, realistic, and timely. The supervisor will discuss the standards and expectations for each goal or duty with the employee. The supervisor will list these goals and duties in section 1 of the performance-appraisal form. The standards and expectations may either be included on the appraisal form or documented on a separate worksheet.

The supervisor will select the job-specific competencies that are most relevant to the employee's goals and duties. The supervisor will discuss the standards and expectations for each competency with the employee. The supervisor will list the competencies in section 2 of the performance-appraisal form. The standards and expectations may either be included on the appraisal form or documented on a separate worksheet.

Next, the supervisor will discuss with the employee standards and expectations for university values. University values address behaviors common to all library employees that are necessary to perform any job and include examples of behavior covering such things as initiative, attendance, safety, and teamwork. The university's values are expressed in the Strategic Plan. These values guide and support employees in achieving the library's mission. University values are listed in section 3 of the performance-appraisal form. The standards and expectations may either be included on the appraisal form or documented on a separate worksheet.

Performance Feedback

A productive, effective work environment is achieved when each supervisor clearly communicates job requirements and expectations and provides support for each employee to meet those expectations. The supervisor will observe each employee's performance throughout the year and provide regular feedback. Problems that may impact on performance will be addressed in a timely, constructive, and corrective manner.

Written Performance Appraisal

Each supervisor is required to complete a written annual performance appraisal for each employee. The library's performance appraisal is primarily narrative in nature. Narrative appraisals are descriptive and focus specifically on individual employee responsibilities and performance. For these reasons, a narrative appraisal is more meaningful for both the employee and the supervisor. Objective facts are included in the narrative appraisal to support descriptive conclusions. The library's performance-appraisal form includes five sections: 1) goals and duties, 2) job-specific competencies, 3) university values, 4) overall rating, and 5) planning activities.

Goals and Duties At the end of the appraisal period, the supervisor describes how well and to what degree the employee accomplished his or her goals and duties developed at the beginning of the appraisal period. The supervisor should also identify other accomplishments the employee achieved during the appraisal period. An individual rating is assigned to each goal and duty, and a summary rating is assigned to the section.

Job-Specific Competencies At the end of the appraisal period, the supervisor describes how well and to what degree the employee demonstrated the job-specific competencies identified at the beginning of the appraisal period. An individual rating is assigned to each relevant competency, and a summary rating is assigned to the section.

University Values In this section, the supervisor describes how well and to what degree the employee demonstrated each university value listed using standards and expectations developed at the beginning of the appraisal period. An individual rating is assigned to each competency, and a summary rating is assigned to the section.

Overall Rating The three sections goals and duties, job-specific competencies, and university values reflect the three components of job performance. Typically, all three sections are weighted equally in determining the employee's overall performance rating. However, in some circumstances, a supervisor may weigh the sections slightly differently to reflect the specific needs of the employee or the position. If the sections are to be weighted differently, the supervisor will inform the employee at the beginning of the appraisal period when setting goals, performance standards, and expectations. An overall performance rating is assigned to this section. This rating is used to determine merit.

Planning Activities This section is designed to assist the supervisor and employee in planning for the next year and does not require a rating. This section does not contribute to the overall performance rating and therefore does not affect merit. The section covers multi-rater feedback, the employee's career-development plan, management support necessary for success, and goals and duties for the next appraisal period.

Multi-rater feedback. Multi-rater feedback is a process that allows employees to receive performance feedback from their peers, customers, and if the employee is a supervisor, direct reports (the employees who work directly for the supervisor). This process is similar to that used by many departments to assess program effectiveness or level of customer service. Multi-rater feedback is given to the specific employee, whereas department assessments are provided to the department as a whole. Multi-rater feedback is intended to increase awareness and accountability by providing the employee with multiple perspectives. This feedback will allow the employee to be more aware of areas that can be improved. The feedback will be used to assist the employee in creating a development plan that will help the employee work toward continuous improvement and will not be used to determine performance ratings or merit.

Feedback will be collected from all direct reports, as well as from designated peers and customers who have regular contact with the employee. Individuals providing feedback will assess the employee using the university's values. During the feedback period, the manager of the employee being evaluated will select appropriate individuals and solicit feedback. Feedback will remain anonymous. Before individuals can participate in the multi-rater process, they will attend training to assist them in giving useful and effective feedback. Training is also available to assist employees in receiving feedback and developing action plans. The greatest value of multi-rater feedback occurs when an employee uses the feedback to improve performance. The manager will provide the employee with summary feedback of the responses and will assist the employee in interpreting the feedback and creating an action plan. A copy of the action plan should be attached to the performance appraisal.

Career development. The supervisor and employee should use the first three sections of the performance appraisal and the feedback obtained through the multi-rater process to design a career-development plan to assist the employee in accomplishing his or her professional goals.

Management support. The supervisor and employee should identify the resources necessary for the employee to accomplish both the work-related goals and duties and career-development goals. This section should contain specific information on the management support needed.

Planning for the next appraisal period. At this point in the appraisal process, the supervisor and employee should complete the planning portions of sections 1 and 2 on a new performance-appraisal form for the next appraisal period.

Change in Supervisor A supervisor leaving a position is encouraged to document employee performance prior to leaving. If an employee's supervisor changes, the employee will normally be reviewed on the goals and duties, performance standards, and expectations stated in the last written performance appraisal. The new supervisor will meet with the employee to discuss and document any changes to the previously stated goals and duties, performance standards, and expectations.

Finalizing the Performance-Appraisal Form After completing the performance appraisal, the employee and supervisor sign the performance-appraisal form. The supervisor's signature indicates that he or she has followed the process and completed the form. The employee's signature indicates that he or she has read and understood the performance appraisal. The employee's signature does not necessarily indicate agreement.

Disagreement with Written Appraisal If a postprobationary employee disagrees with his or her written performance appraisal, the employee may

- attach a response to the performance appraisal,
- request reconsideration by the next level supervisor, or
- contact the dispute resolution department for assistance. The dispute resolution department will act as a neutral party in identifying and clarifying relevant issues in an attempt to resolve concerns about the performance appraisal.

The final decision is made by management taking into consideration any attached responses, reconsideration, and guidance from the dispute resolution department.

Recognition

Performance recognition can take many forms, both monetary and nonmonetary. To reward employees who have demonstrated excellence as reflected in their written performance appraisals, the administration may designate funds for performance increases. In addition to merit pay, there are various ways to recognize employees for their achievements. These can include career-development opportunities, certificates of appreciation, subscriptions to professional journals, and memberships in professional organizations.

Records Retention

Copies of performance appraisals will be maintained in the employee's official personnel file.

SAMPLE STAFF-APPRAISAL FORM

The following performance-appraisal form for library staff is adapted from the form in use by staff at the University of New Mexico.

PERFORMANCE APPRAISAL

Employee name
Job title
Department
Reviewing supervisor
Review period
Review date

1 GOALS AND DUTIES
- At the beginning of the review period, list goals and duties for the upcoming review period in the first column.
- At the time of the written review, describe how well and to what degree the employee accomplished the goal or duty in the second column, "Description of Results."
- In the third column, assign a rating, using the definitions that follow, for each goal or duty, based on the answers given under "Description of Results."
- Provide a summary rating for goals and duties on the line that follows.

Goal or Duty	Description of Results	Rating: E, M, I, U

Provide the appropriate summary rating of goals and duties:

Exceeds Expectations (E)	Meets Expectations (M)	Needs Improvement (I)	Unsatisfactory (U)
Achievement clearly and con-sistently exceeded requirements.	Consistently achieved goals or performed duties.	Sometimes, but not consistently, achieved goals or performed duties.	Did not achieve goals or perform duties.

2 JOB-SPECIFIC COMPETENCIES
   • At the beginning of the review period, choose the most relevant competencies from the "Knowledge, Skills, Abilities" section of the job description and list them in the first column.
   • At the time of the written review, describe how well and to what degree the employee demonstrated the competency in the second column, "Description of Results."
   • In the third column, assign a rating to each competency, based on the answers given under "Description of Results."
   • Provide a summary rating for job-specific competencies on the line that follows.

Competency (from the "Knowledge, Skills, Abilities" section of the Job Description)	Description of Results	Rating: E, M, I, U

Provide the appropriate summary rating of goals and duties:

Exceeds Expectations (E)	Meets Expectations (M)	Needs Improvement (I)	Unsatisfactory (U)
Demonstrated competencies clearly and consistently above what is required.	Consistently demonstrated competencies.	Sometimes, but not consistently, demonstrated competencies.	Did not demonstrate competencies.

3 VALUES

- The values are derived from the strategic plan. The values guide and support us in achieving our mission. All employees are expected to demonstrate behaviors that support the values that are listed in the following areas. Under each value are examples of behaviors that reflect that value.
- At the time of the written review, describe how well and to what degree the employee demonstrated the listed behavior in the second column, "Description of Results."
- In the third column, assign a rating to each behavior, based on the answers given under "Description of Results."
- Provide a summary rating for values on the line that follows.

Values and Examples of Behaviors	Description of Results	Rating: E, M, I, U
Excellence The library values excellence and creativity in its people, programs, and facilities. Excellence is demonstrated by customer service, teamwork, and quality work.		
Example 1. Provides quality customer service to students, patients, colleagues, and the public. Consistently demonstrates effective face-to-face, telephone, and electronic interaction with all patrons. Meets or exceeds the needs or requests of the patrons so that the number of complaints is reduced from that of the review period before. Accomplishes these goals throughout the current review period.		
Example 2. Works effectively and productively as a team member. Treats others with respect and confidence and uses initiative to support and help coworkers when their workload allows.		

Values and Examples of Behaviors	Description of Results	Rating: E, M, I, U

Example 3. Produces high-quality results; learns from mistakes. Uses all means and re-sources to meet patron needs; listens to and thoroughly understands patron inquiries. Recognizes that making mistakes is inevitable; applies lessons learned from these experiences to future job performance.

Diligence and Initiative The library encourages initiative and rewards diligence and hard work, which are demonstrated by productivity, resourcefulness, attendance, and safety.

Example 4. Consistently engages in work-related activity and makes productive use of work time. Completes assigned duties in a conscientious and timely manner. Shows self-reliance in accomplishing tasks.

Example 5. Seeks out new job assignments; suggests ways to improve work. Demonstrates awareness of work flow and opportunities for career advancement with potential new job duties. Provides suggestions to improve duties when workload allows.

Example 6. Arrives to work on time, is prudent in use of leave, and adheres to leave policies.

Example 7. Follows safe work practices and participates in required safety training. Is concerned with and informed about following established safety practices in the workplace. As such, participates in all required safety training and safety-policy reviews.

Integrity and Professionalism The library strives to ensure a climate of trust, which is demonstrated by accountability, responsible stewardship, and positively representing the library.

Example 8. Consistently engages in work-related activity and makes productive use of work time. Completes assigned duties in a conscientious and timely manner. Shows self-reliance in accomplishing tasks.

Values and Examples of Behaviors	Description of Results	Rating: E, M, I, U
Example 9. Seeks out new job assignments; suggests ways to improve work. Demonstrates awareness of work flow and opportunities for career advancement with potential new job duties. Provides suggestions to improve duties when workload allows.		
Example 10. Demonstrates ability to solve problems independently.		
Diversity The library values the diversity of its people and their ideas. A diverse community is based on tolerance and treats all individuals with the highest regard.		
Example 11. Treats people with respect and civility. Consistently shows through both language and demeanor an ability to foster a nonjudgmental atmosphere for both employees and library patrons. Actively encourages others to refrain from activities that may be considered disrespectful or uncivil.		
Example 12. Demonstrates tolerance and acceptance of differences.		
Example 13. Adapts well to change in the work environment. Supports, implements, and adapts to changes in a diverse work environment by fully discussing implications and procedures with supervisors and team members to minimize obstacles, maximize communication, and promote consensus within the team throughout the current evaluation period.		
Inquisitiveness and Academic Freedom The library protects and fosters an environment of open-mindedness and encourages the exploration of new ideas. These values are demonstrated by contributing to an environment that respects inquiry and supports continuous improvement and innovation.		
Example 14. Demonstrates an interest in learning; keeps current in field. Participates in career development or training sessions. Reads job-related literature for reference. Stays current with automation updates.		

Values and Examples of Behaviors	Description of Results	Rating: E, M, I, U
Example 15. Works to identify, explore, and share innovative and creative ideas. Identifies and explores these by attending at least one academic or professional meeting, training session, or product demonstration or by sharing with the department at least one idea gathered from an article, discussion, or other working group some time within the calendar year.		

Provide the appropriate summary rating of goals and duties:

Exceeds Expectations (E)	Meets Expectations (M)	Needs Improvement (I)	Unsatisfactory (U)
Demonstrated values clearly and consistently above what is required.	Consistently demonstrated values.	Sometimes, but not consistently, demonstrated values.	Did not demonstrate values.

4 OVERALL RATING
- Use the information from sections 1 to 3 to develop an overall rating. This rating is used to determine merit. Provide a narrative summary and select an overall rating from the following chart below that best expresses the summary.

Exceeds Expectations (E)	Meets Expectations (M)	Needs Improvement (I)	Unsatisfactory (U)
Clearly and consistently exceeded the requirements of the job.	Consistently met the requirements of the job.	Sometimes, but not consistently, met requirements of the job.	Did not meet the requirements of the job.

5 PLANNING ACTIVITIES

| A. Multi-rater feedback | Did the employee participate in multi-rater feedback? Yes   No
If yes, please summarize and attach supporting documentation. |
|---|---|
| B. Career-development plan | Did the employee complete a career plan? Yes   No
If yes, please summarize and attach supporting documentation. |
| C. Management support | Describe what management actions will be taken to assist the employee during the coming year. |

D. Planning for next review period	Start planning for the next review period by completing the first columns in sections 1 and 2 of a new performance-appraisal form. List goals and duties, job-specific competencies, and standards to be evaluated during the next review period.

I have had the opportunity to review this document and discuss its contents with my supervisor. My signature acknowledges that I have been informed of my performance ratings but does not necessarily indicate agreement.

Employee Signature _____

Date _____ /_____ /_____

Supervisor Signature _____

Date _____ /_____ /_____

Employee Comments (*Additional sheets may be attached*)

BIBLIOGRAPHY

American Health Lawyers Association. *Compensation Survey: In-House Government and Academic Positions*. Washington, DC: American Health Lawyers Association, 1999.

American Production and Inventory Control Society. *1999 APICS Salary Survey: Compensation Information for the Resource Management Professional*. Alexandria, VA: American Production and Inventory Control Society, 1999.

Baker, Kermit, and Pradeep Ramesh Dalal. *Compensation at U.S. Architecture Firms: 1999 AIA Report*. Washington, DC: American Institute of Architects, 1999.

Baubles, Kimberly, Amber Dolly, Timothy Klatka, and Erica Schaub. *Salary Differences Between Male and Female Physical Therapists at Entry into the Profession*. Research project, Springfield College, 1999.

Bertrand, Marianne, and Kevin F. Hallock. *The Gender Gap in Top Corporate Jobs*. Cambridge, MA: National Bureau of Economic Research, 2000.

Bowen, David E., Stephen W. Gilliland, and Roger Folger. "HRM and Service Fairness: How Being Fair with Employees Spills Over to Customers." *Organizational Dynamics* 27, no. 3 (Winter 1999): 6–23.

Brennan, Nancy, and Carola Cowan. *Where Are the Jobs? What Do They Pay? Annual Covered Employment and Wages*. Casper, WY: Wyoming Department of Employment, 2000.

College and University Personnel Association. *1999–2000 Mid-Level Administrative/Professional Salary Survey*. Washington, DC: College and University Personnel Association, 2000.

————. *2000–2001 Administrative Compensation Survey: The Benchmarking Source for Higher Education Salaries*. Washington, DC: College and University Personnel Association, 2001.

————. *2000–2001 Mid-Level Administrative/Professional Salary Survey*. Washington, DC: College and University Personnel Association, 2001.

Darnay, Arsen J. *American Salaries and Wages Survey: Statistical Data Derived from More Than 200 Government, Business, and News Sources*. Detroit, MI: Gale Group, 2001.

Ding, Mae Lon. *Over 1500 Surveys and Their Sources*. Anaheim, CA: Personnel Systems Associates, 2000.

Educational Research Service. *Salaries and Wages for Professional and Support Personnel in Public Schools*. Arlington, VA: Educational Research Service, 2001.

Federation of Public Employees, American Federation of Teachers, and American Federation of Labor and Congress of Industrial Organizations. *FPE/AFT Compensation Survey, 2000: A Survey of Professional, Scientific and Related Occupations in State Government*. Washington, DC: Federation of Public Employees, American Federation of Teachers, and American Federation of Labor and Congress of Industrial Organizations, 2000.

Feenstra, Robert C., and Gordon Hanson. *Global Production Sharing and Rising Inequality: A Survey of Trade and Wages*. Cambridge, MA: National Bureau of Economic Research, 2001.

Flint, Jacqueline Kay. *Factors Affecting Salaries of Public Administrators*. Master's thesis (MPA), California State University, Northridge, 1999.

Fox, Charlie. "Library Support Staff Salary Survey: 2000." *Library Mosaics* 11, no. 4 (July/August 2000): 8–12.

Global HR Solutions Survey Unit, PricewaterhouseCoopers. *Internet Survey, 2000: A Comprehensive Survey of Base Salary, Annual Bonus and Long-Term Incentives for Key Executive Positions*. Westport, CT: Global HR Solutions Survey Unit, PricewaterhouseCoopers, 2000.

————. *A Study of Compensation in Public Internet Companies, 1999: A Comprehensive Survey of Base Salary, Annual Bonus, and Long-Term Incentives for Key Executive Positions*. Westport, CT: Global HR Solutions Survey Unit, PricewaterhouseCoopers, 2000.

Hay Group. *Study to Assess the Compensation and Skills of Medical Library Professionals vs. Information Technology Professionals*. Chicago: Medical Library Association, 2000.

Hospital and Healthcare Compensation Service. *Hospital Salary and Benefits Report 2000–2001*. Oakland, NJ: Hospital and Healthcare Compensation Service, 2000.

Institute of Electrical and Electronics Engineers. *Salary Benchmarks: A Personal Workbook, a Companion to the IEEE-USA Salary and Fringe Benefit Survey, 1999–2000 Edition*. Piscataway, NJ: Institute of Electrical and Electronics Engineers, 1999.

Minnesota Council of Nonprofits. *Minnesota Nonprofit Salary and Benefits Survey*. Saint Paul, MN: Minnesota Council of Nonprofits, 1999.

Moulder, Evelina R. *Compensation and Benefits for Local Government Employees: Programs and Practices*. Washington, DC: International City/County Management Association, 2001.

National Association for Law Placement. *Starting Salaries: What New Law Graduates Earn—Class of 1999*. Washington, DC: 2000

National Society of Professional Engineers. *Income and Salary Survey*. Washington, DC: National Society of Professional Engineers, 2000.

Nevada Department of Personnel. *Salary and Benefits Survey. Nevada Employers*. Carson City, NV: Nevada Department of Personnel, 2000.

New England Museum Association. *1998/1999 Salary and Benefits Survey*. Boston, MA: New England Museum Association, 1999.

O'Shaughnessy, K.C., David I. Levine, and Peter Cappelli. *Changes in Managerial Pay Structures, 1986–1992, and Rising Returns to Skill*. Cambridge, MA: National Bureau of Economic Research, 2000.

Reynolds, Calvin. *2000 Guide to Global Compensation and Benefits*. San Diego, CA: Harcourt Professional, 2000.

Romac International. *Salary Survey and Career Navigator Information Technology*. Tampa, FL: Romac International, 1999.

U.S. Bureau of Labor Statistics. *Where Are the Markets, Jobs, and Highest Wages?* Washington, DC: U.S. Department of Labor, Bureau of Labor Statistics, 2001.

Washington Software Alliance. *1999–2000 Salary Survey*. Seattle, WA: Washington Software Alliance Press, 1999.

Watson Wyatt Data Services. *Compensation Survey 2000*. Rochelle, NJ: Watson Wyatt Data Services, 2000.

7   LIBRARIAN
PAY STRATEGIES

If we take people as we find them we may make them worse, but if we treat
them as though they are what they should be, we help them to become what
they are capable of becoming.

—JOHANN WOLFGANG VON GOETHE

This chapter examines pay strategies for librarians and library faculty. Issues of
salary, appraisal, merit, and market for library faculty are all quite different from
those of library staff. Too often, salary issues of library staff and librarians become in-
tertwined when in fact the two are often quite distinct. For example, when market
is discussed, librarians' salaries must be compared to a national average, not a local
average. In addition, a large number of library staff members are nonexempt, and
their working conditions are strictly governed by law. All librarians are exempt from
such coverage. All references in this chapter are to librarians or library faculty.

MARKET

Librarians and library faculty members are recruited through national and international searches. The process involves advertising widely and encouraging applications from individuals who meet the posted qualifications. These searches are
normally conducted by committees charged with eliciting applications, screening
the applicant pool for bona fide candidates, and recommending a short list of candidates after conducting telephone interviews with the applicants' references and
others. The committee also arranges for and conducts on-site interviews. Following

the interview, participants are encouraged to submit their recommendations to the committee, who forwards the information to the hiring officer.

After the time and effort spent on recruiting and hiring the best candidate for a position, it is in the best interest of the library to provide an opportunity for that person to successfully earn tenure and promotion and, if a contributing member of the library faculty, be retained. The library has a significant investment in a tenured individual and does not want to lose that person to another library because salaries are not competitive. To be competitive, the library needs to be aware of what other libraries are offering librarians to perform similar work, all other things being equal. One way to maintain that awareness is to conduct salary surveys and use those already in existence.

SALARY SURVEYS

Salary surveys are a common means of gathering data for comparing librarian salaries. Libraries may wish to conduct a survey or use information from existing surveys. An excellent source of existing surveys is the Association of Research Libraries (ARL). ARL is a not-for-profit membership organization comprising the leading research libraries in North America. Its mission is to shape and influence forces affecting the future of research libraries in the process of scholarly communication. ARL programs and services promote equitable access to and effective use of recorded knowledge in support of teaching, research, scholarship, and community service. The association articulates the concerns of research libraries and their institutions, forges coalitions, influences information policy development, and supports innovation and improvements in research library operations. It operates as a forum for the exchange of ideas and as an agent for collective action. There are currently more than 120 member organizations. Salary surveys of ARL members are published annually.

The *ARL Annual Salary Survey* is a compilation of data covering more than 12,000 professional positions in ARL libraries. Tables display average, median, and beginning salaries; salaries by position and experience, sex, and race/ethnic background; and salaries in different geographic regions and sizes of libraries. Additional tables cover law, medical, Canadian, and nonuniversity research libraries.

In addition, demographic information, such as year of birth, years of experience in a specific library, education credentials, and so on, has been occasionally collected. Such information was published for the first time in *The Age Demographics of Academic Librarians: A Profession Apart*, by Stanley Wilder.

NATIONAL AVERAGE SALARIES FOR LIBRARIANS

The *ARL Annual Salary Survey 2000–2001* reports on 8,882 professional staff members for the 112 ARL university libraries (including law and medical libraries) and 3,731 staff members for the 10 nonuniversity ARL libraries. It reports that ARL librarians' salaries are barely keeping up with inflation. The median salary for combined U.S. and Canadian salaries increased only 3.3 percent over 2001, compared with the 3.7 percent and 3.0 percent rise in U.S. and Canadian consumer price indexes, respectively. Overall, the median ARL university library salary was reported at $49,068, and $62,521 for ARL nonuniversity library staff. Only ARL nonuniversity salaries increased at a rate higher than the rate of inflation (4.2 percent). Salaries in private U.S. ARL university libraries continue to exceed those paid in publicly supported U.S. university libraries, an average of 4.5 percent more.[1]

FACULTY RANK, STATUS, AND TENURE FOR LIBRARIANS

The Association of College and Research Libraries (ACRL), a division of the American Library Association (ALA), is a professional association of academic librarians and other interested individuals. It is dedicated to enhancing the ability of academic library and information professionals to serve the information needs of the higher-education community and to improve learning, teaching, and research. The ACRL is the largest division of the ALA. The ACRL's current membership is approximately 11,000, accounting for nearly 20 percent of the total ALA membership. The ACRL provides a broad range of professional services and programs for a diverse membership.

The ACRL supports faculty rank, status, and tenure for librarians to ensure that their rights, privileges, and responsibilities in all institutional settings reflect that they are an integral part of the academic mission of the institutions in which they serve. In a recent survey of more than 900 member libraries, the ACRL asked questions about faculty rank, status, and tenure, as well as whether librarians had salary equivalency with teaching faculty. The following is the summary data from that survey, in which libraries were asked to indicate the degree to which the following standards applied to their institutions.[2]

	Not at All	Partially	Fully	Total
Degree to which librarians have the following:	% (Number) of Libraries	% (Number) of Libraries	% (Number) of Libraries	% (Number) of Libraries
Professional responsibility	24.7% (198)	29.2% (234)	46.1% (370)	100% (802)
Governance structure	21.5% (189)	25.7% (226)	52.8% (464)	100% (879)
Eligible for governing bodies	30.4% (243)	39.1% (313)	30.5% (244)	100% (800)
Salary equivalency	43.3% (365)	18.1% (152)	38.6% (325)	100% (842)
Tenure	35.5% (300)	20.9% (176)	43.6% (369)	100% (845)
Peer review	35.2% (291)	19.4% (160)	45.4% (375)	100% (826)
Leave	21.1% (168)	40.0% (267)	47.9% (400)	100% (835)
Research funding	13.0% (104)	15.6% (124)	71.4% (569)	100% (797)
Academic freedom	.3% (3)	91.6% (894)	8.1% (79)	100% (976)

Of the 976 responding libraries, 894, or 91.6 percent, reported that they had partial academic freedom, but 43.3 percent (365) reported that they did not have salary equivalency to teaching faculty.

PERFORMANCE EVALUATION

Annual increases in librarian salaries are almost always tied to an assessment of the previous year's performance. This section looks at specific performance-appraisal processes for librarians.

Depending on the library's orientation, librarians may be subjected to stafflike evaluations or to faculty reviews. In either instance, however, the fit is not a good one. If required to participate in an annual evaluation like staff because they have 12-month appointments like staff, librarians likely feel that the process does not work very well. The staff evaluation is often focused on clerical or nonprofessional duties. If they are required to participate in the teaching faculty review process, the fit may be even worse. Unfortunately, some campuses have little in the way of faculty review except that provided through the tenure and promotion process, post-tenure, or student evaluations of teaching.

In response to the need for an annual review apart from, or instead of, a regular tenure and promotion process, it is a good idea to have a separate system in place. Libraries that have effective performance-appraisal processes can counter accountability demands that are occasionally made by legislatures. The library is usually one of the largest single staff employers on campus, and the human resources department will expect that the library will evaluate all of its staff.

PERFORMANCE APPRAISAL FOR FACULTY LIBRARIANS

The 45 to 50 ARL members who have faculty status for librarians often face a dual system for evaluation. The tenure and promotion process provides for a schedule of reviews leading to tenure and to promotion, and a separate appraisal process provides for annual assessments. Libraries with a combination of faculty and nonfaculty status or an equivalent status also often have dual evaluation systems.

The tenure and promotion process is beyond the scope of this book, so this chapter will focus on the annual review process. Anyone who has investigated the review processes for librarians will acknowledge that it is a difficult issue in many libraries. One cannot evaluate a librarian using a staff form or staff expectations. One also cannot evaluate a librarian based on student evaluations. It must be accepted that the work of librarians is different from both staff and teaching faculty.

PERFORMANCE MANAGEMENT

One approach to evaluating librarians is to use a performance-management system. That process provides for the individual to identify the goals and objectives for the coming year and to discuss them with the individual who will complete the assessment form. The result is a negotiated list of objectives that are in keeping with the library's stated priorities and strategic plan. In the system used at the University of New Mexico, librarianship, research, and service objectives are included. During the year, these objectives are updated as necessary in response to change. At the end of the year, the librarian provides a written assessment of the objectives to the supervisor, who writes a final assessment. The supervisor and the librarian meet to discuss and finalize the assessment and agree on a merit rating for librarianship. The librarian provides a committee of peers with a complete listing of service and research accomplishments during the year. It will then recommend merit points in the two areas to the dean. Added together, the librarianship points (60 percent), research points (25 percent), and service points (15 percent) make up the merit point value for the year. The complete policy used at the University of New Mexico is given in the appendix to this chapter.

DETERMINING FACULTY RAISES BASED ON MERIT

Under a merit system, the next step in the evaluation process is to determine faculty raises based on merit points. An easy calculation is to divide the dollars available by the total number of points assigned to all librarians. Next, multiply each librarian's points by the value of each point.

Problems inherent in this system are the same as those found in every system. In order for pay for performance to be successful, an organization must pay attention to the following issues:

- A reasonable amount of funds must be allocated to merit so that performance differences translate into meaningful differences in pay increases. If sufficient funds are not available for meaningful merit increases, these points can be banked and used in successive years when funds are available.
- Supervisors must be trained to discriminate among employees' performance in the assignment of librarianship points. The supervisor of librarians who has the philosophy that all librarians must be "10" fouls up the system for everyone else. When libraries are aware that a particular supervisor is applying this errant philosophy, it may have to employ the system differently for those persons who report to that supervisor than for those who do not in order to minimize the impact when assigning points.
- Supervisors must be willing and able to provide feedback to employees about performance. To have a successful merit system requires that everyone use the same general scale. The system's credibility is damaged when it is generally known that a supervisor does not give lower points to a nonperformer.
- The supervisor must have a supportive environment in which to make these decisions.
- It is crucial that these practices be adhered to consistently over time.

SALARY REVIEW

One effective approach to ensuring some measure of fairness in the distribution of merit is to have a committee of peers determine the merit points for individuals. Another approach is to establish a library salary review board made up of peers to field concerns and complaints about equity. One such board has been in place at the University of New Mexico General Library since the early 1990s. The salary review board is composed of both faculty and staff members and deals with both faculty and staff salary issues. The individual faculty or staff member is encouraged to submit a written request to the board. Members then compile data or refer to existing tables in writing its recommendation to the administration. In addition to responding to requests, the board initiates salary studies and reviews in preparation for dealing with faculty and staff concerns. The board is not involved in setting salaries, but it does advise the administration when asked about starting salaries or specific salary issues. The members of the board are appointed for indeterminate terms by the library administration.

APPENDIX

ANNUAL ASSESSMENT OF GENERAL LIBRARY FACULTY

Summary

The purpose of the annual evaluation of all library faculty is to assess the performance of the individual faculty member. The dean and associate dean are reviewed under separate policy. An assessment will be conducted in February and/or early March to review job performance during the previous calendar year. The basis of the review will be a negotiated list of job objectives that expands on the faculty member's individual statement of job responsibilities and that includes activities in the areas of job performance, research and scholarship, and service. The review will take into account individual differences in job responsibilities and in professional abilities. An open, ongoing dialog between the faculty member and the supervisor is critical to the success of the assessment process. The assessment will include a merit recommendation. The assessment process is complemented by the activities of the mentor. A separate process, tenured review of untenured faculty, provides feedback on progress toward code 3, tenure, and promotion.

Purpose

- To assess job performance.
- To measure employee's contribution to the library.
- To identify individual objectives to be used for evaluating job performance.
- To determine merit recommendations.
- To provide feedback on employee's performance.
- To determine training and development needs.

Procedure Guidelines

Documents

An expanded Annual Supplement to the Biographical Record packet is the core documentation used in all faculty reviews. The expanded Annual Supplement to the Biographical Record includes (1) the Annual Supplement to the Biographical Record form provided by the University Secretary's Office with any added sheets as needed and (2) a list of proposed objectives for the current calendar year. (The Annual Supplement to the Biographical Record will be referred to as the Biographical Supplement from this point forward.)

In Section 1 "Teaching" of the Biographical Supplement, all faculty should include (1) primary job responsibilities (ex: science reference librarian, coordinator for CSEL library instruction, and selector for mathematics) and (2) accomplishments for the previous year related to the previous years' objectives. Sections 2–9 should be completed following the given instructions. As noted on the form, additional sheets can be added as needed. Attachments that are continuations of sections 1–9 of the form will be forwarded to the University Secretary unless noted otherwise. Faculty members may also attach a written self-evaluation. [The list of proposed objectives for the current calendar year and the self-evaluation (if provided) should be labeled as such and will not be forwarded to the University Secretary's Office.]

Schedule

- Library-wide Supervisor Assessment Process. Due mid-January.
- The assessment of supervisors is completed as part of the Library-wide supervisor assessment process. All library staff and faculty are encouraged to participate in the performance assessment of supervisors. The submission process must be completed by mid-January with an exact date announced each year by the director of budget and personnel.
- Faculty Annual Review Packet. Due January 31.
- Each faculty member sends an expanded Biographical Supplement packet to the supervisor. See Documents section.
- The faculty member also sends a copy of Biographical Supplement (without proposed list of objectives and self-evaluation, if provided) to the Dean's Office.
- The Dean's Office makes a copy for review by the Faculty Merit Points Committee and a copy for the Library Personnel file. The Dean's Office forwards the Biographical Supplement to the University Secretary in compliance with University guidelines.
- Code 1, 2, 4 and 5 Faculty Review Packet. Due January 31.
- Code 1, 2, 4 and 5 library faculty will turn in a review packet to the director of budget and personnel. The packet includes
    (1) the Expanded Biographical Supplement,
    (2) current resume, and
    (3) offprint or similar copy of any new published or creative work or evidence of work in progress.

- Annual Review Conducted by Supervisor. Due mid-March.
- The supervisor reviews the expanded Biographical Supplement and reaches agreement with supervisee on negotiated objectives for the current calendar year, writes an annual review document for signature by both parties, and includes a merit recommendation for librarianship. Reviews including list of negotiated objectives are submitted to Library Personnel by mid-March with the exact date announced each year by the director of budget and personnel.
- Review of Untenured Faculty by Tenured Faculty. Completed by third week in February.
- The tenured faculty meets and reviews Code 1, 2, 4, and 5 faculty review packets. The Faculty Convener is responsible for coordinating these reviews by tenured faculty.

Reviews

Faculty Annual Review

- During February and/or early March, all faculty members will meet with their supervisors for annual reviews. Supervisors and supervisees will meet to review performance during the previous year and to negotiate objectives for the current calendar year. The Expanded Biographical Supplement packet will be the basis for the review.
- During the meeting, the supervisor and supervisee will review the negotiated list of objectives from the previous calendar year. At this meeting, the supervisee will describe to what extent the objectives have been met. In case an objective was not met, the supervisee has the opportunity to explain why. The supervisee can also identify other accomplishments that were not listed on the previous year's list of objectives. The performance evaluation process recognizes that opportunities may occur during the year that were not included on the previous year's list.
- The list of objectives for the current calendar year is a negotiated product. The objectives should be specific. It is important that the supervisor and the supervisee mutually understand each objective and how the objective will be accomplished and measured. It is the supervisor's responsibility to include objectives reflecting the library's goals. It is the supervisee's responsibility to identify objectives that are appropriate for his or her statement of job responsibilities.
- Objectives may be revised at any time during the year in consultation with the supervisor and/or department head.
- During the meeting and as described in the Faculty Merit Criteria Guidelines document, the supervisor will assign a numerical value to librarianship. [The Faculty Merit Points Committee will assign a numerical value to the two other categories: (1) research, scholarship and creative works, and (2) service, based upon the Biographical Supplement.]

- Based on the discussion with the supervisee, the supervisor will prepare a final copy of the annual review document by early March for signature by the supervisee and supervisor.
- This document along with the Biographical Supplement and the list of negotiated objectives will be sent to Library Personnel by mid-March with exact due date announced each year by the director of budget and personnel.
- During merit discussions, Library Personnel will give a copy to the Library administrative group. Merit points for librarianship may be adjusted during the administrative group discussion.
- If the supervisor and the supervisee cannot come to an agreement about a performance assessment, a mediation committee will be formed at the request of the supervisee. This committee will consist of individuals who are familiar with the supervisee's performance. The supervisor and the supervisee will select the committee members. The mediation committee will consist of at least two library faculty members, all of whom are agreeable to both the supervisor and the supervisee. The mediation committee will prepare its own assessment document after meeting with the supervisor and the supervisee. The committee will then present its document to the supervisor and the supervisee. Based on the assessment document submitted by the mediation committee, the supervisor may revise his or her assessment document. The committee's document will be attached to the supervisor's report. If the mediation committee cannot resolve the disagreement, other options can be explored with the director of budget and personnel.

The following reviews apply only to faculty members in the specified group—supervisors, untenured faculty, and tenured faculty.

Assessment of Supervisors

The annual performance evaluation includes a supervisor assessment component.

- All staff and faculty are encouraged to complete these forms for supervisors and department heads.
- The evaluation forms are forwarded by the associate dean to the supervisor's department head; in the case of a department head, to the appropriate Dean's Cabinet member; and in the case of a Dean's Cabinet member, to the appropriate administrator.
- The supervisor assessment should be part of the respective supervisor's annual review meeting with his/her supervisor as described in "Faculty Annual Review" section and taken into consideration in preparing the annual review document.

Review of untenured faculty by tenured faculty.

- By January 31, each untenured faculty member in code years 1, 2, 4, and 5 will provide the director of budget and personnel with a review folder to be placed in the Dean's Office. The folder will consist of the following material:

a.   current resume;

b.   expanded biographical supplement (as described earlier under Documents); and

c.   offprint or similar copy of any new published or creative work or evidence of work in progress from the previous year.

- The tenured faculty will meet during February to review each individual's packet and to prepare a progress report.
- Copies of each progress report will be distributed by the Faculty Convener to the individual, the supervisor, the supervisor's department head if applicable, the Dean of library services, the sponsor, and the library personnel file. The progress reports will become part of the individual's code 3 and tenure packets.
- The Dean or associate dean will meet with the individual, the sponsor, and the supervisor to discuss the report.

Tenured faculty.

"The Post Tenure Review Policy ensures that all tenured faculty members will receive an annual review and that those with either exceptionally good performance or deficiency in one or more areas will be identified. Special achievement shall be rewarded in a manner determined by each college/school. For a faculty member who receives two successive annual reviews with identified uncorrected deficiencies, the Post-Tenure Review policy provides a mechanism to either (a) overturn the findings of deficiency in the annual reviews or (b) establish a remedial program for correcting the deficiencies." *Section 4.9.1, page B-24, UNM Faculty Handbook Policy on Academic Freedom and Tenure, approved 12/98*

Tenured faculty are reviewed under the Faculty Annual Review section of this document. The annual review document shall be made available to the Dean by Library Personnel for review and retained in the faculty member's official personnel file.

Dean and associate dean evaluations.

The procedures in the existing policy, Dean and associate dean annual progress review, will be followed. [Discontinued].

This policy was revised on January 11, 1993 and administratively reviewed on February 22, 2000. Latest revision approved by Library Faculty on November 13, 2000.

http://www.unm.edu/unm.html
The University of New Mexico
Albuquerque, New Mexico
Copyright © 2000 The University of New Mexico.

Faculty Merit Criteria Guidelines

The categories for merit recommendations are the same as those used for promotion and tenure.

1. Librarianship/Teaching
2. Scholarship, Research, and Creative Work
3. Service

Librarianship/Teaching

- The faculty member should show evidence of performing above average in this area. Performing one's job at a minimal level is not considered meritorious.
- Each faculty member must have a statement of job responsibilities, which will be the starting point for evaluating that faculty member. During the evaluation period each year, the faculty member and the supervisor will review the statement of job responsibilities and set up objectives to be achieved in the coming year.

The statement of job responsibilities and the agreed upon objectives will form the basis for determining how well the individual has performed in the area of librarianship.

Some suggestions for the supervisor to consider in evaluating the fulfillment of objectives established for the previous year are listed below. Since job responsibilities differ, care should be taken to apply these criteria as they relate to the faculty member's job responsibilities and objectives.

- Development and implementation of teaching methods which result in significant improvements in services or operations in the library.
- Ability to perform functions in a creative and innovative fashion and/or to introduce innovative procedures, techniques, etc.
- Productivity combined with quality.
- Contribution of job performance to the overall performance and enhancement of the unit.
- Evaluation of the faculty member based on feedback from library patrons, colleagues, and library employees.
- Honors and awards presented to the faculty member (awards are not included if only for travel, i.e., Professional Enrichment Awards).
- Grants received for library materials, facilities, equipment, and supplies.
- Job-related library committees.

If any of the activities listed below are stated as job objectives, they will be included under the category of librarianship/teaching.

- In-house reports and guides.
- Relevant activities which enhance knowledge of new developments in areas related to the person's job such as credit courses, seminars, workshops, short courses.
- Teaching of courses.

- Consulting, for example, review and assessment of programs in other institutions; providing instruction or conferring with off-campus visitors about specific library operations or services within the individual's statement of job responsibilities.

Scholarship, Research, and Creative Work

The quality of work in any one year is not the determining factor in the evaluation. The crucial factors are the quality of work and its research or creative value as demonstrated by publication, public display, or performance. Scholarship in library science or in subject specialties is to be considered. Scholarship, research, and creative work are of equal value. Work in progress is also to be considered. The statement of job responsibilities and the agreed-upon objectives will form the basis for determining how well the individual has performed in the area of scholarship, research, and creative work.

A suggested ranking follows:

- Books authored or co-authored
- Refereed journal articles authored or co-authored
- Books edited
- Invited essays or chapters
- Chapters authored or co-authored
- Refereed proceedings (full paper or abstracts)
- Presentations of papers
- Research grants
- Awards and honors for research activities (awards are not included if only for travel, i.e., Professional Enrichment Awards)
- Non-refereed journal articles authored or co-authored
- Reviews of manuscripts for scholarly publications
- Editing, compiling, and indexing of substantial published works
- Working papers
- Book reviews
- Contributions to abstracts and indexes
- Articles in newsletters
- Letters to the editor
- Works in progress (ranked according to the type of work, amount of accomplishment to date, and potential for publication)

Other areas which may be considered as part of the evaluation of research and other creative activities are:

- Participation in scholarly activities of an academic or professional organizations, such as conducting lectures, workshops, seminars, and poster sessions
- Advanced degrees earned
- Bibliographies or databases for publication or dissemination
- Translations

Service

Service may include: service to the University community, activity in professional organizations on an international, national, regional, state, or local level, and service to the civic community. The statement of job responsibilities and the agreed-upon objectives will form the basis for determining how well the individual has performed in the area of service.

Considerations in this area:

- Quantity and quality of the individual's contribution to the functioning of the university or professional organization. (Weight should be given to type of participation as officer, chairperson, committee member, etc.)
- Credit should also be given for membership on committees or attendance at meetings

Weighting of the Criteria

The goal of the document is to establish a range of criteria which would allow for 0 merit raise to exceptional merit raise. Librarianship will be considered the most heavily weighted of the three major areas. An individual must achieve the minimum standard of excellence in librarianship before they may be considered for merit in any other area. Merely a standard performance in this area will result in a 0 merit raise. Scholarship and service should not offset inadequate job performance by failure to publish and/or perform service activities during any one year. (However, it is expected that faculty will over time show progress in all three areas.)

In order to accomplish this purpose the following range of weights has been established.

Criteria	Weight
Librarianship	60%
Research	25%
Service	15%

Note: After this proposal has been in place for three years, it would be desirable each year to average the person's percentages over a three-year period. This would avoid penalizing a faculty member who was exceptionally meritorious in a year in which the amount of money available for merit was very small.

This guideline was approved by the Library Faculty on September 17, 1990 and administratively reviewed on February 21, 2000

http://www.unm.edu/unm.html
The University of New Mexico
Albuquerque, New Mexico
Copyright © 1995 The University of New Mexico.

NOTES

1. Association of Research Libraries, *ARL Annual Salary Survey 2001–2002* (Washington, DC: Association of Research Libraries, 2001), 18.
2. Shannon Cary, "Faculty Rank, Status, and Tenure for Librarians: Current Trends," *College and Research Library News* 62, no. 5 (May 2001): 510–11.

BIBLIOGRAPHY

American Association of Law Libraries. *How to Hire a Law Librarian*. Chicago: American Association of Law Libraries, 1998.

American Association of University Professors. *More Good News, So Why the Blues? The Annual Report on the Economic Status of the Profession, 1999–2000*. Washington, DC: American Association of University Professors, 2000.

American Health Lawyers Association. *Compensation Survey: In-House, Government, and Academic Positions*. Washington, DC: American Health Lawyers Association, 1999.

American Society of Corporate Secretaries. *Directors: Selection, Orientation, Compensation, Evaluation, and Termination*. New York: American Society of Corporate Secretaries, 2001.

Association of Academic Health Sciences Libraries. *Annual Statistics of Medical School Libraries in the United States and Canada, 1999–2000*. Seattle, WA: Association of Academic Health Sciences Libraries, 2000.

Association of Research Libraries. *ARL Annual Salary Survey 2000–2001*. Washington, DC: Association of Research Libraries, 2001.

Blessing, Laura K. "Using Statistical Techniques to Reduce Salary Inequities Among Librarians at the University of Texas at Arlington." *Library Administration and Management* 15, no. 2 (Spring 2001): 80–4.

Brown, Patricia Q. *Salaries and Tenure of Full-Time Instructional Faculty on 9- and 10-Month Contracts, 1997–1998*. Washington, DC: U.S. Department of Education, Office of Educational Research and Improvement, National Center for Education Statistics, 1999.

Cary, Shannon. "Faculty Rank, Status, and Tenure for Librarians: Current Trends." *College and Research Library News* 62, no. 5 (May 2001): 510–11.

College and University Personnel Association. *2000–2001 Administrative Compensation Survey: The Benchmarking Source for Higher Education Salaries*. Washington, DC: College and University Personnel Association, 2001.

———. *2000–2001 Mid-Level Administrative/Professional Salary Survey*. Washington, DC: College and University Personnel Association, 2001.

———. *2000–2001 National Faculty Salary Survey by Discipline and Rank in Private Four-Year Colleges and Universities*. Washington, DC: College and University Professional Association for Human Resources, 2001.

———. *2000–2001 National Faculty Salary Survey by Discipline and Rank in Public Four-Year Colleges and Universities*. Washington, DC: College and University Professional Association for Human Resources, 2001.

Council on Foundations. *Grantmakers Salary and Benefits Report*. Washington, DC: Council on Foundations, 2000.

Educational Research Service. *Salaries and Wages for Professional and Support Personnel in Public Schools*. Arlington, VA: Educational Research Service, 2001.

Employers Group. *The National Compensation Survey on Information Technology Professionals*. Los Angeles: Employers Group, 1999.

Gaskell, Carolyn, and Allen S. Morrill. *Travel, Sabbatical, and Study Leave Policies in College Libraries*. Chicago: Chicago Library Information Packet Committee, College Libraries Section, Association of College and Research Libraries, 2001.

Gregory, Vicki Lovelady. "Beating Inflation Now." *Library Journal* 124, no. 17 (October 15, 1999): 36–42.

Hay Group. *Study to Assess the Compensation and Skills of Medical Library Professionals vs. Information Technology Professionals*. Chicago: Medical Library Association, 2000.

Hoppe, Katherine Sutton. *The Relationship Between Faculty Reward Structures and Instructional Technology Initiatives: An Exploratory Investigation*. Ph.D. thesis, University of North Carolina at Greensboro, 2000.

International City/County Management Association. *Compensation 99: An Annual Report on Local Government Executive Salaries and Fringe Benefits*. Washington, DC: International City/County Management Association, 1999.

Larue, James. "Can't Get No Satisfaction: Library Pay in the 21st Century." *American Libraries* 31, no. 3 (March 2000): 36–8.

Matarazzo, James M. "Who Wants to Be a Millionaire (Sic Librarian!)." *Journal of Academic Librarianship* 26, no. 5 (September 2000): 309–10.

McFadden, John J. *Executive Compensation*. Bryn Mawr, PA: The American College, 2001.

National Center for Education Statistics. *Background Characteristics, Work Activities, and Compensation of Faculty and Instructional Staff in Postsecondary Institutions: Fall 1998*. Washington, DC: GPO, 2001.

Nettles, Michael T., Laura W. Perna, and Ellen M. Bradburn. *Salary, Promotion, and Tenure Status of Minority and Women Faculty in U.S. Colleges and Universities 1993 National Study of Postsecondary Faculty (NSOPF:93)*. Washington, DC: U.S. Department of Education, Office of Educational Research and Improvement, National Center for Education Statistics, Educational Resources Information Center, 2000.

Overton, Bruce B. *Executive Compensation Answer Book: 1999 Supplement*. New York: Panel, 1999.

Pitzer, Rob. *SLA Annual Salary Survey 2000*. Washington, DC: Special Libraries Association, 2000.

Rubenstein, Hymie. *Rewarding University Professors: A Performance-Based Approach*. Vancouver, British Columbia: Fraser Institute, 2000.

Schneider, Karen G. "All the Basic Issues Come Back to—Money." *American Libraries* 31, no. 3 (March 2000): 35.

Seaman, Scott, Nancy Carter, and Carol Krismann. "Market Equity Tempered by Career Merit: A Case Study—Librarian Salaries at the University of

Colorado at Boulder." *Journal of Academic Librarianship* 26, no. 4 (July 2000): 225–32.

State of Washington, Department of Personnel. *Compensation Plan for Higher Education.* Olympia, WA: State of Washington, Department of Personnel, 1999.

Sutton, Terry P., and Peter J. Bergerson. "Faculty Compensation Systems: Impact on the Quality of Higher Education." San Francisco: Jossey-Bass, 2001.

University Professionals of Illinois. *Revenue, Budget Priorities, and Higher Education Spending in the Fifty States: A Report.* Chicago: University Professionals of Illinois, 2001.

Waters, Richard Lee. "How Much Do We Pay Our Public Library Directors? Part 1." *Public Library Quarterly* 19, no. 1 (2001): 47.

———. "How Much Do We Pay Our Public Library Directors? Part 2." *Public Library Quarterly* 19, no. 2 (2001): 23.

Wilder, Stanley. *The Age Demographics of Academic Librarians: A Profession Apart.* New York: Haworth Information Press, 1999.

8   WAGE GAP
   AND PAY EQUITY

If you treat people right, they will treat you right—ninety percent of the time.

—FRANKLIN D. ROOSEVELT

PAY EQUITY

Pay equity is a policy that seeks to eliminate sex and race bias from the wage-setting process. Jobs held predominantly by women and minorities have been historically undervalued and underpaid. Pay equity is achieved when the average compensation for predominantly female job classes is equal to the average compensation for the predominantly male job classes of comparable skill, effort, responsibility, working conditions, and other relevant work-related criteria. Pay equity also means that equitable pay relationships exist among all employees of one organization. The criteria used to value jobs and set wages should be sex and race neutral.[1]

Background

In the 25 years between 1876 and 1900, library work changed from a predominantly male profession to one dominated by females. A study from 1876 revealed that 19 percent of the 1,612 librarians in the United States were female. By 1900, there were 4,184 librarians, 3,125 (74.7 percent) of whom were women. By 1930, 91.5 percent of all librarians were women. Like teaching and nursing, librarianship had become a predominantly female profession with salaries that were lower than in male-dominated occupations. Employers could pay women less than men were paid during the nineteenth century because it was legal to do so. It was argued that female library workers saved the taxpayers money and provided the nurturing care that libraries gave to its users. Is it any wonder then that when pay equity became an issue in the 1970s, librarians became leaders in lobbying for equal treatment and were involved in actions to remedy the inequitable pay differences between librarianship and predominantly male professions?

The state of Minnesota was among the first to enact a comprehensive pay-equity program for state employees. The state also required local governments to conduct job-evaluation studies and correct inequities between predominantly male and female jobs. The Oregon pay-equity struggle was one of dozens of such campaigns in the 1980s, mostly in the public sector, that attempted to upgrade wages for undervalued female-dominated jobs, and that experience illustrates the achievements and disappointments of these campaigns. Most of the campaigns resulted in pay increases for women, but the upgrades often fell short of original expectations. Because each state's pay-equity campaign was waged independently, it was difficult to translate gains from one jurisdiction to another. The reforms occasionally bogged down in technical classification and job-evaluation issues or stalled because of recalcitrant management or because of the need to protect wages for men even as states upgraded women's wages.

Two basic approaches have been employed to address the inequities: equal employment opportunity and pay equity. Equal employment opportunity focused on preventing discrimination against women as well as affirmative action to move women into higher-paying jobs. Affirmative action helped establish the notion of discrimination in the job market and the need for remedial efforts. It also gave a push to eliminating occupational segregation by race and gender.

Pay equity, also known as comparable worth, continued where affirmative action left off. Instead of being directed at individuals, it was a collective reform targeted at the sex segregation of jobs and the undervaluation of women's jobs. It held the promise of upgrading wages in the jobs where women actually worked, as opposed to affirmative action hiring, and took aim at the wage gap between male- and female-dominated jobs. It attempted to expand the reach of the Equal Pay Act, which had been interpreted to require equal pay only for the same jobs and therefore did not have a major impact on the gap between men's and women's jobs. Instead, comparable worth sought equal wages for jobs that might be dissimilar but of equal value.

Most experts conclude that pay equity, as it has been practiced, has been relatively disappointing. Wage gains were not widespread, and pay equity has not been a factor in reducing the gender wage gap.

Fading Interest?

When concern with pay equity first became a public issue toward the end of the 1970s in the United States, advocates cited the gap between the average pay of men and women as evidence of pay discrimination. Women earned less than

60 percent of the male average until the early 1980s. As of 1999, women were earning 72 percent of the male average. Under the Equal Pay Act, employers are required to pay employees performing the same work on the same basis—equal pay for equal work. Some states have gone beyond that standard to requiring equal pay for work of equal value. For states to make that determination, job-evaluation systems are needed to determine each job's value. Critics of pay equity argue that the job-evaluation systems are subject to bias and are unreliable. Despite that, public employees in some states made significant gains during the 1980s. In the most recent report by the National Committee on Pay Equity (NCPE), 42 states were reported to have conducted pay-equity studies in state government.[2]

Support for pay equity waned in the 1990s, partly because organizations were addressing the issue of equity in the absence of pay-equity studies and partly because some of the pay-equity efforts had failed. Although there is a valid argument that female-dominated jobs are underpaid, is it still true that females and males in equal jobs today are paid significantly different wages?

WAGE GAP

The NCPE reports that the wage gap for 2000 was 73 percent.[3] The wage gap is a statistical indicator often used as an index of the status of women's earnings relative to men's. It is also used to compare the earnings of people of color to those of white men. The wage gap is expressed as a percentage and is calculated by dividing the median annual earnings for women by median annual earnings for men. To calculate the wage gap for each race and sex group, median annual earnings are divided by those of white males, who are not subject to race- or sex-based discrimination. The following lists give the details in the wage gaps for the year 1999.[4]

2000 Median Annual Earnings for Year-Round, Full-Time Workers

Men	$37,339
Women	$27,355
Wage Gap	73%

2000 Median Annual Earnings by Race and Sex for Year-Round, Full-Time Workers

Race/Gender	Earnings	Wage Gap
White men	$38,869	
White women	$28,080	72%
Black men	$30,409	78%
Black women	$25,117	64%
Hispanic men	$24,638	63%
Hispanic women	$20,527	52%

GAINS IN THE PAY GAP

Since the Equal Pay Act was signed in 1963, the wage gap has been closing at a very slow rate. In 1963 women made 59 cents on average for every dollar that men

---

FROM THE NATIONAL COMMITTEE ON PAY EQUITY[5]

The Wage Gap over Time:
In Real Dollars, Women See a Widening Gap

Over the past 38 years, since the Equal Pay Act was signed in 1963, the real median earnings of women have fallen short by a total of $497,319—nearly half a million dollars. Thus, on an annual basis the average woman earns approximately $13,087 less than the average man does.

The wage gap narrowed from 64% in 1986 to 73% in 2000, but some of this is due to a decrease in men's real wages rather than an increase in women's real wages. In fact, since last year, the wage gap has narrowed slightly by 1% due to a decline in men's earnings and a leveling off among those of women.

Source: Census Bureau, 2000 Current Population Reports

Note: All figures in 2000 Dollars

Updated September, 2001

---

earned. "The State of Working America," a report by the Economic Policy Institute, a Washington, D.C.–based think tank, states that women have made pay gains on men.[6] Based on an analysis of median hourly wages, it found that in 2000 women earned 73 cents for every dollar men earned, up from 66 cents in 1989.

According to the study, the median wage for all workers grew 7.3 percent from 1995 to 1999. For male workers, the median rose 5.5 percent; for female workers, it rose 5.8 percent. For the 1989–99 period, median wages for all workers rose a more modest 2.4 percent, whereas median male wages were down 1.2 percent and median female wages rose 4.0 percent. Male workers with just a high school degree earned 6.3 percent more at the end of the four-year period; women high school graduates earned 6.2 percent more.

CHANGES IN THE WAGE GAP

The wage gap is most severe for women of color (see table 8.1). Note that numbers are not available for Hispanic men and women in 1970.

NCPE analysis shows that women in the same occupation as men, with the same work experience and in the same firm, made 89 cents on the dollar compared with men in 1999. Nonwhite and Hispanic workers made 95 cents compared with their white counterparts when controlling for these same factors.

Although interest in pay equity lags, partly because of the current pay practices of organizations and partly because of the costs associated with making the needed changes in a conservative political environment, that women earn 72 per-

Table 8.1 Median Annual Earnings of Black Men and Women, Hispanic Men and Women, and White Women as a Percentage of White Men's Median Annual Earnings

Year	White Men	Black Men	Hispanic Men	White Women	Black Women	Hispanic Women
1970	100%	69.00%	N/A	58.70%	48.20%	N/A
1975	100%	74.30%	72.10%	57.50%	55.40%	49.30%
1980	100%	70.70%	70.80%	58.90%	55.70%	50.50%
1985	100%	69.70%	68.00%	63.00%	57.10%	52.10%
1990	100%	73.10%	66.30%	69.40%	62.50%	54.30%
1992	100%	72.60%	63.35%	70.00%	64.00%	55.40%
1994	100%	75.10%	64.30%	71.60%	63.00%	55.60%
1995	100%	75.90%	63.30%	71.20%	64.20%	53.40%
1996	100%	80.00%	63.90%	73.30%	65.10%	56.60%
1997	100%	75.10%	61.40%	71.90%	62.60%	53.90%
1998	100%	74.90%	61.60%	72.60%	62.60%	53.10%
1999	100%	80.61%	61.63%	71.58%	65.05%	52.11%

cent of what men earn doing the same work is clearly inequitable. We can learn much from the efforts of pay-equity activists in libraries during the 1970s and 1980s. One important outcome of the pay-equity movement is the heightened interest in job-evaluation systems.

DEVELOPING A PAY-EQUITY CAMPAIGN

Successful campaigns for pay equity have had similar elements. In each an organized group of advocates have become educated about pay-equity issues and adopted strategies for pursuing their goals. They have developed and followed tactical plans with timetables that lay out the step-by-step activities. Successful campaigns have achieved pay-equity goals in phases over the course of several years. The key is planning.

The ALA's Committee on Pay Equity developed a pay-equity manual that provides a step-by-step process for gaining pay equity.[7]

Briefly, the steps are as follows:

1. Organize and educate a core group of activists.
2. Plan strategy and tactics for a pay-equity campaign.
3. Conduct preliminary research, such as a workforce analysis or a simplified pay-equity study, to identify sex segregation and wage inequities.
4. Campaign for adoption of recommendations for correction of pay inequities using the strategy plan.

PAY EQUITY IN MINNESOTA

Minnesota is often cited as an example of a successful pay-equity campaign. The state's Women's Commission took up the issue in the early 1970s and provided leadership for the campaign. The commission worked to organize and educate a group of unions, women's groups, and supporters to lobby the legislature for passage of pay equity acts. This group then developed tactics for achieving the established objectives for pay equity in state and local positions. Members conducted research into the problem and informed the public and the legislature about existing inequities. They pointed out, for example, that the mostly female workers who cared for mentally handicapped people made less money than the mostly male zookeepers who cared for animals in the state's zoo. A statewide Hay Associates study of positions in state government provided data for a study of male- and female-dominated positions that revealed a clear and consistent pattern of lower pay for women's jobs. The coalition of unions, women's groups, and supporters lobbied the state legislature for passage of the State Employees Pay Equity Act in 1982. The Local Government Pay Equity Act was passed two years later. The effect of these two acts was to provide pay-equity adjustments to underpaid, predominately female state and local government job classes. From the Minnesota's Hay study in 1979 to the implementation of the local government act in 1984, the planning and persistence of the campaign's leaders took time but also paid off in the end. It is important to recognize that this process takes time and commitment.

IDENTIFYING WAGE DISCRIMINATION BASED ON SEX

Do you suspect that predominately female jobs in your organization are paid less than predominantly male jobs? Is that suspicion based on fact? Whose problem is it if women are paid less than men? It is quite simply a human resources issue that requires examination and, if there is a problem, requires that the organization address it.

The segregation of male and female workers, with women being concentrated in jobs that traditionally have not been highly valued, forms the basis for pay inequities. The first step in documenting sex segregation in your organization is to gather workforce data by sex. Using this data, you can identify the salary distribution for men and women in your library and isolate the sex-segregated jobs.

It is important to gather data on all of the employees in your organization, not just the library. The following data are needed:

- a listing of all job titles or classes
- the number of employees in each job title or class
- the number and breakdown by percentage of males and females in each job title or class
- the salary range for each title or class

The best source for overall workforce data is the Equal Opportunity Commission report EEO-4. All public institutions are required to file this report annually.

Another source is the employer's affirmative action plan, which usually contains a workforce analysis. To obtain a breakdown by sex of employees in each job title, contact your human resources department or ask that the library administration make the request on your behalf. Public employers are covered by freedom-of-information laws, which require that such data be made available upon request. You may be able to obtain much of the information through publicly available budget documents, although in some instances—for example, a document that lists last name and first initial only—they will not be useful for identifying gender.

Private organizations are required to file an Equal Opportunity Commission report EEO-1, which is similar to the public institution's EEO-4. They should also have an affirmative action plan, especially if government funds are sought by the institution; employee rosters or directories may provide needed information. You may need to persevere in your search for salary data. Know what your rights are to the information and assert those rights if told you cannot have what you ask for. Once you have obtained the information, you will have to analyze it and put it into usable tables and charts. It is not likely that anyone will provide you with precisely the information you need in the form you want it.

PERFORMING A WORKFORCE ANALYSIS

The key in identifying potential wage discrimination is to collect data on the nominal employer's total workforce. If you are in a municipal library, you will gather data on the city's workforce. If you work in an academic library, you will gather data from the whole college or university. Then you can finally examine the data.

The first way to look at the data is to analyze the distribution of female and male employees by job title or class and by pay level. Using the job-title information, determine the percentage of male and female incumbents. Categorize this list by pay grade and calculate the percentage of males and females in each grade, as shown in table 8.2. This sample table shows that females are primarily in the lower pay grades.

Next, analyze the number of males and females in each pay grade to determine the earnings distributions by sex, as shown in table 8.3. This table shows that women are concentrated at the lower end of the pay grades.

Graphing the information in a different form shows clearly that there are pay-equity issues to be addressed (see figures 8.1 and 8.2).

On the other hand, if you were to find the kind of distribution shown in figure 8.3, you could assume that pay equity is not an issue in your organization.

IDENTIFYING SEX-SEGREGATED JOBS

With the information you have gathered, you are now ready to determine to what extent each job title or class is female- or male-dominated. All of the organization's job titles or classes should be grouped into three categories: male-dominated, female-dominated, and integrated titles. One note of caution: When you identify job titles, make certain that the titles are those recognized by your organization's

Table 8.2 Sample Distribution of Female and Male Employees by Percentage

Pay Grade	Annual Salary	Percentage of Females	Percentage of Males
1	$14,000	80	20
2	$16,000	65	35
3	$18,000	60	40
4	$20,000	58	42
5	$22,000	40	60
6	$24,000	34	66
7	$26,000	30	70
8	$28,000	26	74
9	$30,000	20	80
10	$32,000	15	85

Table 8.3 Sample Distribution of Female and Male Employees by Number

Pay Grade	Annual Salary	Number of Females	Number of Males
1	$14,000	8	2
2	$16,000	13	7
3	$18,000	19	12
4	$20,000	29	21
5	$22,000	18	26
6	$24,000	11	21
7	$26,000	9	21
8	$28,000	6	17
9	$30,000	5	20
10	$32,000	2	11

job-evaluation system. Some organizations classify employees according to an established list of titles and then assign them more meaningful titles. For example, the job title of Library Assistant III may be a grade 9 position, but the individual may be listed in directories as a reference assistant, a title not found in the job list. Budget documents and human resources listings may be more reliable sources for titles than directories in organizations that use a multitude of titles.

DETERMINING WHEN A JOB CLASS IS PREDOMINANTLY MALE OR FEMALE

If 70 percent or more of the individuals in a job title are of one gender, you can assume that the job is predominantly male or predominately female. Although this number may vary slightly for state to state, 70 percent is a good rule of thumb. Once a target is identified, group the job titles by the three categories. An example of the titles is shown in table 8.4. Shown are types of jobs that are dominated by

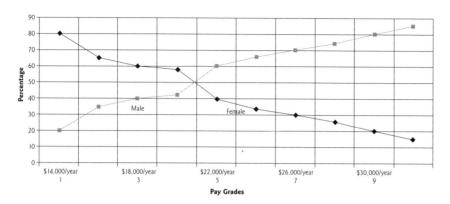

Figure 8.1 Sample Distribution of Female and Male Employees by Percentage

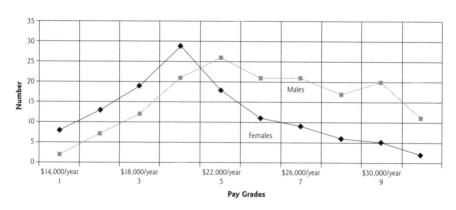

Figure 8.2 Sample Distribution of Female and Male Employees by Number

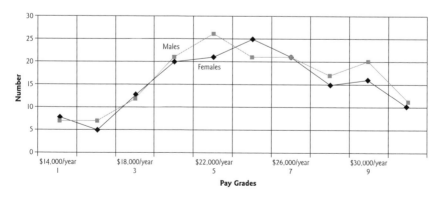

Figure 8.3 Sample Distribution of Female and Male Employees by Number

Table 8.4. Sample List of Job Titles by Category

Type of Job	Incumbents	Female	Male	Percentage Female	Percentage Male
Female-Dominated Job Titles					
Clerk typist	15	15	0	100%	0%
Receptionist	13	13	0	100%	0%
Data entry operator	9	8	1	89%	11%
Social worker	6	5	1	83%	17%
Registered nurse	4	4	0	100%	0%
Librarian	2	2	0	100%	0%
Male-Dominated Job Titles					
Custodian	9	2	7	22%	78%
Maintenance technician	9	0	9	0%	100%
Corrections officer	8	1	7	13%	88%
Computer analyst	6	1	5	17%	83%
Security guard	4	0	4	0%	100%
Engineer	3	0	3	0%	100%
Construction equipment operator	3	0	3	0%	100%
Accountant	2	0	2	0%	100%
Investigator	2	0	2	0%	100%
Integrated Job Titles					
Computer operator	9	5	4	56%	44%
Recreation therapy aide	8	3	5	38%	63%
Mail room clerk	6	4	2	67%	33%
Motor vehicle clerk	5	3	2	60%	40%
Personnel assistant	4	2	2	50%	50%
Single-Incumbency Titles (Female)					
Nurse administrator	1	1	0	100%	0%
Office administrator manager	1	1	0	100%	0%
Public information director	1	1	0	100%	0%
Senior librarian	1	1	0	100%	0%
Single-Incumbency Titles (Male)					
Data operations manager	1	0	1	0%	100%
Personnel manager	1	0	1	0%	100%
Director of social services	1	0	1	0%	100%

(continued)

Table 8.4. Sample List of Job Titles by Category *(continued)*

Type of Job	Incumbents	Female	Male	Percentage Female	Percentage Male
Single-Incumbency Titles (Male) *(continued)*					
Manager of plant and maintenance	1	0	1	0%	100%
Finance director	1	0	1	0%	100%
Attorney	1	0	1	0%	100%
Mail services supervisor	1	0	1	0%	100%
Director of motor vehicle services	1	0	1	0%	100%
Pharmacist	1	0	1	0%	100%
Taxpayer services representative	1	0	1	0%	100%
School superintendent	1	0	1	0%	100%
Transportation planning aide	1	0	1	0%	100%
Psychologist	1	0	1	0%	100%

Table 8.5. Breakdown of the Job Titles for the Sample Workforce by Male and Female

	Number of Classes	Number of Employees	Number of Women	Number of Men
Female-dominated job classes	10	53	51	2
Male-dominated job classes	24	63	4	59
Integrated job classes	5	32	17	15
Total	39	148	72	76

female incumbents, male incumbents, integrated or both male and female incumbents, and jobs that have one incumbent (single-incumbency), male or female.

Note that the sample shown in table 8.4 is highly segregated by sex. Table 8.5 shows how the list breaks down. The pie chart in figure 8.4 illustrates the percentage breakdown of female- and male-dominated job titles and integrated job titles. It clearly shows that the job titles in the hypothetical workforce are male dominated—evidence of sex segregation.

The workforce analysis can be used in a number of ways. First, using the job titles that are predominantly female or male with more than one incumbent, you can identify job titles for comparison in your pay-equity study. Second, you can

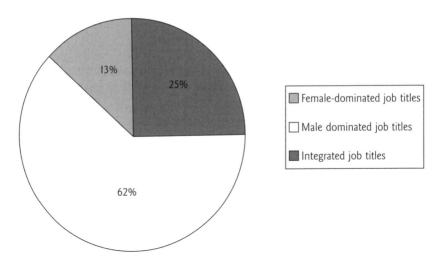

Figure 8.4 Composition of Job Titles in Sample Workforce

use your analysis and graphs in your pay-equity report to describe employment patterns in your organization. Note that sex segregation is not really the problem in pay equity. Women choose to do certain types of jobs, and men choose to do other types. The problem has been that the types of jobs that women have traditionally chosen have not been valued fairly or paid appropriately through the years. The goal of pay equity is not to end sex-segregated jobs but to ensure that all jobs are valued fairly and paid an amount commensurate with their value to the organization. One effect of pay-equity adjustments over time may be the blurring of male- and female-dominated job titles, with more individuals choosing traditionally other-sex jobs.

FIXING THE PROBLEM

If the data gathered and analyzed clearly point to sex segregation and pay inequity, some administrators may attempt to correct the problem by holding men's salaries down in order for women to catch up. The goal of pay equity is to use average male salaries to raise underpaid predominantly female job classes. Pay for men should not be frozen or lowered in order to achieve pay equity. Raises given to traditionally underpaid females in certain job classes should always be in addition to regular cost-of-living and merit increases. The goal should be to adjust the pay scale for identified job titles through a thorough job-evaluation process (see chapter 2).

Job evaluation is one strategy for correcting pay inequities that can provide evidence of those inequities and a process for correcting them. An organization that has not undergone a thorough job-evaluation process will likely discover many anomalies in its classification system. Either there are wholesale reclassifications because the jobs are poorly designed and there is little difference between one grade and the next, or there is an uncomfortable freeze on changes because the organization cannot afford the possible consequences of opening the floodgates.

If you are developing a plan of action for pay equity, be sure to review chapter 2.

WRITING A PAY-EQUITY REPORT

You have gathered all of the data and analyzed it. You believe you have convincing evidence of pay inequity. The next step is to make an effective argument. Your objective is to convince the decision makers to act on your recommendations. For this, you need to write a pay-equity report.

First, define the report's purpose. Ask yourself who will read the report, how the report will be released, and what the ultimate purpose of the document is. Written materials by themselves rarely effect change, so how the report is presented is extremely important. You have already invested many hours in gathering and analyzing the relevant data. If there has also been a job-evaluation study, many more hours of work were invested. Now is not the time to have your pay-equity plan fizzle.

The primary audience for the report will be the decision makers. Make sure you know who those people are. Determine what information will influence them. Learn how they conduct their meetings and how new issues are brought to them. If you are in an academic environment, you will first need to have the support of the library director and the library's administration. The next step is to get the support of the person to whom the library director or dean reports. Who will present the recommendations to the director's boss? Will it need to be approved by the dean's cabinet or another administrative group before being presented to the ultimate decision makers, the board of education or regents? Is the president the person who decides what goes on the board's agenda?

If you have the support of the library director, that person should be able to present and defend the pay-equity recommendations, but you may find that it will be your job to carry these recommendations to higher authorities. It is therefore even more important that you draft an effective report. It is conceivable that you will be allowed to make a brief oral presentation and that the printed document will be used to make final decisions. Your report must be free of errors. Persons who are not inclined to approve such recommendations could easily point to errors or omissions in the document to delay or dismiss the recommendations.

Who else will read your report and potentially influence its success or failure? In addition to the decision makers, the other audience is the peer group in the library and other workers in predominately female job classes who are potential allies. People in this group will likely have their salaries impacted by these recommendations and can be very helpful. Enlist their aid. Do not forget that males could either support or oppose pay equity, out of fear for their own salaries. Your report should include a recommendation that no jobs be downgraded or lowered in pay and should emphasize that point at every opportunity. If the report is viewed as a feminist attempt to take money away from men, it will certainly fail.

149

The report will also be read by persons outside of your organization, including library users, members of the media, and taxpayers.

The timing and location for the release of the report is critical. First, you must get approval from all of the administrative levels in your organization before the report can be presented to the ultimate decision makers. The report should not be disseminated widely until it is clear that it is appropriate to release it. Does it become part of the public record when it is placed on an agenda for final decision? Will it have been shared with library employees, persons in predominately female job classes, persons in predominantly male job classes, or others? Once again, you must learn how the system works. Do not leave anyone out who could impact the report's success.

If appropriate, you should attend several of the decision makers' regular open meetings to see how they conduct business. Familiarize yourself with open-meeting laws in your area. Talk with individuals who are familiar with the workings of the body. Will you need to have the report approved by a subcommittee of that body before it is brought to the whole group? Who are the members of the subcommittee and the whole group? Are they likely or unlikely to agree with the recommendations? What about timing? What time of year is best for presenting the recommendations? Do you want to present your recommendations when the decision-making group is working on a reduction-in-force plan or is searching for a way out of budget deficits? Is it better to present the report during the summer or spring? Are they more likely to approve such a plan at the beginning of the fiscal year or at the end? At the beginning of a meeting or the end? Many very good projects have been killed by decision-making bodies because they were poorly presented or proposed at the wrong time.

Will your report be given to the board in advance of the meeting, distributed at the meeting, or disseminated after the meeting? Will it be given to decision makers who missed the meeting? Will the report stand on its own, or will it need explanation? Your report must be designed to speak to those who hear an oral presentation as well as to those who do not.

What is the report's strategic objective? It should be a part of the strategy for pay equity and should advance the goals of the plan. In addition to defining the problem, the report should include a set of recommendations. Pay-equity supporters can then lobby decision makers to approve and act on those recommendations. Always remember that the easiest thing to do is nothing. You must get them to act.

THE PAY-EQUITY REPORT

Answers to all of the questions in the previous section will determine the content, theme, and format of the pay-equity report or reports. The campaign for getting approval for pay equity is a long process. Your strategic plan may involve several reports that serve different purposes. It is extremely important that they all contain consistently accurate information. The last thing you need is for someone to hold up two reports that contain conflicting data.

Your reports should contain the following elements: executive summary, introduction and background, methodology, findings, recommendations, and appendixes. The executive summary should provide an overview of the report. Because many persons will read only the summary, it should clearly communicate the main points of the report and be complete enough to be published separately. The executive summary should be written to stimulate readers to review the entire report and should present the most compelling and persuasive arguments, as well as the major recommendations. As with all reports, you must be sure that it contains no errors.

The full report need not be lengthy, but it should expand on the information presented in the executive summary. In the introduction, explain the purpose of the study and what led up to it. Tell the reader why the study was conducted and why it is needed. The methodology section should simply explain how the study was conducted and the data were collected. You may wish to cite here other studies that used the same methodology. In the findings section, present factual data and the conclusions that have been drawn from them. This section should also contain charts that illustrate the findings and present the information in a visually pleasing format. Decide what information to present and how it can best be presented. Do not overwhelm the reader with repetitious data or with data that do not strongly present your positions and support your recommendations.

The next section of the report should include the recommendations that flow directly from the data presented in the findings section. Be sure that some of your recommendations are easy to implement to allow you to press for immediate action. Other recommendations will be more substantial, and this section should suggest timelines for implementation. Recommendations should specify what action is to be taken, by whom, and by what time. Do not forget to include a recommendation that whatever action is taken, it should not adversely impact other individuals not covered by the recommendations, notably males in predominately male job classes.

The last section of the report includes the appendixes and list of sources. You may wish to include charts in this section or additional material that supports the findings and recommendations. The list of sources should be a concise list of readings relevant to the report. The whole document should not be more than seven or eight pages. Most people will read the executive summary, but those who read the entire report will not likely wade through a long document.

The main objective of the report is to present clear and persuasive evidence of pay inequities and to recommend actions that are rational, logical, and doable. With your report, you want to bring the reader to the same conclusions you have reached and then tell them what those logical conclusions are. Even a decision-making body that is faced with fiscal difficulties will see that they are obligated to make pay equity a priority if the study and the report lead them to that conclusion. Generally speaking, employers do not oppose pay equity. Often they are not aware of the issue, and when presented with a logical argument, they are supportive of change.

DISTRIBUTION OF PAY-EQUITY FUNDS

At least two academic libraries in the past few years have obtained pay-equity funds to distribute to librarians. Librarians at the University of Colorado at Boulder and at University of Texas at Arlington were awarded pay-equity funds to correct inequitable salaries.

In 1997, University of Colorado at Boulder libraries were awarded $300,000 in market equity to be made over four years at $75,000 each year.[8] Awards were to be made with case-by-case justification based on merit rather than simply dividing the award by the number of faculty. The actual process of determining the specific market-equity increase for each position consisted of two steps. The first placed each faculty member into a job classification that most closely matched those in the ARL "Comparison of Mean Salaries."[9] The second required the use of an internal merit process to measure career performance. Assigning faculty to an ARL classification immediately determined a market-salary mean for that position. Factors considered in determining the career merit score included quality of librarianship, publication record, service contributions, and years of experience. Although partly a subjective assessment, one consequence of the annual internal merit-equity evaluation was that a score was calculated for each librarian's career merit. This part of the process was well understood and had been approved by the library faculty. Because increases to these market salaries were to be distributed over a period of four years, the annual increase was one-quarter of the total increase.

One outcome of the University of Colorado experience was that the dean was able to successfully obtain equity funds. In addition, a library task force was able to quickly implement an accepted strategy for distribution of funds.

At the University of Texas at Arlington, the libraries' administration allocated $40,000 for salary equity increases for librarians and archivists in 1999–2000 to ensure that the professional staff was compensated fairly.[10] The University of Texas at Arlington used the University of Colorado's "Professional Experience Score," which included weighted ratings for longevity, prior performance, and research experience to identify salary inequities among the professional staff. The three measurements used to create the University of Texas's Libraries' Professional Experience Score were average merit scores, career-status rank, and longevity. Each librarian's score, along with current salary, was plotted on a scatterplot. Multiple regression analysis was used to identify librarians whose actual salaries did not match their anticipated ones and who therefore were deserving of an increase.

At both libraries, the distribution of funds was accomplished fairly and equitably. Both caution, however, that any library contemplating a salary-equity study needs to examine its own unique situation to decide which factors and ratings will make up their professional experience score.

PAY EQUITY IS EVERYONE'S CONCERN

Pay equity is not just a women's issue. Men in traditionally female job classes also benefit from pay increases when those classes are upgraded. And everyone in the organization benefits when employees believe they are being treated fairly, especially when it comes to salaries.

NOTES

1. Heather Antecol, "Why Is There Interethnic Variation in the Gender Wage Gap?" *Journal of Human Resources* 36, no. 1 (Winter 2001): 119–44.
2. Carolyn Kenady, *Pay Equity: An Action Manual for Library Workers* (Chicago: American Library Association, 1989), 3.
3. Ibid.
4. U.S. Bureau of the Census, *Current Population Survey* (Washington, DC: U.S. Commerce Department, 2001).
5. National Committee on Pay Equity, "The Wage Gap over Time" Fact Sheet, http://www.feminist.com/fairpay/f_change.htm.
6. Economic Policy Institute, *The State of Working America* (Washington, DC: Economic Policy Institute, 2000).
7. Kenady, *Pay Equity*.
8. Scott Seaman, Nancy Carter, and Carol Krismann, "Market Equity Tempered by Career Merit: A Case Study," *Journal of Academic Librarianship* 26, no. 4 (July 2000): 225–32.
9. Association of Research Libraries, *ARL Annual Salary Survey 1996–97* (Washington, DC: Association of Research Libraries, 1997).
10. Laura K. Blessing, *Using Statistical Techniques to Reduce Salary Inequities Among Librarians. Library Administration and Management* 15, no. 2 (Spring 2001): 80–4.

BIBLIOGRAPHY

Acker, Joan. *Doing Comparable Worth: Gender, Class, and Pay Equity.* Philadelphia: Temple University Press, 1989.
———. "Sex Bias in Job Evaluation: A Comparable Worth Issue." In Christine Bose and Glenna Spitze (eds.), *Ingredients for Women's Employment Policy,* 183–96. Albany, NY: State University of New York Press, 1987.
American Council of State, County, and Municipal Employees. *We're Worth It: An AFSCME Guide to Understanding and Implementing Pay Equity.* Washington, DC: American Council of State, County, and Municipal Employees, 1998.
Antecol, Heather. "Why Is There Interethnic Variation in the Gender Wage Gap?" *Journal of Human Resources* 36, no. 1 (Winter 2001): 119–44.
"Are Women's Wage Gains Men's Losses? A Distributional Test." *American Economic Review:* 90, no. 2 (May 2000): 456–61.
Arnault, E. Jane. "An Experimental Study of Job Evaluation and Comparable Worth." *Industrial and Labor Relations Review* 54, no. 4 (July 2001): 806–15.
Association of Research Libraries. *ARL Annual Salary Survey 1996–97.* Washington, DC: Association of Research Libraries, 1997.

Baldwin, Marjorie L., Richard J. Butler, and William G. Johnson. "A Hierarchical Theory of Occupational Segregation and Wage Discrimination." *Economic Inquiry* 39, no. 1 (January 2001): 94–111.

Blessing, Laura K. "Using Statistical Techniques to Reduce Salary Inequities Among Librarians at the University of Texas at Arlington." *Library Administration and Management* 15, no. 2 (Spring 2001): 80–4.

Blum, Linda M. *Between Feminism and Labor: The Significance of the Comparable Worth Movement.* Berkeley, CA: University of California Press, 1991.

Chen, Shih-Neng, Peter F. Orazem, and J. Peter Mattila. "Measurement Error in Job Evaluation and the Gender Wage Gap." *Economic Inquiry* 37, no. 2 (1999): 181–94.

Clain, Suzanne Heller, and Karen Leppel. "An Investigation into Sexual Orientation Discrimination as an Explanation for Wage Differences." *Applied Economics* 33, no. 1 (January 15, 2001): 37–48.

DeLeire, Thomas. "Changes in Wage Discrimination Against People with Disabilities: 1984–93." *Journal of Human Resources* 36, no. 1 (Winter 2001): 144–59.

Economic Policy Institute. "The State of Working America." Washington, DC: Economic Policy Institute, 2000.

Erbe, Bonnie. "Pay Equity, Corporate Style." *Working Woman* 25, no. 3 (February 2000): 22–23.

Evans, Sara, and Barbara Nelson. *Wage Justice: Comparable Worth and the Paradox of Technocratic Reform.* Chicago: University of Chicago Press, 1989.

Feldberg, Roslyn L. "Comparable Worth: Toward Theory and Practice in the United States." *Signs* 10, no. 2 (1984): 311–28.

Figart, Deborah M. "Equal Pay for Equal Work: The Role of Job Evaluation in an Evolving Social Norm." *Journal of Economic Issues* 34, no. 1 (2000): 1–19.

Figart, Deborah M., and Peggy Kahn. *Contesting the Market: Pay Equity and the Politics of Economic Restructuring.* Detroit: Wayne State University Press, 1997.

Gunderson, Morley. "Male-Female Wage Differentials and the Policy Response." *Journal of Economic Literature* 2 (1989): 46–72.

Hallock, Margaret. "Pay Equity Outcomes in the Public Sector: Resolving Competing Interests." *Policy Studies Journal* 18, no. 2 (1990): 421–32.

———. "Pay Equity: What Is the Best Union Strategy?" *Labor Studies Journal* 25, no. 1 (Spring 2000): 27–45.

Hartmann, Heidi, and Stephanie Aaronson. "Pay Equity and Women's Wage Increases: Success in the States, a Model for the Nation." *Duke Journal of Gender Law and Policy* 1 (1992): 69–87.

Horrace, William C., and Ronald L. Oaxaca. "Inter-Industry Wage Differentials and the Gender Wage Gap: An Identification Problem." *Industrial and Labor Relations Review* 154, no. 3 (April 2001): 611–20.

Kenady, Carolyn. *Pay Equity: An Action Manual for Library Workers.* Chicago: American Library Association, 1989.

Lofstrom, Asa. "Can Job Evaluation Improve Women's Wages?" *Applied Economics* 31, no. 9 (1999): 1053–60.

Milken, Michael. "Amid Plenty, the Wage Gap Widens." *Wall Street Journal* 236, no. 45 (September 5, 2000): A34.

Minnesota Public Employment Study. *Recommended Job Content Evaluation and Salary Plan for the State of Minnesota.* St. Paul: Minnesota Department of Finance, 1979.

National Committee on Pay Equity. *Collective Bargaining for Pay Equity: A Strategy Manual.* Washington, DC: National Committee on Pay Equity, 1989.

———. *Erase the Bias: A Pay Equity Guide to Eliminating Race and Sex Bias from Wage Setting Systems.* Washington, DC: National Committee on Pay Equity, 1993.

———. *The Intersection Between Pay Equity and Workplace Representation.* Washington, DC: National Committee on Pay Equity, 1996.

———. "The Wage Gap over Time" Fact Sheet. http://www.feminist.com/fairpay/f_change.htm. September 2001 (last accessed December 2002).

Okuda, Sachiko. "Pay Equity: What's It All Worth? Public-Sector Librarians in Canada Agitate for Pay Equity" *Feliciter* 46, no. 6 (2000): 314–17.

Rogers, Michael. "Female Special Librarians Finally Achieve Pay Equity." *Library Journal* 124, no. 19 (November 15, 1999): 12.

Seaman, Scott, Nancy Carter, and Carol Krismann. "Market Equity Tempered by Career Merit: A Case Study." *Journal of Academic Librarianship* 26, no. 4 (July 2000): 225–32.

Smith, Paul. "Diversity Pays, Doesn't It?" *Management* 47, no. 1 (February 2000): 24–8.

Sorenson, Elaine. *Wage and Employment Effects of Comparable Worth: The Case of Minnesota.* Washington, DC: Urban Institute, 1990.

St. Lifer, Evan. "Women Directors at Research Libraries Earn More Than Men." *Library Journal* 123, no. 6 (April 1, 1998): 14.

Steinberg, Ronnie. "Job Evaluation and Managerial Control: The Politics of Technique and the Techniques of Politics." In Judy Fudge and Patricia McDermott (eds.), *Just Wages: A Feminist Assessment of Pay Equity,* 193–218. Toronto: University of Toronto Press, 1991.

———. "Emotional Labor in Job Evaluation: Redesigning Compensation Practices." *Annals of the American Academy of Political and Social Science: Emotional Labor in the Service Economy* 561 (January 1999): 143–57.

U.S. Bureau of the Census. *Current Population Survey.* Washington, DC: U.S. Commerce Department, 2001.

"Wage Gap Narrowing Between Women, Men." *Indianapolis Business Journal* 21, no. 28 (September 25, 2000): 39–43.

Whalen, Charles J. "A Wage Gap Too Wide." *Business Week* no. 3744 (August 6, 2001): 22–7.

"Women Rise in Workplace but Wage Gap Continues." *Wall Street Journal* 235, no. 82 (April 25, 2000): A12.

9 ADDRESSING PAY ISSUES IN LIBRARIES

You win some, you lose some, and some are rained out.

—HENRY FORD II

LIBRARIANS' SALARIES

John N. Berry III, *Library Journal's* editor-in-chief, has been one of the few actors in librarianship calling for a change in the leadership of professional associations to bring salaries to the top of the agenda, where they belong. He writes that "there is no more urgent professional issue facing our profession or our association."[1] Librarians have to ask themselves if the salaries of the top library administrators, who also head library associations, are high enough that salaries are not an issue to them. Berry also calls on librarians to devote creative thought to the salary crisis to bring about change. "Until we fix the profession's most glaring weakness, libraries will remain ill-equipped to compete for and attract the 'best and the brightest' to a library future."[2] That is not to say that many library directors do not work independently for better salaries, just that it is not the priority it should be for librarians' professional associations.

Librarians' salaries have been historically low. As noted in chapter 8, for many years librarianship has been a female-dominated profession. Almost 75 percent of all librarians in 1900 were women; by 1930 91.5 percent were women. Like teaching and nursing, librarianship had become a predominantly female profession with salaries that were lower than predominantly male occupations. Employers could legally pay women less than men. Fortunately, discrimination legislation has outlawed the practice.

In fact, women and men working as special librarians and information professionals are paid the same for the first time in history, according to the *1999 Annual Salary Survey of the Special Libraries Association*.[3] The change has occurred over several decades, with women receiving relatively higher percentage increases in pay than men. From 1976 to 1999, female special librarians' salaries rose 237 percent, while men's increased 169 percent.

The overall gender balance in ARL university libraries (including law and medical) has remained essentially steady since the early 1980s. For fiscal year 2000–2001, women made up 64.57 percent of staff, and men 35.43 percent, according to the *ARL Annual Salary Survey 2000–2001*.[4] The salaries of men surpassed the salaries of women in most ARL job categories. Overall, female professionals earn an average salary that is still only 93.9 percent that of men, despite corresponding experience levels (women with an average 17.0 years of experience versus 16.8 years for men). This pattern is repeated for minority librarians. The average salary for minority women is lower than that for minority men in 9 of the 10 experience cohorts. The average salary in 2000–2001 for minority women was $49,065, and $53,456 for minority men. The combined average salary for minorities was 95.09 percent that of nonminority librarians (U.S. only).

However, for the fifth year in a row, the average salary for female directors in university libraries was slightly higher than that for male directors. Additionally, the number of women in top administrative library positions continues to grow (51 of 112 ARL libraries have female directors). Although women running research libraries have bridged the gender gap in pay, the same cannot be said for their subordinates. The library profession still faces gender equity issues. University teaching faculty face similar problems.

TEACHING FACULTY SALARIES AND DISTRIBUTION

From the *Fact Sheet 2000–2001*, a report prepared for the American Association of University Professors Committee on the Status of Women in the Academic Profession, comes the following statistics:[5]

- Full-time women faculty account for 36 percent of faculty overall.
- The salary advantage held by male faculty over female faculty holds across all ranks and all institutional types. On average, women earn 91 percent of what men earn.
- The earnings gap between men and women is largest at the rank of full professor and smallest at the rank of instructor. For all institutional types combined, women earn

  - 90 percent of what men earn at the rank of lecturer,
  - 96 percent of what men earn at the rank of instructor,
  - 93 percent of what men earn at the ranks of assistant and associate professor, and
  - 88 percent of what men earn at the rank of full professor.

- The earnings gap between female and male faculty is largest at private-independent institutions and smallest at church-related institutions. For all ranks combined, women earn on average 93 percent of what men earn at church-related institutions, 92 percent of what men earn at public institutions, and 91 percent of what men earn at private-independent institutions.
- The earnings gap between male and female faculty is largest at doctoral-level institutions and smallest at two-year colleges without rank. For all ranks combined, women earn on average 96 percent of what men earn at two-year colleges without rank; 95 percent of what men earn at comprehensive, general baccalaureate institutions, and two-year colleges with rank; and 92 percent of what men earn at doctoral-level institutions.
- Women are most well represented at institutions without rank and least well represented at doctoral-level institutions.
- Women are most well represented at church-related institutions and least well represented at private-independent (non-church-related) institutions.
- Among tenured or tenure-eligible faculty, women are most well represented among assistant professors and least well represented among full professors.

GAINING EQUITY

Do you know whether salaries in your library are inequitable, or do you just have a feeling that they are? The easiest thing for anyone to do is to complain about their salaries. Find out. Review the library's budget. Track down the regional, state, and national salary data. What if your salary or the salaries of your peers in the library fail to come close to those of your colleagues in the faculty or in other departments, of the librarians in other libraries, or of your peers in other related professions? What can you as an individual do?

Whether you are interested in raising average librarians' salaries to those of the teaching faculty, other librarians, or other occupations, the steps are similar. Significant data on all of these groups are available. No one will do it for you—you must do it for yourself.

The process for gaining equity with other faculty, other librarians, or other professions is similar to the process spelled out by the ALA's Committee on Pay Equity for gaining pay equity based on sex (see chapter 8):

1. Organize and educate a core group of activists.
2. Plan a strategy and tactics for a pay-equity campaign.
3. Conduct preliminary research, such as a workforce analysis or a simplified pay-equity study, to identify wage inequities.
4. Campaign for adoption of recommendations for correction of pay inequities using your strategy plan.

The first step is to gather data that proves that your salaries need to be addressed.

SOURCES OF DATA

Faculty salary data is available in the annual publication of faculty salaries in the *Chronicle of Higher Education* and in *Academe, The Journal of the Association of University Professors*. In addition, the *ARL Annual Salary Survey* provides information on more than 12,000 professional positions in ARL libraries.

Chronicle of Higher Education

Tables provided in the *Chronicle of Higher Education* give teaching faculty data by discipline based on nine-month salaries, but be aware that they do not contain salaries for librarians. If your librarians' salaries are 12-month salaries, you will need to convert them to 9-month salaries for comparability. If you want to compare your librarians' salaries to faculty on your own campus, the *Chronicle of Higher Education* salary data is quite useful. Local librarian salary information will have to be found in budget data for your own institution.

Academe, The Journal of the Association of University Professors

The *Annual Report on the Economic Status of the Profession* is published by the American Association of University Professors each spring and contains extensive faculty salary data.

Association of Research Libraries (ARL)

The *ARL Annual Salary Survey* provides tables that display average, median, and beginning librarian's salaries; salaries by position and experience, sex, and race/ethnic background; salaries in different geographic regions and sizes of libraries, including law, medical, Canadian, and nonuniversity research libraries.

Other Sources

Demographic information, such as year of birth, years of experience in a specific library, education credentials, and so on, has been occasionally collected in addition to the categories already mentioned. As noted in chapter 7, Stanley Wilder's *The Age Demographics of Academic Librarians: A Professional Apart* was the first publication that included this information for libraries.

Salary data for various occupations can be located in many sources. Overall occupational salary data can be found in the *Occupational Outlook Handbook* and in other government publications. In gathering salary data, you must take care to report comparable data. Be sure you have comparable year data, that is, 9-month, 10-month, or 12-month data. Be sure you are reporting gross income for all groups. And also take care that you have comparable reporting year data. Comparing data from two different years will result in inaccuracies.

A SUPPORTIVE GROUP

Once gathered and found convincing, the salary data can be shared with others. Generally, it is a good idea to work in ever-expanding circles to gain support. You must know who will ultimately be in a position to approve or reject any changes to salaries.

If your colleagues do not agree that you have a convincing argument, you will not win over others. If your library administration does not believe you have a convincing argument, you will not convince the organization's management. Test your data and your argument with your colleagues. Enlist their support in presenting your case to the library's administration. Obtain their advice on how to proceed or even if to proceed.

WRITING A REPORT

The advice provided in the section on writing a pay-equity report in chapter 8 should be followed in developing recommendations on raising librarian salaries to the averages of teaching faculty, other librarians, or other occupations.

CONDUCTING SALARY STUDIES

Market equity is achieved when local salaries approximate those of peers at a group of comparable institutions. Not only does market equity acknowledge the moral, judicial, and economic equality of employees; it also recognizes that the ongoing health of an institution depends on paying fair-market value to attract qualified individuals and prevent high turnover.

Most organizations have identified peer institutions for comparative purposes. For example, a university will have a peer group of universities selected based on their similarities in mission, curriculum, student body, research, and budgets. The libraries can use those same peer institutions for comparative purposes. You can extract salary data from national data for those peer institutions. If the data is not as specific as needed, you may consider developing a brief set of questions to pose to your colleagues at peer institutions. Often, if you are willing to share the data you have collected with those you survey, they will gladly participate. One group of library personnel that is particularly interested in salary information is the personnel and staff development officers at these libraries. If you are interested in conducting such a survey, it is a good idea to speak with the personnel officer in your library to advise you. That person may be interested in conducting the survey with colleagues at other libraries. Many are members of the ACRL Personnel and Staff Development Officers Discussion Group.

If you are considering a survey of peers, be certain that you have carefully thought out what you intend to learn from it. The questions must be clear and concise. The ideal is two to three questions that would yield the kind of information that you cannot glean from other salary data and that can be reported without bridging confidentiality. An e-mail or phone survey is the most effective method.

Before conducting your own survey, check to see if local or state library associations have already done similar studies. In many cases, other groups are gathering longitudinal data that can be useful.

PRESENTING A PAY-EQUITY CASE

Thus far the discussion has focused on how librarians may be paid less on average than teaching faculty, librarians in other libraries, and those in other occupations. What about the situation in which you believe you are paid less than your peers in the same library? How do you correct that problem?

First, make sure that what you believe is true and that you can prove that it is true. Using reliable data taken directly from the budget, compare your salary with that of your peers. By peers, you must use individual salaries of persons who have the same job as yours who have essentially the same job history. For example, if you are a reference librarian, do you have the same number of years of experience as those to whom you are comparing your salary? Are those years of experience comparable? For example, a librarian who has 12 years of experience in reference cannot be compared directly with a librarian who has 12 years of experience but 9 years in a staff position and only 3 as a librarian. Can the difference in salary be explained by work history?

Next, make sure that what you believe about salary history is accurate. For example, is the merit history comparable? Have you gotten average merit, whereas the person you are comparing yourself with has received highest merit over a period of time? Can the difference in salary be explained by merit history?

Next, can the difference in merit history be explained? Does the other librarian have a different supervisor who is known as an "easy grader"—someone known for giving higher merit points or someone who goes to bat for employee salaries? Has your salary history been impacted by a less-than-aggressive supervisor? How significant is the difference in salaries? Is there enough of a difference to risk the possibility that the relationships with your coworkers and supervisor might be impacted?

If you have a case for correcting an inequity that cannot be explained by work history or salary history, you should put together a brief report that documents the inequity and present it to your supervisor, who should advise you on how to proceed.

RESPONDING TO INDIVIDUAL SALARY CONCERNS

It cannot be stressed enough that salaries are important. How many times have you talked with librarians who resigned to take other positions, explaining that they left because of salary? How many of those individuals who left did more than write a letter of resignation? How many took their salary offers to the decision makers to see if the offer could be matched? How many simply assumed that in order to get more money, they had to leave? How many administrators would prefer to find the small sums needed to keep experienced librarians than to go through the time-consuming and costly recruitment and hiring process? Yes, of course there are administrators who would not make an attempt to match a reasonable salary and others whose hands are tied. But it is always in a librarian's best interest to discuss a new job offer with the administration if that person has any interest in staying. Leaving for promotion, fame, and fortune are different matters altogether.

Administrators normally have salary data available to them. The budget data detail how librarians are paid, and national salary surveys tell administrators how their librarians stand nationally. Most librarians do not have that data near at hand, however. That information should be made readily available and should be shared with a salary review board composed of librarians and staff, as an effective means of addressing and responding to individual salary concerns in the organization.

MAKING SALARIES A PRIORITY

A library has many competing demands for its budget, not the least of which is personnel. Many libraries expend more than half of their budgets on personnel. Effective management of the personnel budget is key to the success of the library's collections and services. If a library has librarians and staff who are dissatisfied with their salaries, all of the library's services are impacted. Impressing on the librarians and staff that the library is doing all it can to pay them fairly and equitably will go a long way to improve morale. Making salaries a priority for the library and making that known to the librarians and staff will help the administration gain support for its efforts.

STAFF SALARIES

Issues regarding staff salaries are quite distinct from and often more challenging than faculty and librarian salaries. One reason is that the staff represents a tremendously diverse group of people performing a wide variety of duties. Whereas faculty members often only have titles of instructor, lecturer, assistant professor, associate professor, and professor, there are hundreds of staff titles. Library faculty have those five ranks, which have well-established guidelines for promotion to higher ranks. Staff often find themselves in positions without career ladders. Faculty members also tend to have more options for moving to better-paying, more-prestigious positions than staff. Faculty are often represented by relatively strong bargaining units and make valid claims to be integral to university success or failure. Quite simply, faculty members have more opportunities to make salary claims. All of these benefits normally accrue to the librarians and the library faculty in the library.

What can individual staff members do? You must ask the same types of questions that the librarian who senses inequity should ask. Do you know whether salaries in your library are inequitable, or do you just have a feeling that they are? Is that inequity based on different salaries being paid to persons doing the same work or similar work? What about experience? Do those you are comparing your salary with have the same or similar work history? Years of experience at that level, years of education, and reclassification or promotion history? What about years of education? Do education and experience count the same in meeting job-qualification requirements? Can experience be substituted for education or vice versa? What about merit history? Have you received highest merit and still find yourself paid less?

Depending on the organizational culture and the expressed policies on handling salary questions, you would be wise to begin with your supervisor. Lay out what you consider to be an inequity, and ask for your supervisor's advice. If your supervisor does not agree, you may decide, again depending on the organizational culture, to inform your supervisor that you wish to take this issue up the chain of command, to the supervisor's boss. Or perhaps your supervisor agrees with you and will support your request. In any case, you must be sure of your facts and be prepared for counterarguments. Go over the potential arguments beforehand. Find out if your complaints about your salary are justified. Review the library's budget. Review the university's budget for similar positions. Track down the regional, state, and national salary data. What if your salary or the salaries of your peers in the library fail to come close to those of your colleagues in other departments or staff in other libraries, or to your peers in other related professions?

ASKING FOR A RAISE

"Ask for a raise" is the obvious response to the question "How can I get more money?" Sure, you could use some extra cash, and you might actually deserve it. Why wait for your boss to come to the same conclusion? First, if you work in a public-sector setting, giving and getting raises often only occurs at the beginning of a fiscal year. Your boss may be unable to give you a raise even if it was agreed that a raise would be a good idea. But if you are in a situation in which you could potentially receive a raise in the middle of the year, what must be considered? Do the following:

- Research. Find out what others in your field earn so you can support the numbers you bring to the table.
- Flaunt it. Be prepared to recount your major responsibilities and accomplishments and to list your goals for the future. This is not the time to be modest.
- Time it right. If business is slow, or the company is being reorganized, the odds of getting a larger paycheck are against you.
- Be specific. Come in with a dollar figure in mind, and begin negotiating from there.
- Show respect. Do not present your argument as an ultimatum. Your goal is to demonstrate that you are an asset to the team.

LIBRARY STAFF CONCERNS

In 2000 the ALA Support Staff Interests Round Table (SSIRT) released three task force reports on issues of concern to library staff.[6] These reports are the culmination of almost four years of work that resulted from a SSIRT strategic planning process that began in 1996. Following a nationwide survey in 1997, with more than 2,000 responses, the top three issues of concern to library support staff were determined. The issues are

- career ladders (few opportunities for advancement),
- compensation not appropriate to the level of education, experience, and responsibilities, and
- access to continuing education and training opportunities.

The survey revealed what most library administrators already know: Staff members who work in libraries are concerned with their salaries, and they often believe they are not being adequately compensated for their contributions.

LIBRARY SUPPORT STAFF SALARY SURVEY

In January 2000, *Library Mosaics* sent 400 survey questionnaires to U.S. libraries selected from the top 100-ranked metropolitan areas, based on population.[7] Within these areas, four different types of libraries were contacted: public libraries, academic four-year college or university libraries, academic two-year college libraries, and special libraries.

Each survey packet contained a cover letter outlining some general definitions, classifications, and descriptions to avoid confusion among the many job titles and descriptions found in libraries. Standard definitions included the following:

- Support staff: All employees working in non-MLS (master's in library science) positions. Examples include assistants, associates, clerks, aides.
- Clerk: Entry-level library position requiring a high school diploma, previous library experience, or both. Examples include circulation clerk, processing clerk.
- Assistant: Any position requiring at least one to two years of previous library experience and some college education.
- Technician: Any position requiring at least an associate's degree or two or more years of previous library experience. May include more sophisticated or responsible positions. Examples include area supervisors, head of staff.
- Other: High-level position of responsibility or expertise requiring a bachelor's or specialized degree, specified relevant experience, or both. Examples include video specialist, computer specialist, program coordinator.

Of the 400 questionnaires mailed, 282 responses were tabulated (68 percent). Libraries in the west reported the largest number of salaries over $30,000, but a number of positions in the west paid in the $20,000–$29,000 ranges. Unlike previous *Library Mosaics* surveys, the lowest salary range was found not in the south but in the midwest, where 36 of the libraries had salaries in the $0–$19,000 range.

The responses also revealed that public libraries generally pay support staff the highest median salaries. Median ranges for public libraries ranged from assistants at $26,007 to "other" at $42,550. Academic two-year college libraries paid the highest median range for the clerk category, at $21,486. Academic libraries paid a range from clerks at $20,600 to "other" at $34,350. Special libraries' and academic libraries' median salary ranges were $19,639–$35,800 and $21,486–$36,600, respectively.

The following list outlines some of the survey's highlights:

- Public libraries pay the highest median salaries for clerks, assistants and technicians.
- The western United States has the highest number of salaries over $30,000.
- The southern United States has the lowest median salary ranges.
- Special libraries have the lowest median salary ranges for all categories.
- The lowest median salary is for a clerk working in the south, at $19,436.
- The highest median salary is for "other" working in the west, at $46,500.

RAISING AVERAGE STAFF SALARIES TO LOCAL MARKET SALARIES

Organizations' human resources departments are usually charged with conducting market surveys to ensure that their staff salary schedules are competitive with other jobs in the local market. If there is agreement in the library that compensation is not appropriate to the level of education, experience, and responsibilities possessed by staff, a market-salary survey may be warranted.

Market surveys report data on a large number of jobs. The U.S. Department of Labor's Bureau of Labor Statistics collects wage and salary data for the federal government. These findings are available in area and industry wage surveys as well as in the publications *Monthly Labor Review* and *Occupational Outlook Quarterly*. State and local governments also collect data, which is available in state documents or from the local chamber of commerce. One drawback of government data is that they are often dated. Another is that the data are often for nonexempt jobs rather than exempt.

SELECTING SALARY SURVEYS

Increasingly, employees are coming across detailed salary survey information. Without knowledge about finding and using reputable data, these individuals are at risk of misinterpreting or misusing this information. Survey data should be supplemented with thoroughly researched government labor statistics. In selecting surveys, one needs to make sure that the surveys reflect the correct labor market and job category.

You should examine surveys for the following characteristics. A good survey

- has an adequate sample size,
- readily identifies the key elements, including effective date of the data, term definitions, clarity of statistics, and position descriptions,
- identifies sources and sample sources, and
- is timely and up-to-date, particularly for new, "hot-skill" technology positions.

SALARY SURVEYS ON THE INTERNET

A number of Web sites can be accessed to locate salary and wage surveys and data. In 1997 Vice President Gore announced the first version of America's Career InfoNet (ACINet), a component of America's Career Kit sponsored by the U.S. Department of Labor. ACINet allows Internet searchers to access America's Labor Market Information System (ALMIS) and find an array of occupational, demographic, and labor market information at the local, state, and national levels (http://www.acinet.org/acinet). The database contains information pulled from a variety of state and federal government agencies, such as the U.S. Bureau of Labor Statistics and various individual state departments of labor.

The ACINet Web site allows searchers to access salary and wage data either by a keyword or menu search. The menu search contains a list of 22 general job families derived from the U.S. Bureau of Labor Statistic's Occupational Employment Statistics occupation list. Within each job family exists a more detailed list of occupational titles. Like many classification schemes, trying to determine which category contains the job title you need can be cumbersome. Thus it is more straightforward to use the keyword search feature. You can then define the search by geographic area, such as state, district, or territory. For instance, if a recent college graduate wants to find the average salary for a librarian in New Mexico, a search in ACINet would reveal the average salary for librarians in the state was $32,800 in 1998, compared with the national average of $38,500. If the job seeker then wants to compare the average salary for a librarian with that of an architect, he or she can make a detailed wages report by comparing this salary to the entire job family or similar occupations and a local metropolitan or "balance of state" area. The job seeker can also find out that there were 40 new librarian positions in New Mexico in 1998.

The *Wall Street Journal* publishes *Careerjournal* (http://www.careers.wsj.com), a portal of salary- and job-search-related information. The site provides data on salaries organized by industry. The staff screens the news and trade journals for mention of salary surveys and trends and then publishes the articles on the site.

The Economic Research Institute publishes wage, salary, cost-of-living, human resource, and demographic information as it relates to employee pay (http://www.erieri.com).

The Salary Wizard (http://www.salary.com) is a free, comprehensive salary tool enabling users to research salary ranges for thousands of job titles in a large set of career fields, sorted by occupation and region. Salary.com gathers data from proprietary research and published reports. It also links to related salary surveys that are provided on the search results page. It also contains news and feature articles on compensation and workplace trends and issues, a compensation glossary, and a list of frequently asked questions.

CompGeo.com is a "Geographic Salary Survey Research Site with forecasting options, best suited for salary and compensation survey research for a small number of jobs or job families" (http://www.compgeo.net). It provides Online Standard Reports for each industry or sector breakout and a particular area or job.

Each report includes projected mean and median, low and high individual wage and salary estimates, estimated competitive salary ranges, quartile-based range, tercile-based range, and salary differentials for 10 U.S. regions. A variety of more-detailed reports are available from the site, available in PDF format and delivered in secure password-protected files.

Business and trade publications available on the Internet are excellent sources of salary surveys, and using the databases' controlled subject vocabulary allows searchers easier access to the data. The Gale Group databases such as General BusinessFile, Trade and Industry Index, and PROMT use the subject headings "Wages" and "Wage Surveys." ABI/INFORM, ProQuest Direct, and Northern Light use the subject heading "Wages and Salaries."

Many sites are offering fairly good free access to private and public salary data and have done some of your research for you in terms of providing links to specific salary surveys on the Internet. On the other hand, because many salary surveys are complex and the result of an economic study or model, some companies do charge for them. Most of the fee-based sources of salary data provide a sample or portion of the study for free, but users should not be surprised if they are asked to pay for the rest of the survey.

DEVELOPING YOUR OWN SALARY SURVEY

As stated previously, when salaries are in question, your library should conduct a market salary survey if one is not already being conducted by the organization's human resources department. As a last resort, you can conduct your own salary survey by following these steps:

- Develop a list of libraries that your library would compete with for employees.
- Use professional directories or the Internet to identify a person in each organization who has a position similar to your own. Contact the individuals by telephone or e-mail to see if they would be willing to participate in a survey. They are likely to respond favorably if you promise to tabulate the results in an anonymous fashion and share the results.
- Fax or e-mail the survey to the contact person. Include a brief job description to verify that the person you are surveying is in a job similar to yours.
- Tabulate the results, removing all clues to the data sources, and calculate the median value. Report the anonymous results to the survey participants together with a thank-you note.

OUTSIDE OFFERS

A risky, but sometimes effective, means of improving your salary is to get a job offer elsewhere. Such an offer could be viewed as strong evidence of your market value. For ethical reasons, you should look for another job only if you are genuinely interested in taking another job. You should not seek another job just to get a pay increase from your current employer; organizations spend a great deal of money recruiting, and such games are unfair to serious applicants. Getting an outside offer is risky because it is entirely possible that rather than making a counteroffer, your present employer will simply wish you well in your new job. In addition, your employer may well conclude that you will leave the minute you get a better offer, hampering future promotion possibilities. All in all, getting an outside offer has many potential problems, but it is a means of establishing your market value.

SUMMARY

Addressing pay issues for both librarians and staff depends on many factors. Chief among them is that the library has a pay structure and a salary policy. If salaries are a concern, individuals can take certain steps to improve salaries, both for the organization and individually. As an employee, you can elevate your performance to become more meritorious, upgrade your current job by taking on new tasks, upgrade your capabilities through additional education and training, and assess your market value to determine whether you are paid fairly. If salaries are found to be inequitable, there are options for individuals to address these concerns.

NOTES

1. John N. Berry, "Governed by Administrators," *Library Journal* 125, no. 19 (November 15, 2000): 6.
2. John N. Berry, "The Compensation Crisis," *Library Journal* 125, no. 3 (February 15, 2000): 100.
3. Special Libraries Association, *SLA Annual Salary Survey: A Research Publication of the Special Libraries Association* (Washington, DC: Special Libraries Association, 2001), introduction.
4. Association of Research Libraries, *ARL Annual Salary Survey 2000–2001* (Washington, DC: Association of Research Libraries, 2001), 14–16.
5. Marcia Bellas, *Fact Sheet 2000–2001* (American Association of University Professors Committee on the Status of Women in the Academic Profession). The data in this fact sheet is based on the "Annual Report on the Economic Status of the Profession," *Academe* 87, no. 2 (March–April 2001): 27–98.
6. Martha Parsons, "SSIRT Task Force Update: Career Ladders, Compensation, and Continuing Education," *Library Mosaics* 11, no. 6 (November/December 2000): 11.
7. Charlie Fox and Raymond G. Roney, "Library Support Staff Salary Survey," *Library Mosaics* 11, no. 4 (July/August 2000): 8–12.

BIBLIOGRAPHY

Association of Research Libraries. *ARL Annual Salary Survey 1999–2000*. Washington, DC: Association of Research Libraries, 2001.

Bellas, Marcia. *Fact Sheet 2000–2001*. American Association of University Professors Committee on the Status of Women in the Academic Profession. Washington, DC: Association of University Professors, 2001.

Berger, Lance A., and Dorothy R. Berger. *The Compensation Handbook: A State-of-the-Art Guide to Compensation Strategy and Design*. New York: McGraw-Hill, 2000.

Berry, John N. "The Compensation Crisis." *Library Journal* 125, no. 3 (February 15, 2000): 100.

———. "Governed by Administrators." *Library Journal* 125, no. 19 (November 15, 2000): 6.

Fox, Charlie, and Raymond G. Roney. "Library Support Staff Salary Survey: 2000." *Library Mosaics* 11, no. 4 (July/August 2000): 8–12.

Gregory, Vicki Lovelady, and Sonia Ramirez Wohlmuth. "Better Pay, More Jobs: Placements and Salaries 99." *Library Journal* 125, no. 17 (October 15, 2000): 30–6.

Hebel, Sara, and Jeffrey Selingo. "For Public Colleges, a Decade of Generous State Budgets Is Over." *Chronicle of Higher Education* 47, no. 32 (April 20, 2001): A10–A13.

Johnson, Albie. "How Are We Doing? Compensation for Librarians in the Fenway Library Consortium: Survey Results." *Technicalities* 20, no. 1 (January/February 2000): 6–8.

Line, Maurice B. "Does Low Pay Have to Be Associated with High Boredom?" *Library Management* 22, no. 1/2 (2001): 98.

Lynch, Mary Jo. "Librarian Salaries: Annual Increase Drops Below U.S. Average." *American Libraries* 32, no. 8 (September 2001): 64.

Milliot, Jim. "Salary Survey." *Publishers Weekly* 247, no. 27 (July 3, 2000): 35–40.

Pack, Thomas. "Are You Earning What You're Worth? Salary Web Sites." *Link-Up* 18, no. 3 (May/June 2001): 27.

Parsons, Martha. "SSIRT Task Force Update: Career Ladders, Compensation, and Continuing Education." *Library Mosaics* 11, no. 6 (November/December 2000): 11.

"Public and Private Sector Pay: Unfair Comparison?" *Worklife Report* 12, no. 4 (2000): 3–5.

Seaman, Scott, Nancy Carter, Carol Krismann, and David Fagerstrom. "Market Equity Tempered by Career Merit: A Case Study—Librarian Salaries at the University of Colorado at Boulder." *Journal of Academic Librarianship* 26, no. 4 (July 2000): 225–32.

Smallwood, Scott. "MLA Survey Reveals Wide Discrepancy in Part-Time Faculty Members' Earnings." *Chronicle of Higher Education* 47, no. 17 (January 5, 2001): A15.

———. "The Price Professors Pay for Teaching at Public Universities." *Chronicle of Higher Education* 47, no. 32 (April 20, 2001): A18, A23.

Special Libraries Association. *SLA Annual Salary Survey: A Research Publication of the Special Libraries Association*. Washington, DC: Special Libraries Association, 1997.

Stock, Wendy A., and John J. Siegfried. "So You Want to Earn a Ph.D. in Economics: How Much Do You Think You'll Make?" *Economic Inquiry* 39, no. 2 (April 2001): 320–35.

Tudor, Jan Davis. "Executive Compensation Surveys Available on the Web." *Econtent* 23, no. 5 (October/November 2000): 72–4.

———. "Salary Surveys on the Web" *Econtent* 23, no. 6 (December 2000): 68–70.

U.S. Department of Labor. *Occupational Outlook Handbook*. Washington, DC: U.S. Department of Labor, 1949–.

Waters, Richard Lee. "How Much Do We Pay Our Public Library Directors? Part 1." *Public Library Quarterly* 19, no. 1 (2001): 47.

———. "How Much Do We Pay Our Public Library Directors? Part 2." *Public Library Quarterly* 19, no. 2 (2001): 23.

Wetzel, Karen A. "ARL Salary Survey 2000–2001 Released." *ARL: A Bimonthly Newsletter of Research Library Issues and Actions* no. 214 (February 2001): 9.

Wilder, Stanley. *The Age Demographics of Academic Librarians: A Profession Apart.* Washington, DC: Association of Research Libraries, 1995.

10 INDIRECT COMPENSATION

You can only drink thirty or forty glasses of beer a day, no matter how rich you are.

—ADOLPHUS A. BUSCH

What have traditionally been referred to as *fringe benefits* are seldom called that any more because they have become such a critical part of the compensation package. These benefits are also called *supplemental compensation* or *indirect compensation*. The fringe benefits of yesterday have become the employee benefits and services program of today. The following are the main causes of this transition:

- Organizations were forced during the imposition of wage ceilings during World War II to offer more and greater benefits in place of wage increases in order to attract and keep workers.
- Instead of autocratic management using threats or other forms of pressure to get work done, organizations have used indirect compensation to gain employee loyalty and compliance. This was necessary because the former had become unacceptable to today's workers.
- The steady increase in wages has led employees to believe that their basic needs are being satisfied leading to increased interest in improving indirect compensation.
- Inflation, rising wage levels, and higher taxes have increased interest in tax shelters and in improving disposable income. Employers are providing a greater number of benefits that employees do not have to purchase with after-tax dollars.

Although the interest in indirect compensation is relatively recent, many companies were providing insurance programs in the early twentieth century. During the depression of the 1930s, the federal government provided workers with economic security when they were unable to work because of lack of employment, health problems, or old age. Today, organizations assume a social obligation for the welfare of employees and their dependents by offering a wide range of employee benefits. Employees are more satisfied and therefore, it is reasoned, more productive when there is a sense of security.

Even though organizations employ benefits specialists to manage the wide array of indirect compensation available today, it is incumbent on other managers to be aware of and understand the indirect compensation package offered to the employees they supervise.

Indirect compensation provides employee protection without regard to performance, flexibility, or changing challenges to organizations. Every year since 1985, benefits (excluding those provided to retirees and former employees) have ranged between 36.2 and 39.3 percent of the total payroll. Because indirect compensation is driven by tenure and entitlement, it is difficult to make adjustments in response to change. Indirect compensation is usually determined by what other similar organizations are doing.

WHAT ARE INDIRECT PAY BENEFITS?

Employee indirect pay benefits or compensation are those compensation components made available that provide protection in case of health-related problems and income at some future date or occasion such as retirement, or termination. Employee services are compensation components that may or may not be included within a benefits program. These services contribute to the welfare of the employee and usually enable the employee to enjoy a better lifestyle or to meet social or personal obligations while minimizing employment-related costs. The following sections explore both types of benefits in more detail.

EMPLOYEE INDIRECT COMPENSATION

The six major categories of indirect pay benefits for employees are disability income continuation, loss-of-job income continuation, deferred income, spouse or family income continuation, health and accident protection, and property and liability protection.

Disability Income Continuation

When an employee cannot work because of an accident or other health-related reason, disability income continuation provides weekly or monthly payments in lieu of the regular paycheck. There are a number of different disability income continuation programs.

• Sick leave allows employees to receive their regular pay when they are unable to work because of illness. Most organizations allow for a specific number of days of leave each year, with 12 days being fairly common. Many organizations limit the number of sick days that are allowed to accumulate, and some pay the employee for unused sick leave. There is an argument to be made that buyback of unused sick leave amounts to double payment just to ensure that employees come to work. When organizations feel that sick leave is encouraging absenteeism, they may institute such measures as requiring a doctor's written explanation, not paying for the first day, or even reducing the number of allowed days.

• Short-term disability or accident and sickness plans provide payment while the injured person is absent from work, up to 26 weeks. Indirect compensation provided usually ranges from 50 to 75 percent of the employee's base pay. There is often a waiting period before the employee collects any pay, often seven days for sickness and three days or less for accident.

• Long-term disability (LTD) insurance is a method of providing incapacitated employees with long-term security. Many LTD plans provide payment for up to five years and are funded in conjunction with the pension plan or offered as optional insurance plans. Benefits provided usually replace between 50 and 75 percent of base pay.

• Workers' compensation is an insurance program, paid for by the employer, designed to protect employees from expenses incurred for a work-related injury or disease. This coverage is provided by state law. Although benefits differ from state to state, most pay lifetime benefits. The formula for two-thirds of average weekly wage to calculate disability payments is common. The employee is covered, regardless of fault in an accident. Each state has its own schedule of income benefits for various types of injuries.

• Nonoccupational disability is offered to employees in a select number of states and Puerto Rico, providing partial disability payments. Payments for nonoccupational illnesses and injuries usually are limited to 26 weeks, and the plan is funded through employee contributions.

• Social Security provides that totally and permanently disabled employees may be eligible for payments under the Social Security Act of 1935. To qualify, workers must have spent a period of time in covered employment or self-employment and must be disabled as defined by the law. Payments may begin after five months and continue until age 65. The money to pay these benefits comes from contributions by employers, employees, and self-employed people during their working years. As contributions are paid in each year, they are immediately used to pay the benefits to current disabled beneficiaries, as well as all of the retirees. Many retirement plans also offer some form of disability retirement benefits.

• Supplemental disability, accidental death and dismemberment, and total permanent disability offered through group life programs are also offered as disability income continuation options. Some are paid for by the organization and others are offered as employee contribution options. In addition, some organizations provide travel accident insurance for employees who are required to travel frequently. All provide payment in the event of injury, disability, or death.

Loss-of-Job Income Continuation

Several programs provide a continuation of some income if an employee loses a job.

- Unemployment insurance is designed to assist workers during short-term period of unemployment stemming from layoffs and termination. The provisions of state-sponsored coverage through the Social Security Act of 1935 typically provide up to 26 weeks of payments of 50 to 66.7 percent of base pay. Coverage is extended under certain conditions, including periods of high unemployment. Employers pay federal and state employment insurance tax; employees usually pay nothing.
- Supplemental unemployment benefit plans have been developed through collective bargaining and are usually coordinated with unemployment insurance programs. Eligible employees may receive up to 95 percent of their base pay.
- Guaranteed annual income (GAI) plans and individual account plans are normally found within collective-bargaining situations. GAI plans provide for guaranteed pay to covered employees for a specific number of hours worked per year. Individual account plans require the employer to make predetermined contributions to the account of each covered employee that would provide payments when there are work suspensions.
- Severance pay of two to three days or up to a year's pay is provided by some organizations when an employee is terminated, often depending on the length of employment. Severance pay is not as common as some of the other loss-of-pay income continuation plans.
- Job contracts sometimes provide for guaranteed payments if the employer terminates employment under certain conditions.

Deferred Income

Deferred income programs provide employees with retirement income.

- Social Security provides millions of Americans with retirement income. Social Security allows an employee to retire at 62, with the maximum benefits provided to employees who retire at 65. It is possible to slightly improve the level of benefits by working until the age of 72. Note that as the Social Security Fund balances change, adjustments are made to the ages at which people may collect benefits. The amount of retirement benefits depends on the age of retirement, the number of years the individual has worked, the average earnings during that period, and the number of eligible dependents. Employees pay into the Social Security system through payroll deduction. Social Security is an employee's most portable or vested plan. There are no penalties for changing jobs.

• Pension plans in most organizations are designed to allow employees to accumulate capital and meet future financial goals. Some organizations provide for the total funding of their group pension plans, but most require some share of employee contributions. All pension plans deal with four main issues: standard retirement age, early retirement, size of benefits, and vesting.

The standard retirement age is 65, but some organizations have developed plans to allow retirement at an earlier age. Any retirement before age 60 is considered early and often results in reduced benefits. Early retirement opens jobs to younger employees, which is good. The size of retirement benefits has been steadily increasing, partly because many plans are tied to the cost of living. Vesting refers to earned pension rights that cannot be forfeited by the employee. The amount of time required to become vested varies from one organization to another.

• Keogh plans, individual retirement accounts (IRAs), 403(b)s, and simplified employee pension plans (SEPs) have all been established by Congress to enable employees meeting certain conditions to supplement their employers' existing retirement plans.

• Stock purchase plans, stock option plans, and stock grants are all intended to promote employee savings and stimulate increased interest and employee identification with the company through stock ownership. Tax-sheltered annuities provide for deferred income and income tax shelters.

Spouse and Family Income Protection

Programs are available to employees that ensure that survivors will continue to receive income if covered employees die.

• Pension plans often contain features that provide monthly income payments to the spouse and sometimes the children of a deceased worker with joint and survivor life income coverage.

• Social Security provides beneficiaries of deceased workers with certain payments. Those covered may include the spouse, dependent children, dependent parents, and under certain conditions, a divorced spouse. The amount of the payments depends on the worker's earnings, length of time in Social Security system, the worker's age at the time payments begin, the age and number of recipients, and the recipients' state of health.

• Life insurance may be provided to workers as part of a group plan that permits employees to benefit from lower rates based on the total value of the group plan. Among the standard features are that all employees, regardless of health or physical condition, are included and that an employee is usually permitted to convert the policy to an individual policy upon leaving the organization. Often group life insurance plans provide continuing coverage for retired employees. The ratio of employer/employee contribution to this insurance varies from one organization to another.

• Workers' compensation insurance provides for burial expenses and income benefits to survivors. In addition, accidental death and dismemberment policies and travel insurance coverage provides income protection to family members.

Health and Accident Protection

When asked to identify which element of indirect compensation is most important, employees usually point to heath care protection. This is because health care is the most-used benefit, but it is also the benefit that is most quickly increasing in cost. In most cases, health care involves protection for expenses related to hospitalization, surgery, and general medical expenses. In some instances, these plans also cover dental care, eye care, and prescriptions.

• Basic medical, hospital, and surgical insurance plans are offered by organizations to provide employees with a wide variety of coverage for accidents and illness. These basic health care plans are either commercial insurance plans or hospital service plans. Commercial plans typically pay the employee for costs of medical care, who then pays the doctors and hospitals. Hospital service plans typically provide service rather than direct payments to the insured. The plan pays the doctors and hospitals for the employee's care. Coverage tends to expand each year, with payments for such things as diagnostic visits, annual physicals, psychiatric care, and alcohol and drug rehabilitation services.

• Postretirement health insurance has been extended to retired employees in recent years.

• Health maintenance organizations (HMOs) were established as part of the Health Maintenance Organization Act of 1973. HMOs focus attention on providing health care with an emphasis on preventative medicine at a specific site for a monthly fee. Many organizations provide access to several health care options, including HMOs.

• Workers' compensation laws in various states provide medical benefits and hospital care for insured and disabled employees.

• Dental care, vision care, and hearing aid plans are often optional coverages that employees may elect.

• Social Security, through its Medicare program, provides health care benefits to persons aged 65 and older. This program protects persons against the costs of extended hospitalization, convalescent care, and major medical costs.

Property and Liability Protection

Various insurance plans are offered to employees, which vary among organizations. Group purchases sometimes permit large savings for individuals.

• Group insurance for auto, home, legal, and umbrella liability are becoming more prevalent. Mass purchase through an employer can provide for significant savings for employees with premium payments made through payroll deduction.

• Legal insurance plans permit employees to either seek attorneys who will perform the work for the scheduled fees or provide employees with a number of approved attorneys from which to select.

• Group umbrella liability policies are being offered by some employers to provide employees with coverage beyond that found in normal auto and home-owners' policies. Employees are provided with this coverage through minimal charges handled through payroll deduction.

EMPLOYEE SERVICES

There are two major categories of employee services: pay for time not worked and tax-free benefits.

Pay for Time Not Worked

Employers provide employees with services that assist them in improving their lifestyles. From an employee's perspective, one of the most important and valued benefits is time off with pay. Employees usually receive their daily base pay during these time-off periods.

• Holidays usually number from 9 to 12 days each year. Some organizations offer up to three floating holidays that may be taken at the discretion of the employee. Some organizations allow employees to take their birthdays off as holidays. If required to work on a holiday, employees may be given compensatory time off or paid a premium for the day worked.

• Vacation benefits vary from one organization to another, but most offer from one to four weeks, sometimes depending on length of service.

• Most employers grant time off with pay to employees for jury duty. Employees usually receive the difference between their regular pay and the amount they receive for each day of jury duty. When employees are required to appear as witnesses in court, they are also granted leave with pay.

• Some employers grant time off to vote for local, state, and national elections. Employees working as election officials are often paid the difference between their base rate of pay and the amount received when working as an election official. Some organizations provide a specified number of days off with pay to employees who are providing services to civic organizations.

• Military obligations of up to two weeks are usually provided to employees with pay.

• Funeral leave and family illness leave are usually provided to employees with pay. One to five days may be provided to employees to care for members of their immediate families.

• Personal leave may be granted in some organizations for a variety of special circumstances at the discretion of management.

• Marriage leave of up to five days is provided by some organizations to employees who are planning to continue employment after marriage.

• Maternity leave is normally handled through accrued sick and annual leave. Few organizations actually provide for paid time off while on maternity leave.

Paternity leave, on the other hand, is granted by some employers for up to five days to help the father assist his wife after the birth of a child.

• Sick leave is a time-off-with-pay benefit that is described in the section on disability income continuation. Wellness leave is a more recent addition aimed at combating absenteeism. For example, each employee may receive a half-hour of paid leave for each week of perfect attendance during regular work hours. Time off to donate blood is also sometimes provided to employees. The time off may vary depending on how far an employee must travel to donate.

• Grievance and contract negotiations time is provided by most unionized organizations to employees involved in a grievance procedure or in certain union activities as specified in the contract.

• Lunch breaks of 30 minutes to an hour and coffee breaks of 10 to 15 minutes twice daily are granted by most employers.

• Sabbatical leaves of a semester, two semesters, or a year are granted to some employees, especially faculty in academic institutions. Leaves granted to faculty librarians permit professional growth and enhance the professional qualifications of librarians.

Tax-Free Benefits

• Educational subsidies have been provided to public and private college employees and dependents for many years. In public institutions, this normally consists of free tuition for the employee and spouse. In private colleges and universities, the children of employees are often provided with a tuition-free education.

Parking is often a scarce commodity on campuses. Some organizations provide free parking for employees, but in many instances, faculty and staff compete with students for spaces. Parking is often available through payroll deduction. Because parking has become an increasingly irritating problem, employees give this benefit a high priority.

• Travel expenses are often reimbursed for work-related travel. In addition to airfare and mileage, most organizations reimburse for lodging, meals, registration, and all other costs associated with approved travel.

• Relocation expenses are often reimbursed to new faculty hires. The amounts vary from one organization to another, but it is often an important part of the negotiations for hiring new faculty. Typically, staff members are hired from the local area and do not receive this benefit.

• Credit unions provide financial services to employees in most state and federal jobs. Credit unions often have offices on campuses.

• Discounts are often available to employees for campus-sponsored events including athletic and cultural events. Employees can also take advantage of recreational facilities and activities.

COSTING OF INDIRECT COMPENSATION

Employers devote a great deal of effort assembling and managing benefits packages for employees. Employees, on the other hand, frequently take them for granted and do not see them as an incentive to improving work performance. Often employers have failed to communicate the value of the indirect compensation they provide and have never performed a cost analysis of their program to determine their value. There are at least four ways to express the value of the indirect compensation package. First, the organization can calculate the annual cost of benefits and services for all employees. In a public institution, the release of this information could well lead to an effort by legislative bodies to seek a reduction in these costs, which are considerable. Second, the organization could calculate the cost per employee per year. The costs of pay for time not worked and employee health benefits would be relatively easy to ascertain. Many of the other services and benefits are self-selected by employees and would be harder to calculate except in the very broadest sense. Third, percentage of the benefits to the total payroll can be calculated. Most organizations expend more than 35 percent of total payroll costs on benefits. The number may not actually have much meaning for employees but again may raise a red flag to cost-conscious legislators.

The last method for expressing the value of indirect compensation is cents per hour. Although this may also be difficult to calculate given the variety of benefits selected by employees, it is the method most often used and the one which employees can most easily relate to their pay. An employee earning $40,000 annually can see that a $15,000 annual benefits cost is significant.

Most organizations receive information annually about benefits available and are given an opportunity to make decisions about various options. Informing employees about not only the kinds of options available but also the value of these benefits and services could be useful not just once a year but on a more regular basis. Unfortunately, in some organizations, the view of benefits as "fringe" still prevails. With the costs of indirect compensation becoming such a large part of payroll costs, the value of these services should be made known. The flexible benefits packages offered by many organizations allow employees to tailor their packages to meet their individual needs. This allows the employees to see what the employer is attempting to do in improving the quality of their work lives.

THE BENEFITS AND SERVICES PACKAGE

Dividing the wide variety of benefits and services into the required and optional items allows you to see how the entire package is individualized. Required items include the government-required Social Security, workers' compensation, and unemployment insurance. Other nonoptional items are the group life, heath, and pension plans that require full participation before an insurance company will provide them. The optional items include all of the other components. Although not required by law, many of these components are given to all employees as benefits of employment. For example, employees could refuse to take time off for holidays, but why? Employees could certainly elect not to take advantage of discount basketball tickets even though it is an option available to everyone. Quite simply stated, fringe benefits are no longer fringe. They are an important part of the total compensation package.

INDIRECT COMPENSATION ADMINISTRATION

Three basic decisions must be made in setting up a benefits program: 1) Who should receive the benefits, 2) how much choice should be offered among the various benefits, and 3) how should benefits be financed?

Who Should Receive Benefits?

A number of questions need to be answered to determine whether an employee is eligible for certain benefits:

- In order to be eligible, what probationary period, if any, should new employees serve? Should there be different probationary periods for different benefits?
- Should only full-time employees be covered?
- Which dependents of employees should be covered?
- Which benefits, if any, should be made available to retirees?
- Which benefits, if any, should be made available to survivors of employees (and retirees)?

How Much Choice Should Be Offered Among the Various Benefits?

Indirect compensation packages vary from the standard package that is made available to everyone based on the "average" employee to the other end of the spectrum represented by the cafeteria-style plans, in which individual employees receive a set number of dollars and are permitted to select benefits according to their attractiveness and cost. In between is the flexible offering of a range of options without going to a full cafeteria style.

A standard package is easiest to administer, but it has a high likelihood of not meeting all employees needs, leading to dissatisfaction. Giving employees options appears to be the most effective way to provide benefits. The advantages are that employees can choose options to best satisfy their unique needs and that the increased involvement by employees leads to a greater understanding of the indirect compensation package. For the employer, flexible benefits help meet the changing needs and wants of employees and make the introduction of new benefits less costly. Among the disadvantages of having employees select from among options is that they sometimes make bad choices and find themselves without needed coverages. Also, the administration costs of providing a wide variety of choices increase with a flexible benefits program.

How Should Indirect Compensation Be Financed?

Indirect compensation can be financed totally by the employer (noncontributory), with costs shared by the employer and employees (contributory), or with the costs paid completely by employees (by law, the employer must bear the cost of some benefits). The advantages of a noncontributory system are that all eligible employees are covered after probationary periods are met and that there are economies in group purchasing when all are covered. This form of financing is also the most easily administered. The greatest disadvantage is the cost. In a contributory system, employee contributions can result in more coverage or higher benefits, possible greater employee understanding of a plan they are helping to fund, and possible lessening of employee abuse if it means potential higher costs. An employee-pays-all financing plan could lead to greater numbers of options, but the disadvantage of this system is that the organization would not be in the least bit competitive in its field. By far the most prevalent form of financing of indirect compensation packages today is having the employer and the employees share the costs of indirect compensation, with the share being negotiable.

THE COSTS OF BENEFITS

For employers, benefits eat up a greater share of employee compensation costs for blue-collar workers than white-collar workers. Higher insurance and workers' compensation are mostly to blame. The following data from the U.S. Bureau of Labor Statistics for March 2001 shows the percentage of total employee compensation that goes to various benefits for both white-collar and blue-collar workers.[1]

Employee Benefit	White-Collar	Blue-Collar
All benefits	26.4%	30.6%
Life, health, and disability insurance	6.2%	7.7%
Paid leave	7.4%	5.8%
Workers' compensation	0.8%	3.0%
Sick leave	1.2%	1.6%

CHANGING EMPLOYEE INDIRECT COMPENSATION

Making changes to employee benefits is a challenge for administrators. Communicating and conducting annual reviews of indirect pay and making necessary changes are important. Annual reviews that are made known to employees will communicate to them that benefits are not forever and can be changed. In reality, organizations seldom let employees know that their indirect pay may change. When changes are needed that either reduce the level of benefits or require higher employee contributions, employees often view these actions as a breach of promise. Honest and frequent communications with employees are needed in order to develop credibility on indirect pay issues.

It is advisable to have employee involvement and input when conducting annual reviews of the indirect compensation package. If changes are required, employee involvement in decisions relating to those offerings is very important. Supervisors should also be more involved in communicating benefit changes to employees. If supervisors have a greater understanding of the package and its features, they can provide their employees with that information instead of simply sending people to other offices.

Changes to indirect compensation could be made by "grandfathering" senior employees and changing the benefits of those with less tenure. This is a less-desirable approach if it then appears that the organization is creating "have" and "have-not" employee groups. Incremental change is also an option for benefit changes but is also less desirable if it means drawing out a change that could be more effectively made all at once. The preferred approach to change is to get employees involved and prepared for change so they become partners in the changes in indirect compensation.

INDIRECT COMPENSATION AS PART OF COMPENSATION

The indirect compensation package needs to meet the tests of internal consistency, external competitiveness, employee contribution, and administrative effectiveness. It must be perceived by employees to be fair and consistently applied within the organization. The benefits and services must be competitive with those who will compete with the organization for its employees. Because benefits are such a large portion of the compensation package, the organization must be aware of what others are doing and continue to perform cost analyses of its own offerings. Although it has not been shown conclusively that the availability of benefits increases retention, one can assume that benefits play a part in attracting and retaining employees. Communication between the indirect compensation administrators and employees and supervisors is critical. It is also important that first-line supervisors be willing to share employees' views with the indirect compensation administrators as well as participate in surveys of employees to determine their benefit needs and wants. The indirect compensation program must be effectively administered, responding both to employee and employer needs and also complying with governmental and institutional requirements for financial management.

This is a time for cost containment and cost sharing. Organizations need to evaluate the advantages of indirect compensation plans and to manage employee indirect pay like any other aspect of the budget.

NOTE

1. Sheridan Prasso, "The Bite from Benefits," *Business Week* no. 3747 (September 3, 2001): 10–16. Information here is based on data from 3,800 business and government offices, collected from the U.S. Bureau of Labor Statistics, March 2001.

BIBLIOGRAPHY

Barbeito, Carol L., and Jack P. Bowman. *Nonprofit Compensation and Benefits Practices*. New York: Wiley, 1998.

Beam, Burton T., and John J. McFadden. *Employee Benefits*. 6th ed. Chicago: Real Estate Education, 2001.

"Beyond Salaries." *Journal of Accountancy* 186, no. 4 (October 1998): 24.

Black, Ann. *New Era of Benefits Communication*. Brookfield, WI: International Foundation of Employee Benefit Plans, 2001.

Brody, Lawrence, Louis R. Richey, and Richard C. Baier. *Compensating Employees with Insurance*. Washington, DC: Tax Management, 2001.

Cowart, Greta E. *What You Need to Know in Employee Benefits for 2001–2002*. St. Paul: Minnesota Continuing Legal Education, 2001.

Cravens, Karen S., and Elizabeth Goad Oliver. "The Influence of Culture on Pension Plans." *International Journal of Accounting* 35, no. 4 (2000): 521–38.

Dennis, Anita. "Risks and Rewards in Employee Benefits." *Journal of Accountancy* 185, no. 4 (April 1998): 57–60.

Ding, Mae Lon. *Survey Sources for U.S. and International Employee Pay and Benefits: Over 1500 Surveys and Their Sources*. Anaheim, CA: Personnel Systems Associates, 2001.

Fronstin, Paul. *Defined Contribution Health Benefits*. Washington, DC: Employee Benefit Research Institute, 2001.

Frost, Julie. "Narrowing the Perception Gap; A Study in Employee Benefit Communications." *Compensation and Benefits Management* 14, no. 2 (Spring 1998): 22–29.

Gaskell, Carolyn, and Allen S. Morrill. *Travel, Sabbatical, and Study Leave Policies in College Libraries*. Chicago: College Library Information Packet Committee, College Libraries Section, Association of College and Research Libraries, 2001.

Golub, Barbra, and E. Dina Rand. *Employee Benefits: What Are Wages?* New York: Research Institute of America Group, 2001.

Graig, Laurence A., and Valerie Paganelli. "Phased Retirement: Reshaping the End of Work." *Compensation and Benefits Management* 16, no. 2 (Spring 2000): 1–9.

Guitar, Suzanne. "Paperless Administration of Employee Benefits Plans: A Practical Analysis of the Unresolved Issues." *Tax Lawyer* 53, no. 4 (Summer 2000): 887–919.

Hackleman, Paul, and Bill Tugaw. *Deferred Compensation, Defined Contribution: New Rules/New Game for Public and Private Plans*. Brookfield, WI: International Foundation of Employee Benefit Plans, 2001.

Hyun, Jonathan E. "Compensation and Fringe Benefits." *Journal of Corporate Taxation* 27, no. 1 (Spring 2000): 70–80.

International Foundation of Employee Benefit Plans. *Web Strategies for Communicating Employee Benefits: Survey Results, January 2001*. Brookfield, WI: International Foundation of Employee Benefit Plans, 2001.

Irving (Texas) Human Resources Department. *City of Irving Retiree Medical Insurance: Human Resources Director's Report*. Irving, TX: Irving (Texas) Human Resources Department, 1999.

Kennan, Brian. "Internet Technology and Employee Benefits." *Journal of Pension Planning and Compliance* 25, no. 16 (Summer 1999): 16–41.

Laffe, Lesli S. "Domestic Partner Benefits Taxable to Employee." *Journal of Accountancy* 192, no. 2 (July 2001): 74–76.

Lineberry, Joe, and Steve Trumble. "The Role of Employee Benefits in Enhancing Employee Commitment." *Compensation and Benefits Management* 16, no. 1 (Winter 2000): 9–15.

Lucke, Stephen P., Leslie J. Anderson, and Michael Iwan. "What Employee Benefits Practitioners Should Know About the New EEOC Enforcement Guidance." *Journal of Pension Planning and Compliance* 27, no. 2 (Summer 2001): 41–54.

Mace, Don. *Federal Employees Handbook*. Alexandria, VA: Fedweek, 2000.

Mamorsky, Jeffrey D. *Health Care Benefits Law*. New York: Law Journal Press, 2001.

Mcghie, G. Neff, and Michael E. Callahan. *Defined Benefit Answer Book*. New York: Aspen, 2001.

Miller, Nolan. *Health Benefits and Wages: Minimizing the Total Cost of Compensation*. Cambridge, MA: Research Programs, John F. Kennedy School of Government, Harvard University, 2001.

Oliver, Elizabeth Goad, and Karen S. Cravens. "Cultural Influences on Managerial Choice: An Empirical Study of Employee Benefit Plans in the United States." *Journal of International Business Studies* 30, no. 4 (1999): 745–63.

Pennsylvania Bar Institute. *Creative Compensation Techniques: Options Are Not the Only Option*. Mechanicsburg, PA: Pennsylvania Bar Institute, 2001.

Potter, Edward E. "Putting a True Price Tag on Paid Family Medical Leave." *Employee Benefit News* 14, no. 12 (October 2000): 82–87.

Prasso, Sheridan. "The Bite from Benefits." *Business Week* no. 3747 (September 3, 2001): 10–16.

Project Management Institute. *Study of the Feasibility of Providing Wage Replacement to State Employees for Family and Medical Leave Absences: Report of the Department of Human PMI Project Management Salary Survey*. Newtown Square, PA: Project Management Institute, 2000.

Rosenbloom, Jerry S. *The Handbook of Employee Benefits: Design, Funding, and Administration*. New York: McGraw-Hill, 2001.

Social Security Administration. *How State and Local Government Employees Are Covered by Social Security and Medicare*. Washington, DC: Social Security Administration, 2000.

Thompson, Jane, and Mary Wright. *Fringe Benefits Survey, Arkansas Public Libraries: September 1999*. Little Rock, AR: Extension Services, Arkansas State Library, 1999.

Thompson, Jon M., and Debra A. Draper. "Revisiting Employee Benefits Managers." *Health Care Management Review* 24, no. 4 (Fall 1999): 70–80.

U.S. Department of Labor, Bureau of Labor Statistics. *Employee Benefits in State and Local Governments, 1998*. Washington, DC: GPO, 2000.

U.S. Office of Personnel Management. Office of Merit Systems Oversight and Effectiveness. *The 3Rs: Lessons Learned from Recruitment, Relocation, and Retention Incentives*. Washington, DC: U.S. Office of Personnel Management, 1999.

Warner, Peter E. "Employee Benefits Outsourcing Solutions: Strategic Options and Fiduciary Issues." *Compensation and Benefits Management* 15, no. 3 (Summer 1999): 1–13.

Wood, Stephen. "Family-Friendly Management: Testing the Various Perspectives." *National Institute Economic Review* no. 168 (April 1999): 99–117.

11 LAWS AFFECTING LIBRARY COMPENSATION

In all affairs it's a healthy thing now and then to hang a question mark on the things you have long taken for granted.

—BERTRAND RUSSELL

HISTORY OF COMPENSATION LAWS

It is easy to forget that before government regulations, an employee had no real guarantees that he or she would be paid at all. During the depression era, the federal government stepped in to establish when employees were to be paid, where employees had to be paid, how much extra employees had to be paid for working especially long hours, how long employees could be made to work, and under what circumstances children could be employed. For example, in 1914 a majority of the workers in cotton mills were under the age of 16, some as young as 6 or 7. They worked 12 hours a day at a daily wage of 22 cents, while women were earning 39 cents and men were earning 57 cents.[1] When the Fair Labor Standards Act (FLSA) was first enacted in 1938, the minimum wage was 25 cents per hour. This act, which has been amended numerous times, controls minimum wages, overtime, equal pay, and the employment of minors.

CHILD LABOR LAWS

When the FLSA was passed into law in 1938, child labor was a serious social problem in the United States. Today, children are protected by child labor laws.

Under federal law, minors under 18 may not work in any job that is considered hazardous by the U.S. secretary of labor. Included in those jobs specifically designated are coal mining, logging, slaughtering and meat packing, wrecking and demolition, and roofing and excavation. Also included are working in explosives plants and any job involving radioactive substances.

Minors under 16 may not work in mining, manufacturing and processing, the operation of motor vehicles, or in public messenger service or hazardous occupations. Exceptions include delivering newspapers and agricultural jobs. In addition, minors under 16 may be employed as actors or other performers. Minors under 12 cannot be employed except on a family farm. Federal law does not restrict the number of hours that children between 16 and 18 may work, but it does state that minors between the ages of 14 and 16 may not work during school hours. They may not work more than 8 hours a day or 40 hours a week when school is not in session or more than three hours a day and 18 hours a week when school is in session. Children between the ages of 14 and 16 may not work anytime between the hours of 7:00 P.M. and 7:00 A.M., except from June 1 through Labor Day, when evening hours are extended to 9:00 P.M. Different rules apply in agricultural employment. Minimum wage laws regulate the wage that children must be paid.

Fines of up to $10,000 per violation may be assessed against employers who violate the child labor provisions of the law. This law prohibits discriminating against or discharging workers who file a complaint or participate in any proceedings under the FLSA.

WAGES AND SALARIES

Wages and salaries are simply the payment received for performing work and are probably the single most important incentive for coming to work. Because of this, library managers need to understand how wages and salaries are determined and managed.

As noted previously, although wages and salaries are often used as synonyms, they have slightly different meanings. Wages, or hourly pay, refer to an hourly rate of pay and are the basis for pay used most often for production and maintenance employees or blue-collar workers. Salary refers to a weekly, monthly, or yearly rate of pay. Professional and management employees, as well as faculty, are usually salaried, earning a set salary for the week, month, or year.

Hourly, or wage-earning, employees normally get paid only for the hours they work; salaried employees earn a set salary even though the number of hours they work may vary to pay period to pay period. Salaried employees are normally classed as exempt employees—exempt from the provisions of the FLSA.

EXEMPT EMPLOYEES UNDER
THE FAIR LABOR STANDARDS ACT

Before describing the provisions of the FLSA, it may be helpful to identify the employees who are exempt from its provisions. Exempt workers may include executive, administrative, and professional employees, as well as outside salespeople and computer professionals. There are two tests, one long and one short to determine whether one can be considered an executive, administrative, or professional employee and thus be exempt from the minimum wage and overtime laws. The long form is used primarily to determine whether lower-paid (between $155 and $250 per week) employees qualify, whereas the short test is useful for determining if higher-paid (at least $250 per week) employees qualify.

According to the long test, you are an executive if you

- spend at least 80 percent of your time managing a department or subdivision, directing the work of two or more subordinates, or both;
- have the authority to hire and fire or to give recommendations regarding hiring, firing, and promoting employees;
- routinely rely on your own discretion, and
- are paid at least $155 a week.

You are an administrative employee if you

- spend at least 80 percent of your time doing office work; or
- are on the administration of an educational institution; or
- perform tasks requiring special training or experience with only general supervision or exercise general supervision over others; or
- regularly help your employer or an executive or another administrative employee;
- routinely rely on your own discretion; and
- are paid at least $155 a week.

You are a professional employee if you

- spend at least 80 percent of your time doing work that requires an advanced degree or recognized artistic talent; or
- are a certified teacher in an educational institution; or
- do work that is primarily intellectual;
- routinely rely on your own discretion; and
- are paid at least $170 a week.

According to the short test, executive, administrative, and professional employees are considered highly paid employees. You are highly paid if you

- are paid at least $250 a week and
- spend at least 50 percent of your time performing the duties of an executive, administrative, and professional employee described in the long test.

To qualify as a computer professional who is exempt, you must be paid at least six-and-half times the current minimum wage, and your primary duty has to be one or more of the following:

- Applying systems analysis techniques and procedures, including consulting with users, to determine hardware and software functional specifications.

- Designing computer systems based on and related to user specifications.
- Creating or modifying computer programs based on and related to system design specifications.
- Creating or modifying computer programs related to machine operating systems.

One other major group of exempt individuals are independent contractors. Many universities use independent contractors for specialized work. The independent contractor is sufficiently free from the employer and normally is in a trade, business, or profession independent from that of the person employing him or her. The independent contractor is essentially a nonemployee who is paid for completing a specific task and is not paid any of the employee benefits.

EXEMPT VERSUS NONEXEMPT

Exempt and nonexempt employees differ from one another in a number of ways:

- Nonexempt employees earn an hourly wage.
- Exempt employees earn a salary.

- Nonexempt employee hours are tracked by time clock or recorded on time sheets. Employees report hours worked and hours taken as sick or annual leave on the time sheet.
- Exempt employees do not use time clocks or time sheets. Normally, exempt employees report the hours not worked, to be deducted from hours earned for sick days, annual leave, and so on.

- Nonexempt employees are paid only for the hours reported as worked.
- Exempt employees are paid a salary for the month.

- Nonexempt employees are eligible for daily overtime, call-in pay, and guaranteed overtime.
- Exempt employees are not eligible for overtime or call-in pay.

- Nonexempt employees have a set maximum number of paid sick days, sometimes-cumbersome work rules, and a formal discipline program for tardiness and absences.
- Exempt employees, except in government, do not have a limit on paid sick days, have few work rules, and have no formal discipline program.

Generally, exempt employees have certain benefits or privileges that nonexempt employees do not, such as fewer work rules, but are not eligible for overtime.

VIOLATIONS OF WAGE AND HOUR LAWS

On occasion, employees file charges with the U.S. Department of Labor or a state department of labor to assist them in recovering unpaid overtime, final wages, or pay for accrued but unused vacation. During the course of investigating an employee's claim, investigators often find violations of wage-hour laws that even savvy employers did not know existed. Some of these violations can have substantial ramifications for employers, including requiring employers to pay substantial monies to employees other than the one who filed the charge.

Just because an employee is salaried does not mean the employee is exempt from the overtime provisions of the FLSA. One common misconception employers have is that all employees who are paid on a salary basis are exempt from the overtime provisions of the FLSA. However, only employees who are paid on a salary basis and who meet certain FLSA requirements for exempt status already discussed, such as executives, administrators, and professionals (including certain high-level computer systems analysts), as well as outside salespersons are exempt and need not be paid for overtime. See C29CFR Part 541 of the FLSA for general regulations and interpretations in order to determine whether your employees are exempt.

Private employers should not use compensatory time (comp time) in lieu of paying nonexempt employees for overtime. Federal wage and hour law allows only public-sector employers to substitute comp time for overtime for nonexempt employees. This means that private-sector employers must pay all hourly and salaried nonexempt employees one-and-a-half times their regular rate of pay for all hours worked in excess of 40 hours a week. (Employers are not allowed to substitute comp time even when they correctly allow one-and-a-half hours of comp time for every hour of overtime.) However, there is no prohibition against an employer adjusting hours worked on a weekly basis to control overtime; for example, an employee who works 12 hours on Monday, 8 hours on Tuesday, 8 hours on Wednesday, and 8 hours on Thursday can be scheduled to work only 4 hours on Friday. Adjusting hours over a two-week period also is not allowed.

Docking exempt employees for partial day absences may result in loss of the exemption. As already noted, employers are not required to pay overtime to exempt employees. The Department of Labor takes the position that employers may deduct pay from exempt employees' salaries for full-day absences (or as discipline for major safety violations) without losing exempt status for such employees, but they may not dock exempt employees' salaries for partial day absences or for tardiness. A finding by the Department of Labor that an employer improperly docked even one exempt employee may result in loss of exempt status for all employees who are subject to the employer's docking rules. This, in turn, can result in substantial overtime payments, plus interest and penalties, to all formerly exempt employees who were not paid overtime. Another problem is that employers generally do not keep time records for exempt employees; therefore, the employees' "time records" or guesstimates may be accepted as true in the face of no employer records.

All employers should review their written pay policies and guidelines and communicate with and educate their human resources and personnel departments and payroll staff about proper pay practices. Slipups can be costly. If any of the foregoing situations apply to your library, you may need to immediately consult an attorney to work out a plan for correcting the problems without drawing employees' attention to them.

MINIMUM WAGE

The federal minimum wage is established by legislation enacted by the U.S. Congress. It was last raised to $5.15 per hour effective September 1, 1997. Some states have set minimum wages higher than the federal rate. Employers must pay the higher of the two rates to its minimum wage employees. Any future increase in the minimum wage requires enactment of new legislation passed by Congress. This wage is important to libraries because student employees are directly affected by changes in the minimum wage.

The Department of Labor may recover back wages, either administratively or through court action, for the employees who have been underpaid in violation of the law. Violations may result in civil or criminal action. Fines of up to $1,000 per violation are levied against employers who willfully or repeatedly violate the minimum wage or overtime pay provisions. This law prohibits discriminating against or discharging workers who file a complaint or participate in any proceedings under the minimum wage act.

OVERTIME

The FLSA requires employers to pay time and a half (one-and-one-half times the regular rate of pay) for every nonexempt employee's work over 40 hours in one week or, in some states, for more than eight hours worked in a day. All exempt employees are exempt from the overtime pay requirement. In addition, other groups such as agricultural workers, car salespeople, taxi drivers, people who work on a commission basis, merchant mariners, drivers who work for employers subject to the authority of the Interstate Commerce Commission, anyone whose employer is subject to the Railway Labor Act, and radio and television personnel are specifically exempted from the FLSA's overtime pay requirement. Hospitals and other health care providers are allowed to use a 14-day work period to figure overtime, paying overtime for hours in excess of 80. Firefighters and police can be put on a "tour of duty," which means that they do not receive overtime pay until they work more than 212 hours during a tour.

State and local government agencies may be allowed to give comp time off instead of paying overtime. Unless they are public employees, however, nonexempt employees cannot agree to waive payment of overtime, accepting comp time instead of overtime. FLSA requires that private-sector employers pay nonexempt employees overtime.

REQUIREMENTS FOR EXEMPT POSITIONS

Because groups of employees are exempt from certain requirements of the FLSA, it is important to review the requirements detailed by the Wage and Hour Division of the U.S. Department of Labor as to what is meant by bona fide executive, administrative, professional, and sales personnel. Staffing in libraries can be divided first by exempt and nonexempt, with the nonexempt employees being those individuals meeting production standards—student employees, clerical staff, and individual staff members performing the basic functions—such as lowest-level cataloging, acquisitions, information services, stacks maintenance, and circulation. Persons in this group are sometimes referred to as operative employees and often constitute up to 80 percent of all staff. Librarians are always exempt employees.

Increasingly, libraries need more higher-level staff to perform what at one time were duties and responsibilities assigned to librarians. The exempt group of higher level staff includes two levels of management—senior and operating—and professional, technical, and paraprofessional employees.

Library Managers

Managers in the library include the director or dean, the associate and assistant directors, and division, department, and branch library heads. In addition, there are usually staff members who head units and who are often given manager titles. The Wage and Hour Division of the U.S. Department of Labor defines senior management as being responsible for establishing organization-wide policy, laying groundwork for the strategic operations that enable the organization to meet its objectives, relating organizational activities to external organizations, and serving as the ultimate authority group. Senior management in libraries usually includes the dean/director and associate and assistant deans/directors. Operating managers are those persons at the scene of the action and are responsible for daily operations. They implement operating decisions that enforce established policy. They interpret organizational objectives and relate them to their departmental activities to meet organizational goals. They filter organizational problems, passing on those that need review to the senior management. They are responsible for work schedules and for maintaining the quality and quantity standards of their work groups.

Library Administrators

Administrators, as defined by the Wage and Hour Division of the U.S. Department of Labor, are involved in office or nonmanual work directly related to the management policies or general business operations of the employer or perform work that is directly related to academic instruction or training carried on in the administration of a school system or educational establishment. Administrators normally function in such areas as personnel, accounting, finance, law, medicine, research and development, and planning. Administrators in libraries are often librarians in charge of personnel or budget working with staff specialists who perform the daily personnel or accounting work. Librarians are, by definition, exempt professionals. Typically, in libraries, senior management and administrators are considered as one group.

Professionals in Libraries

The Wage and Hour Division of the U.S. Department of Labor defines professionals as those employees who work requires advanced knowledge in a field of science or learning. Although there may not be specific academic degree requirements, professionals normally have advanced degrees. There are fairly specific standards for professionals, and professionals normally must have some form of license or certification. The MLS is the accepted requirement for librarians. In addition, most libraries require that the degree be from an ALA-approved university. The faculty status of many librarians also establishes their professional status and usually requires that a faculty contract be signed. In libraries, there are many instances of staff members being assigned the highest levels of duties also being performed by librarians. Staff in these positions are required to possess either the ALA-accredited MLS or another advanced degree related to their assigned duties. In accordance with the FLSA, these staff members receive exempt status based on their professional responsibilities and their advanced degrees, sometimes changing the library from 80/20 nonexempt/exempt staff to a 20/80 nonexempt/exempt organization. Library managers are faced with a serious dichotomy: librarians and staff performing the same work while the salary disparity between the groups is quite wide, leading to one of the library's most important compensation problems.

Technicians in Libraries

Libraries are hiring more and more technicians to perform support activities including work with integrated automation systems, networks, staff computers, and computers in public areas. The Wage and Hour Division of the U.S. Department of Labor defines technicians as those employees who provide semiprofessional technical support in their specialized areas. Their activities may involve planning and conducting a complete project or a portion of a larger project in accordance with the objectives, requirements, and methods as outlined by a supervisor. There are limited licensing and academic requirements for technicians, and knowledge acquired on the job or in community college technical courses is often sufficient for entry-level technical jobs. There is an overlap between advanced technicians and paraprofessionals and professionals.

Paraprofessionals in Libraries

Paraprofessionals form the most recent and probably the most dynamic grouping of talent in many organizations. This group is wedged between the technicians and the professionals and is often absent in libraries. There may be a division of professionals and paraprofessionals in a library that divides the librarians from the staff. There may be a third group of professionals who perform some of the librarian's duties and some of the paraprofessional's duties. By definition, the paraprofessionals are not required to have the broad, extensive educational background of the professionals, but they are assuming more of the responsibilities of the professionals in many libraries.

WHAT DO WE CALL THEM?

A library clearly consists of different groups. There are senior management and librarians who have a varying degree of administrative or managerial responsibilities. There is a group of staff who are professionals performing duties that appear to overlap with what the nonmanager librarians do. There are paraprofessionals and technicians whose work appears to overlap with some of the professionals' work. And there are student employees who do all the rest. How do you refer to the staffing in a library? Are they librarians and staff? Yes. Are they professional, technical, and clerical staff? Yes. Are they professional and nonprofessional staff? You will likely always have problems referring to staff as "non"-anything or even "para"-anything. Even if the organization uses the group name of paraprofessionals, they probably should not be referred to as such. If you want staff to act professionally, they should be called professionals or just simply, staff members.

PAYMENT OF WAGES

It is not illegal to pay employees less than they feel they are worth. It is, however, illegal to underpay employees in violation of the FLSA or state wage and hour laws. For example, it is illegal to pay an employee for 30 hours of work when the individual has worked 40 hours. One potential area of abuse is in the misclassification of hourly employees as exempt so as to avoid paying overtime. On the positive side, classifying employees as exempt sometimes gives them additional benefits, such as more annual leave.

PREVAILING WAGE ACT

A government-defined prevailing wage is the minimum wage that must be paid for work done on covered government projects. In practice, these wages are the union rates paid in various geographical areas. The original purpose of prevailing wage was to prevent the government from undercutting local workers. If the government were to pay a wage lower than local rates, it would serve to drive down the pay for other jobs in the area. The main prevailing wage laws are the Davis-Bacon Act (1931), the Walsh-Healey Public Contracts Act (1936), Service Contract Act (1965), and the National Foundation Arts and Humanities Act (1965). All of these acts were aimed at providing coverage to groups of workers either working on public projects or providing services or supplies for government projects. These acts were all passed to address social issues in their time.

In the 1960s, the equal rights movement pushed different social issues to the front, and there was new legislation passed to protect groups of workers. These included the Equal Pay Act, the Civil Rights Act, the Age Discrimination in Employment Act of 1967, and the Pregnancy Discrimination Act of 1978.

EQUAL PAY ACT

An important federal law that specifically addresses equality of the sexes in the workplace is the Equal Pay Act of 1963, which mandates equal pay for equal work. Equal work is that work that requires essentially the same skill, effort, and responsibility, done under similar circumstances. Indirect compensation is also considered as pay under the act, and therefore equal benefits must be provided to both men and women even if the cost of providing those benefits to both is not the same. Employers cannot lower the pay of one sex in order to remedy an unequal situation. The pay of the lower group must be raised. The Equal Pay Act does not require the employer to equalize pay in cases where different wages are paid according to a merit or seniority system, a system based on quality or quantity of production, or any other system not based on sex.

"Comparable worth" is a concept related to the Equal Pay Act. The act requires that people performing essentially the same job receive the same pay regardless of sex, whereas comparable worth states that people performing different jobs having essentially the same value to the employer should be paid the same regardless of sex. The justification is that historically female-dominated job classifications with lower wages should be compared with jobs characterized by the same levels of responsibility or requiring the same skill level or effort under similar working conditions.

THE CIVIL RIGHTS ACT

The most powerful antidiscrimination law governing the workplace is Title VII of the Civil Rights Act of 1964. It outlaws discrimination based on race, skin color, religious beliefs, or national origin. Title VII also created the Equal Employment Opportunity Commission (EEOC) to administer and enforce the antidiscrimination law. Fully 70 percent of the workforce are members of at least one protected group; that percentage does not include those who are protected from reverse discrimination (discrimination against someone who is not a member of any protected group). Among those protected by discrimination laws are females, members of racial minority groups, persons over age 40, and persons from other countries. Individuals are also protected under the law from discrimination based on religion or disability.

Simply stated, Title VII prohibits an employer from refusing to hire or discriminating against an employee on the job because of the employee's race, color, religion, sex, or national origin. Although the law only applies to employers with 15 or more employees, many state laws have extended those prohibitions to smaller businesses.

The 1964 Civil Rights Act, with all of its amendments added during the next 25 years, serves to protect employees from discriminatory acts by employers. It was limited somewhat when in 1989 the U.S. Supreme Court ruled in *Patterson v. McLean Credit Union*[2] that the statute barred discrimination only in the formation of the employment contract, which meant that employees were not protected against discriminatory conduct by their employers, including discriminatory firing once they were on the job. Congress passed the Civil Rights Act of 1991, which served to strengthen the 1964 law by adding the rights for wronged employees to seek damages and to request a jury trial.

Under the Civil Rights Act of 1964, damages could be awarded if an employer could be shown to have intentionally discriminated against an employee because of race or ethnic background. An employee could not sue for damages because of discrimination based on gender, disability, or religion. Reinstatement and back pay were all that were available to individuals found to have been discriminated against because of sex, disability, or religion.

Under the Civil Rights Act of 1991, anyone claiming to have been the victim of intentional employment discrimination can sue for damages, although the law sets limits on the amount that can be awarded to individuals discriminated against because of sex, disability, or religion. The size of the employee workforce determines the maximum amount of damages that may be sought. The amounts range from $50,000 for an organization with up to 100 employees to $300,000 for institutions with 501 or more employees. Victims of discrimination based on race or national origin are not limited by law on the amount for which they may sue. Not only were the amounts raised by the new law, but the Civil Rights Act of 1991 allowed employees suing for race or ethnic discrimination to request a jury trial. Those suing on sex, disability, or religion grounds are still not permitted jury trials. Those cases are heard by judges.

UNDERSTANDING DISCRIMINATION

Most employers are enlightened enough, after more than 30 years of significant antidiscrimination laws, to avoid such comments as, "Oh, we don't hire [fill in the name of a protected group] around here" or "We don't hire [fill in gender name] to do [fill in the name of a job] because [fill in the blank with any old antiquated stereotype]." Employers still run the risk, however, of unintentionally breaking the law through lack of understanding or failure to treat employees fairly.

Terms such as *disparate treatment, adverse impact, perpetuating discrimination, statistical imbalance,* and *reasonable accommodation* should be familiar to anyone who wishes to understand antidiscrimination laws. As will be shown in the following example, these terms can play a major role in legal action related to discrimination.

Suppose that Employee X is considering filing a discrimination lawsuit against his or her employer. In deciding whether to sue, Employee X asks himself or herself three questions:

- "Am I a member of a protected group because of my race, sex, religion, national origin, physical or mental disability, age, or sexual orientation?"
- "Am I being treated differently from other employees who do the same or similar work?" If the answers to 1 and 2 are yes, then,
- "Is it because I'm black, female, over 40, disabled, or a member of any protected group?"

If the answer is "yes" to all three questions: Employee X is probably checking out the yellow pages under "Attorneys." An attorney will advise Employee X that the potential grounds for a lawsuit are disparate treatment, adverse impact, perpetuating discrimination, statistical imbalance, reasonable accommodation, or some combination of these. If the employee believes that the employer treats him or her differently than other employees, the employee may sue for disparate treatment. For example, you are a woman and are paid less than a male counterpart who is performing essentially the same job. If you are getting paid less solely because you are a woman, that is disparate treatment. If the male is paid more because of seniority or any performance-based reason, then you do not have a valid claim of disparate treatment. If the employee or a group of employees believes the employer has a business policy or practice that affects the entire protected group differently than it affects members of other groups, the employee may sue based on adverse impact. An organization may have a policy or work rule that on its face is impartial, but a form of discrimination occurs if the rule falls more heavily on a protected group of workers than on other workers. For example, having a minimum height requirement has been found to adversely affect women and members of certain ethnic groups.

If the employer has a policy or practice that is a continuation of a policy or practice of past discrimination, the employee may sue the employer for perpetuating discrimination. For example, the practice of posting managerial opportunities in departments with only white employees or male employees may amount to discrimination if other employees have no other opportunities to learn about the job openings.

If the employer uses hiring or promotion practices that result in the hiring or promotion of fewer protected class members than other groups, the employee may sue the employer for creating a statistical imbalance. The employer may be guilty of discrimination if, for example, a certain interview process or other selection method creates a statistical imbalance in the workforce to the disadvantage of a protected group. The Civil Rights Act of 1991 requires the employer to show a business necessity for a practice leading to statistical imbalance rather than the less-difficult proof of business justification under the Civil Rights Act of 1964.

Finally, if an employer fails to make reasonable accommodation for an employee with a disability, the employee may sue under the provisions of the Americans with Disabilities Act.

As an administrator, it is important to note that even though there is no longer, it is hoped, any blatant, clearly illegal racial discrimination by employers, certain policies, practices, or rules may exist that unintentionally limit opportunities for protected groups and individuals. Those policies, practices, and rules need to be changed to ensure that they do not discriminate.

ETHNIC DISCRIMINATION

The antidiscrimination laws specifically state that "all persons within the jurisdiction of the United States shall have the same right in every State and Territory to

… the full and equal benefit of all laws for the security of persons and property as is enjoyed by white citizens." In addition, both federal and state laws prohibit race discrimination as well as discrimination against any ethnic minority. No intelligent employer will intentionally discriminate on the basis of race or ethnicity, but an employer may be found guilty of racial bias even if the employer doesn't actively participate in the practice. If the employer knew or should have known about a discriminatory practice, the employer may be found guilty. Any policy, practice, or rule that limits opportunities for minorities or has a disproportionate impact on minorities, even if unintentional, is in violation of the law.

SEX DISCRIMINATION

Discrimination based on sex occurs when an individual is treated differently because of his or her gender. Federal and state laws prohibit discrimination against anyone because of sex. An individual who is refused a job or a promotion, is fired, or is discriminated against in any terms or conditions of employment based on sex may have a discrimination claim. According to the EEOC, the employer may not do any of the following:

- Classify a job as "male" or "female"
- Advertise a job with a preference for "male" or "female"
- Refuse to hire married women
- Refuse to hire a woman because she is pregnant
- Refuse to hire an individual because he or she plans to have a family
- Refuse to hire an individual because he or she is or is not sterile
- Refuse to hire women of child-bearing age for certain hazardous jobs
- Maintain separate career ladders for males and females
- Discriminate in promotions for males and females
- Maintain separate seniority lists for males and females
- Compensate males and females with different wages for the same work done under the same or similar working conditions
- Deny health insurance based on sex
- Offer different health insurance plans to males and females
- Treat pregnancy differently than any other disability
- Deny participation in pension or retirement plans based on sex
- Offer different retirement plans to males and females
- Offer different vacation benefits to males and females
- Offer different holiday benefits to males and females
- Offer different fringe benefits to males and females

The one area in which an employer may specify a preference for a male or female is a bona fide occupational qualification (BFOQ), when the employer can demonstrate that being a male or being a female is crucial to the position. For example, hiring male security guards for an all-male prison or considering only female applicants for an acting role as Cleopatra constitutes a BFOQ. The common theme in all of the prohibitions against sex discrimination is that, with the exception of the BFOQ, the employer cannot treat males and females differently when it comes to employment matters, including pay.

SEXUAL ORIENTATION

Federal court decisions have served to declare that Title VII of the Civil Rights Act of 1964 protects job applicants and employees from discrimination based on sexual orientation, but no federal law specifically addresses the issue. Sexual orientation relates to an individual's preference for heterosexuality, homosexuality, or bisexuality, or identification with one of these preferences. Sexual orientation may also be referred to as *lifestyle*.

The ALA's antidiscrimination policy (54.3) states, "ALA is committed to equality of opportunity for all library employees or applicants for employment, regardless of race, color, creed, sex, age, or physical or mental disability, individual life-style or national origin."[3] By advertising through ALA services, libraries and other organizations agree to comply with this policy. Direct or implied biases are edited out of ads placed in ALA publications.

DISABLED WORKERS

The Vocational Rehabilitation Act of 1973 was passed by Congress to protect the employment rights of disabled workers. The act applied only to federal contractors and subcontractors. Its replacement, the Americans with Disabilities Act (ADA), took effect in 1992 and extends coverage to all employers of 15 or more workers. A disabled individual, for the purposes of the law, is a person who has a physical or mental impairment that limits one or more major life activities, has a record of such impairment, or is regarded by others as having such an impairment. Impairments that limit major life activities must be substantial as opposed to minor and include impairments that limit seeing, hearing, speaking, walking, breathing, performing manual tasks, learning, caring for oneself, and working. An individual with paralysis, substantial hearing or visual impairment, mental retardation, or learning disability would be covered, but an individual with a minor, nonchronic condition of short duration such as a sprain, broken bone, or infection would normally not be covered. A person with a history of cancer or of mental illness would be covered. The third part of the definition protects individuals who are regarded and treated as though they have a substantially limiting disability. For example, the law would protect an individual who is disfigured from adverse employment decisions because the employer feared negative reactions from coworkers. AIDS victims are included in the latter definition as well.

The basic provision of the ADA prohibits discrimination against qualified disabled persons by requiring that the employer make reasonable accommodation for those who can perform the job unless that accommodation would create an undue hardship for the employer. To be a qualified disabled person, the individual must have an impairment that limits one of the major life activities but must be able to perform the essential functions of the job. In other words, the sole fact that an individual is disabled cannot eliminate the individual from consideration. "Reasonable accommodation" requires that the employer modify the job application process to allow disabled persons to apply in the first place and adjust the work environment so that the disabled individual can perform the job. The employer may make pre-employment inquiries into the ability of a job applicant to perform job-related functions. However, the employer cannot ask whether the applicant is an individual with a disability.

A reasonable accommodation might include altering the structure of the work area to make it accessible, acquiring new equipment, modifying work schedules, or simply putting a desk on blocks to accommodate a wheelchair. An undue hardship on an employer depends in large part on the type and cost of the accommodation needed, the size of the organization, and the size of the budget. A large organization would have to go to greater lengths than a small business to make a reasonable accommodation. An accommodation could also be considered an undue hardship if it would unduly disrupt other employees or customers, but not if the disruption is caused simply by fear or prejudice. Even in the case of undue hardship, an employer may be required to provide an alternative accommodation.

The ADA excludes from coverage applicants and employees who are currently illegally using drugs but not those individuals who have been successfully rehabilitated. The act calls largely for commonsense solutions to making accommodations for disabled workers who, with the accommodation, can perform the essential functions of the job. A larger, more difficult problem revolves around those few individuals who would take advantage of a disability to find a way to sue.

AGE DISCRIMINATION

The Age Discrimination in Employment Act (ADEA) protects employees over the age of 40 from discrimination because of age. In addition, state laws have been passed to extend that protection in many cases. The law forbids employers from specifying any age preference in job ads except minimum age requirements, such as for an individual who will serve alcoholic beverages. Employers cannot refuse to hire, pay employees less, or discriminate in any way because of age. Courts recognize four elements necessary for prima facie evidence of age discrimination:

- The individual is in the protected age group—over 40 under the ADEA or younger for some states.
- The individual was terminated, not promoted, or was the object of an adverse employment decision.
- The individual was qualified for the position.
- The adverse decision was made under circumstances that give rise to an inference of age discrimination.

In 1989 the Supreme Court ruled that the ADEA did not apply to employee benefit plans. However, in 1990 Congress passed the Older Workers Benefit Protection Act, which extended age-discrimination prohibitions to benefits. This act states that if an employer has an employee benefit plan, the employer has to expend the same amount of money for the older worker's benefits as for the younger worker, even though the resulting coverage may be less; for health insurance coverage, premiums and benefits must be equal.

Managers must not assume that performance will decline with age. There are variations in performance at all ages. A pay system designed to pay for performance must ensure that performance-appraisal systems are not biased by age.

NATIONAL ORIGIN DISCRIMINATION

The only question relating to citizenship an employer can ask a prospective employee related to country of origin is whether the applicant is authorized to work in the United States. Once hired, the individual must comply with the provisions of the Immigration Reform and Control Act, under which the employer and employee complete applicable sections of the INS I-9 form. Under federal law, employees cannot be discriminated against because of place of origin or because they have physical, cultural, or linguistic characteristics of a certain nationality. Simply put, employees are protected from employment discrimination based on the impression that they "look foreign" or have a "foreign accent."

The prohibitions against harassment on the basis of national origin are the same as for sexual harassment. Title VII of the Civil Rights Act of 1964 protects workers against ethnic slurs or conduct that serve to create a hostile working environment.

RELIGIOUS DISCRIMINATION

Individuals are protected from discrimination based on religion by the First Amendment of the U.S. Constitution: "Congress shall make no law respecting an establishment of religion, or prohibiting the free exercise thereof; or abridging the freedom of speech, or of the press; or the right of the people peaceably to assemble, and to petition the government for a redress of grievances."

The overriding concern in employment is that all individuals be treated equally, whether equally good or equally bad. Inasmuch as more than 70 percent of the employees in an organization are likely to fall into one of the protected groups discussed in this chapter, the minority, in effect, become the majority. Thus, it simply makes sense to treat all employees equally.

JURY DUTY, WITNESS DUTY, AND VOTING TIME

Under the federal Jury System Improvement Act of 1978, an employer cannot discharge an employee for serving on a federal jury. State laws also prohibit employers from disciplining an employee in any way for responding to a summons to serve on a jury in state court. Normally, state employees have the option of either taking their regular pay or the pay offered to jurors, but not both. Federal law prohibits employers from making any deductions from an exempt employee's salary for being absent for less than a week, which would include time spent on a jury. The same rule of thumb applies when an employee is summoned as a witness for a trial. There is no federal law requiring the employer to give employees time off to vote, but some states do make employers give time off if there is not enough time outside of regular working hours to get to the polls.

SCENARIO 1: PERFORMANCE APPRAISALS— PROBLEM RESOLUTION AND PREVENTION

Everything appeared to Patricia to be going smoothly enough. The circulation department was setting new highs each month for checkouts and for reserve materials use. The staff and student workers were working well together, and there was virtually no turnover. But everything was about to change. Patricia carefully read the memorandum from the dean's office stating that performance appraisals were due in 10 days. She reviewed her handwritten schedule. She had asked each staff member to complete a self-appraisal for her. Then she had written a draft appraisal that was discussed in a meeting with each employee set up especially to discuss the draft. Together, employee and supervisor had finalized and signed the appraisals. She was pleased with herself that she had been able to turn them into the office well in advance of the deadline. The appraisal process was usually more of a nuisance than a useful process for Patricia, except for this year. She had been planning for weeks to talk to Anthony about his work, and the appraisal process provided a good opportunity to tell him that he needed to do a better job. He seemed to agree with her assessment. Now Patricia was looking at the stack of papers. The claim of racial discrimination from Anthony Chavez was on her desk. Included in the packet were copies of the previous five appraisals, all giving Anthony "superior" ratings for his work, with only the last one giving two "needs improvement" ratings. Patricia resolved then and there never to give anyone less than a "good" rating.

Patricia scheduled a meeting with the director of library human resources to make certain she understood all of the steps of the performance appraisal system and to review all of the steps she had taken with Anthony. The director of library personnel, Patricia, and the dean would probably receive a series of questions or be interviewed by someone in the Equal Opportunity Programs Offices regarding the complaint. More than likely, the office would want to see what was done in other similar situations; for example, did other employees who were not Hispanic receive similar performance reviews? What documentation was there that showed that the comments on the performance appraisal were justified? What evidence was there that Anthony was being treated consistently with other employees? All Patricia could do is wait for some response from the Equal Opportunity Programs Offices regarding the complaint. She would also have to be sure that she did not take any action against Anthony that could be construed as retaliation. She was also concerned about their friendship.

How can this scenario be prevented? Make sure to take the following steps.

- Document, document, document. At every step of a progressive disciplinary action, each action must be documented, and copies must be provided to the employee.
- The performance-appraisal system has to be clearly understood by all and consistently applied.
- Do not wait for the performance appraisal to take action relating to performance problems. Act when those problems are first evident.
- Maintain good communication with employees on a daily basis.
- Make as sure as you can that there are no surprises.

SCENARIO 2: MERIT DECISIONS— PROBLEM RESOLUTION AND PREVENTION

It was March 10, and the library had done well in its campaign to raise acquisitions funds from private sources, but the legislature has just adjourned, and librarians and staff have learned that it would be another year of almost no increases in salary. Along with the approval of raise monies was the directive to award all of the salary increase monies based on merit. After all, legislators reasoned, there were many in state employment who did not deserve any raises but who, in truth, should be fired. The library was required to determine who would get awards of $795, $545, or $0 increases for the coming year. Dean Rivera wanted to just distribute what little money was available in across-the-board increases. He knew that when there was not enough money for cost-of-living increases, puny merit increases destroyed morale. The dean would await instructions from the provost, but he already knew that salary determinations would be difficult. Dean Rivera reviewed in his head the process for merit determination. Performance appraisals were completed, and attached to each was a merit point recommendation made by the supervisor and department head. Based on those recommendations, the library's department heads would have to get together to agree on how to match those recommendations to the university provost's directions on the awarding of merit. The dean would only need to make some decisions on awarding merit to administrative staff as soon as the guidelines were agreed upon.

On the fourth day of August, Dean Rivera received official notification that he, the head of reference, and the desk supervisor in reference were named in an equal-pay suit by three women in the reference department. When analyzed, it was determined that the males in the library had received an average increase of $691, whereas the females had received an average increase of $548.

Dean Rivera will first meet with the individuals who have filed the complaint for the purpose of sharing relevant information with them. Although the statistical information may indeed point to a sex-discrimination problem, the dean presumes at this point that the merit increases were arrived at in a fair, consistent manner across the library. The individuals should be told how the salaries were arrived at and by whom. If the individuals wish to continue their suit, all the dean can do is make certain that he is confident in the decisions that were made, make adjustments if there were mistakes made, and wait for the next step. Because this action will involve the university attorney's office, he will schedule a preliminary meeting to discuss the issues.

How can this type of scenario be prevented?

- The library must have developed agreed-upon merit criteria for both faculty and staff. Long before merit points are assigned, employees need to know the ground rules. For example, if a merit system is based on five points, everyone needs to understand what it will take to earn five points, four points, and so on. What constitutes "exceeds standards," "meets standards," or "unsatisfactory"?
- The best merit systems are integrated with the performance-appraisal system that requires that appraisals be completed before merit points are assigned. Ideally, employees would know at the beginning of the year what is expected of them, what it will take to earn highest merit, and the schedule for completion of appraisals and merit assignment.
- If merit is assigned based on performance, there should be few disagreements and if there appears to be inequity based on gender, it can be explained.

SUMMARY

There are ongoing debates about the role of government in compensation. Its role in resolving some of this country's early employment and social problems is well established. The government influences compensation practices and wages through laws that set minimum wages and those that prohibit discrimination. The government also influences labor supply and demand, which impacts wages. There is a need, however, for balance between government intervention and the lack of regulations regarding compensation.

Laws prohibiting discrimination require the attention of library managers for several reasons. All employment discrimination law relates to pay in one form or another. These laws regulate the design and administration of pay systems. The definition of pay discrimination, the approaches used by employees to sue under these laws, and the employers' defense of pay practices are continually evolving. Many of the provisions of these laws simply require that managers practice sound pay practices. Decisions on pay should be work related, be connected to the mission of the organization, and provide for a well-communicated appeals process. Knowledge of these laws is essential, and ensuring compliance is the responsibility of all managers working with a pay system that is properly designed and managed.

NOTES

1. Edwin Markham, Benjamin B. Lindsey, and George Creel, *Children in Bondage* (New York: Arno, 1969), 25. Originally published in 1914.
2. *Patterson v. McLean Credit Union*, 109 Supreme Court 2363 (1989).
3. "Career Leads: ALA Guidelines" *American Libraries* 26, no. 8 (September 1995): 832. The ALA's guidelines appear each month in the classified advertisements section of *American Libraries*.

BIBLIOGRAPHY

American Chamber of Commerce. *Employment Discrimination: An Employer's Guide.* Chicago: American Chamber of Commerce, 2001.

"Career Leads: ALA Guidelines." *American Libraries* 26, no. 8 (September 1995): 832.

Kohl, John P., and Paul S. Greenlaw. "The Pregnancy Discrimination Act: A Twenty-Year Retrospect." *Labor Law Journal* 50, no. 1 (March 1999): 71–77.

Markham, Edwin, Benjamin B. Lindsey, and George Creel. *Children in Bondage.* 1914. New York: Arno, 1969.

Sheehan, Michael F., Robert E. Lee, and Lisa Nuss. *Oregon's Prevailing Wage Law: Benefiting the Public, the Worker, and the Employer.* Portland, OR: Oregon and Southwest Washington Fair Contracting Foundation, 2000.

Winfeld, Liz, and Susan Spielman. *Straight Talk About Gays in the Workplace.* 2nd ed. New York: Harrington Park Press, 2001.

12 INCOME REPLACEMENT PROGRAMS

Keep changing. When you're through changing, you're through.

—BRUCE BARTON

WHEN COMPENSATION IS INTERRUPTED

In any discussion of compensation, it is appropriate to discuss what can be done when the employment that provides that compensation is interrupted. In the United States, there are three primary programs that provide for income to individuals whose employment is interrupted. Workers' compensation provides for individuals who cannot work because of work-related injury or illness. Social Security disability insurance furnishes income for individuals who cannot work for at least 12 months because of injury or illness. Finally, unemployment insurance is there for individuals who have lost their jobs through no fault of their own.

UNDERSTANDING THE RISK

The U.S. Bureau of the Census gives some interesting information about working Americans and the risk of income loss:[1]

- Most baby boomers are 38 to 56 years old (in 2002), which puts them in their prime earning years at the time when their responsibilities—mortgages and college—are greatest.
- Single-parent households, which rely on a sole source of income, have doubled in the past 25 years.

- Married-couple households, which depend on dual sources of income, now total 60 percent.
- More than 20 percent fall in the so-called "sandwich generation," caring for both their children and their parents.

Given these figures, it is clear that disability or death could create economic disaster for many employees. Disability is the greater risk for working adults. A 40 year old, for example, is more than three times as likely to suffer a long-term disability than to die before retirement. The same longevity that blesses us during our working years creates financial challenges during retirement. Thanks to medical advancements and lifestyle changes, 60 percent of Americans turning 65 in 2002 can expect to live to age 85, and 21 percent will live to age 95. With the weakening of Social Security, it is no surprise that retirement planning ranks as a top priority for Americans.

WORKERS' COMPENSATION

Prior to the establishment of workers' compensation laws, an employee who was injured at work was simply replaced. The injured employee was forced to file a private lawsuit against the employer to recover medical costs and lost wages. The employers in these lawsuits used one of three defenses: contributory negligence, assumption of the risk, or the fellow servant rule.

Employers used contributory negligence to show that the individual was negligent and was the cause of his or her injury. If the injured employee had been doing the job correctly, they argued, there would not have been an accident. Assumption of the risk implied that the employee knew that the job was a dangerous one and by agreeing to do the job assumed the risk. With the fellow servant rule, the employer could claim that a coworker was the cause of an accident and that the injured employee had to sue the coworker not the employer.

Lawsuits resulted in hardships for the employees and in some cases where the employer was found to be at fault, bankruptcies. Liability lawsuits for on-the-job injuries led to the development of workers' compensation laws. Workers' compensation laws provide that the employee who is injured in a job-related accident cannot sue the employer but will be provided with medical care and continued income while unable to work. Workers' compensation laws require that the employer carry insurance that will pay all of the injured employee's medical expenses and protect the employee against loss of income if the employee is hurt in an on-the-job accident or contracts an illness that is related to the job. These laws also protect the employee against discipline by the employer for filing workers' compensation claims. It is essentially a no-fault system that makes no distinction about who is at fault for the accident.

Workers' compensation laws were enacted and are administered by individual states. The laws and court decisions governing workers' compensation follow a pattern across the United States, although some of the requirements vary from state to state. Generally speaking, workers' compensation laws in all states have the following steps in common:

1. The employer purchases workers' compensation insurance or in some instances is self-insured.
2. The employee is injured on the job or has contracted an illness that is related to the job.
3. The insurance carrier begins immediate payment for medical, hospital, and surgical bills.
4. The employee files a claim for workers' compensation, and the employer's insurance carrier begins paying the employee benefits based on a percentage of the employee's average weekly income (66.67 percent of gross up to a maximum cap in most states).
5. The employee is not required to pay income taxes on workers' compensation benefits.
6. The state workers' compensation board approves the employee's claim if they find it to be work related.
7. The insurance carrier continues to pay the employee's medical bills and income benefits for the duration of the employee's disability.
8. As the employee's condition improves, the employee returns to "light duty."
9. Eventually the employee is back to full duty and off workers' compensation.
10. Or, the employee cannot return to full duty, and workers' compensation makes up the difference between what the employee was able to earn before the accident and what the employee can earn with the disability.
11. If the employee is disabled, the employer must make accommodations in accordance with the ADA.

For most injuries and occupational diseases, workers' compensation laws usually provide

- immediate medical benefits,
- prompt periodic wage replacement for a specified number of weeks,
- if applicable, a death benefit,
- if applicable, payment for loss of function or disfigurement, and
- vocational retraining services if the employee is unable to return to the former job.

In addition, employers in many states are required to

- continue the injured worker's group health and life insurance,
- provide suitable work, if available, when the injured worker is able to return to "light duty,"
- return the recovered worker to the former job or an equivalent job if one is available, and
- refrain from any form of retaliation against the worker for filing a workers' compensation claim.

The workers' compensation laws are administered and enforced by each state's workers' compensation commission or board. This agency establishes rules and regulations regarding how and when claims for benefits must be made, how and when claims may be contested, and how and when hearings and appeals are scheduled. Most states require employers to have workers' compensation coverage for their employees; a few make it elective.

Eligibility for Benefits

An employee is eligible for workers' compensation benefits when an injury or illness arises out of and in the course of employment. For an employee to be eligible, that person must have been injured

- during work time in a place where the employee was supposed to be or at least could have reasonably been expected to have been,
- in the line of duty, and
- under circumstances in which there was a cause-and-effect relationship between the job and the injury.

Common Workers' Compensation Requests

The following are some of the most common situations in which workers' compensation benefits are requested:

- Special hazards. Workers' compensation is designed to cover special hazards presented by the job, such as when an employee is injured in a location because the job required that the employee be in a specific location.
- Dual-purpose trips. Employees are covered if injured on a business trip even if that trip combined business and pleasure. The controlling factor, business or pleasure, determines whether the employee is covered by workers' compensation. If the reason an individual is at a specific place is business, that employee's injury is covered by workers' compensation.
- On call. If an employee is injured when called to work while on call for emergencies, the employee's injury would be covered by workers' compensation. Generally, simply being called to work early or late does not qualify as on call because it lacks urgency.
- Parking lots. Generally, injuries that occur in the employer's parking lot are covered by workers' compensation if the employer owns the parking lot.
- Making deliveries. If injured while making deliveries or while being driven from one job site to another in a company vehicle, employees are covered. If the employee was injured while deviating from the usual route, the determination of coverage is based on the extent of the deviation and its purpose.
- Asleep on the job. Workers accidentally injured while asleep on the job have generally been ruled eligible for benefits.

- Athletic teams. The degree to which the employer is involved determines whether an employee who is injured while playing for a company team is covered by workers' compensation.
- Office parties and picnics. Employees are covered by workers' compensation during office parties and picnics if the employer pays for the party or picnic and employees are expected to attend, if the party or picnic is held on work premises, or the party or picnic is held during work time.

The following are some of the situations which workers' compensation benefits do not cover:

- Commuting. Injuries incurred when traveling to or from work are not generally covered by workers' compensation. Hazards faced by employees on their way to and from work are common to the public at large and are not specifically work related.
- Violation of rules. If injured while acting in violation of company rules, an employee may be excluded from coverage.
- Willful misconduct. An injury may not be covered if it is caused by an employee's own willful and serious misconduct. It would be covered if the cause is a fellow employee's misconduct.
- Alcohol and drugs. An injury caused by an employee's intoxication or addiction to alcohol or drugs is not normally covered by workers' compensation.
- Fighting. Injuries caused by fights between employees may not be covered. However, an injury incurred while protecting the employers' property or interests or if connected to some job duty may be covered.

Occupational Illness or Disease

For workers' compensation, occupational illness or disease requires different proof than accidental injury. Whereas accidental injury is an unexpected occurrence, occupational illnesses really are not unexpected. For example, carpal tunnel syndrome, or repetitive motion disorder, is a reasonably common problem. It is found to be an occupational illness for the purposes of workers' compensation if it results from continued exposure to a recognized hazard of a particular job. In this instance, an individual who is required to work at a keyboard for long hours might reasonably develop carpal tunnel syndrome and have a justifiable workers' compensation claim, whereas an individual whose daily routine involves very little keyboard work may not.

Filing a Workers' Compensation Claim

Because every state has its own workers' compensation laws, the procedures for filing claims differ, although they are similar in their basic requirements. Most states require that the employee notify the employer within a specified period that a claim is being filed. In order to be eligible for disability benefits, the employer must be notified in a timely fashion. Proper notice should include the employee's name, address, occupation, the employer's name and address, the date and site of the accident that caused the injury or the date the employee first noticed symptoms of the occupational disease, and a description of the injury or disease. The claim for workers' compensation benefits should clearly state the connection between the injury or disease and the job. State laws also require that a claim be filed with the state's workers' compensation agency.

The employer has the right to contest an employee's workers' compensation claim, usually within a specified period of time. The employer also has the right to require the employee to submit to a medical examination to determine the extent of the employee's injury or the degree of rehabilitation.

Hearing and Appeals Process

In the case of a contested claim, there is a hearing process and avenues of appeal for workers' compensation claims. First, a workers' compensation commissioner convenes an informal hearing at which the employee and employer state their cases. The commissioner will attempt to mediate an agreement. If not resolved at the first hearing, the workers' compensation commissioner will schedule a formal hearing at which the employee and employer may be represented by attorneys. The commissioner may call witnesses and hear testimony. Although it is a formal hearing, the commissioner is not required to follow rules of evidence or legal procedure. After the hearing, the commissioner normally has up to a couple of months to render a decision. Finally, either party may appeal the commissioner's ruling to the workers' compensation review board. Further appeal may be made to the appellate court, which will hear only questions of law and not questions of fact.

CIVIL LAWSUITS

As already noted, workers' compensation laws were established to provide employees with income replacement for work-related injuries or illnesses and to protect employers from costly lawsuits. If employees are injured or contract an illness that is attributable to the job, they cannot sue the employer but must avail themselves of the workers' compensation laws. However, if an injury or illness is found not to fall within the purview of workers' compensation, the employee may still file a civil lawsuit. Instances in which workers' compensation laws do not apply include injuries caused by a third party, intentional injuries, motor vehicle cases, and ADA violations.

- Third party. If an employee's injury is caused by the negligence of a third party who is not the employee's employer or coworker, the employee may sue that individual but not the employer. For example, an employee making a delivery in a company vehicle who is injured by someone whose car runs a red light may sue the driver.

- Intentional injuries. Employees may bring civil lawsuits against the employer or a coworker for intentional injuries. For example, an employee who is injured in a fight with a coworker may bring a private lawsuit for assault and battery.
- Motor vehicle cases. Some states allow an employee to sue fellow employees for injuries caused by the negligent operation of a motor vehicle.
- ADA violations. Discrimination charges may be made under the ADA if, for example, the employee is a qualified disabled individual as a result of a job-related injury.

SOCIAL SECURITY DISABILITY INSURANCE

When the employee and employer pay into the Social Security program, they are automatically purchasing long-term disability insurance coverage. After paying into the program for a specified period of time, the employee becomes eligible for benefits in the event that he or she is unable to earn a living. In all but the most unusual cases, the Social Security system is not concerned with how an individual became disabled, only that the disability prevents that individual from performing any job or that it is expected to keep the individual out of work for a year or more. For example, an individual who suffers severe injuries in an automobile accident and is unable to work for at least a year would be qualified for coverage under Social Security disability insurance.

Filing a Social Security Disability Insurance Claim

Individuals filing for Social Security disability benefits should file immediately because there is a five-month waiting period before the individual can begin receiving payments. If a Social Security disability claim is approved, the monthly checks for the individual will be roughly equivalent to those received by a retired person whose wage or salary history was similar to the disabled individual in the years just before retirement. Extra benefits may be awarded for dependents. Local Social Security Administration offices have the forms and the formulas required to calculate individual benefit amounts.

Because not all individuals who are injured and unable to work remain disabled for life, the Social Security disability insurance program includes various efforts to help individuals rehabilitate so they can go back to work. At various times, agencies concerned with rehabilitation contact the individual to determine the status of the disability. If the individual's condition shows promise for rehabilitation, these agencies will provide the support and training needed to get the individual back into the workplace. The Social Security disability insurance program provides individuals with the opportunity to try going back to work without canceling the claim. Individuals may go back to work for up to nine months without losing benefits to see whether they can work. If the trial period is successful, the individual continues to receive checks from Social Security disability insurance for two months to assist with the transition period.

Hearing and Appeals Process

If an individual's claim for social security disability benefits is denied, there are four levels of appeals available.

- Request for reconsideration. The individual may review the Social Security Administration's files and submit corrections or additional information that may cause the agency to reverse its decision.
- Administrative hearing. The individual may request a hearing by an independent administrative law judge who may issue a ruling based on the evidence already submitted, issue a ruling based on additional written information submitted, or issue a ruling based on a hearing held to present new or more detailed information.
- Review by appeals council. The individual may request a review by the Social Security Appeals Council in Washington, D.C. The council can decide whether to hear an appeal. If it decides to hear an appeal, the individual may submit a written argument or appear in person.
- Federal court. If the individual fails to get approval at any of the previous levels, a private lawsuit may be filed in federal court to order the Social Security Administration to honor the individual's claim.

UNEMPLOYMENT INSURANCE

One of the least understood of the income replacement programs is unemployment insurance. In a way, the unemployment insurance system is a government-imposed severance-pay policy. It was designed to provide partial income to individuals to tide them over during short periods of unemployment. Employers pay quarterly taxes to finance both state and federal unemployment insurance systems. Founded in 1935, the unemployment insurance system is run jointly by the federal government and the states. State systems provide benefits to qualified unemployed persons for a limited period of time, normally 26 weeks. The federal unemployment insurance system is designed to finance extended benefits in times of high unemployment.

Unemployment insurance covers all employees, including part-time and temporary employees. The employee must have worked for a substantial period and earned a minimum amount to be covered. In most states, the individual must have been employed for at least six months during the year before the job loss. Employees need not be U.S. citizens but must be eligible to work in the United States. Persons not covered by the unemployment insurance system include individuals working for the college or university they attend, individuals employed by small farms, casual domestic workers and babysitters, minor newspaper carriers, children employed by their parents, employees of religious organizations, and elected officials.

Eligibility for Unemployment Insurance Benefits

Individuals must meet two basic requirements to be eligible for unemployment insurance benefits: 1) the employee must be available to be recalled to his or her old job or to work in a similar one, and 2) the employee must be physically able to perform the old job or a similar one. The reasons an individual may be disqualified from receiving benefits vary from state to state. The following are the most common reasons:

- The employee was fired from the job for misconduct.
- The employee was fired for just cause.
- The employee was fired for committing a felony in the course of employment.
- The employee refused to accept a similar job without good reason.
- The employee went out on strike.
- The employee is serving a prison sentence.
- The employee voluntarily retired.
- The employee quit the job without a good reason.

Disputes over unemployment insurance claims often arise because of disagreements over why an employee quit. The following are usually considered good enough reasons to qualify an individual for unemployment insurance benefits:

- Some form of fraud was involved in recruiting an individual for the job. For example, the employee who was promised one salary and given a lower salary could claim unemployment insurance benefits.
- The employee's life or health was being endangered by the employer's failure to maintain a healthful and safe workplace.
- The employee's job was dramatically changed from what the employee was hired to perform.
- The employee's wages and benefits were substantially reduced.
- The employee was being sexually harassed on the job, and the employer failed to take action.
- The employee was constructively discharged. A constructive discharge occurs when the employer deliberately imposes working conditions that are so discriminatory and intolerable that a reasonable person would quit, even if the employer did not specifically intend to force the employee to resign.
- A change in the location of the work made it impractical for the employee to continue.

Once eligible for unemployment insurance benefits, the individual must remain eligible by actively seeking employment and accepting a suitable job when one is offered.

Filing an Unemployment Insurance Claim

Claims for unemployment insurance benefits are accepted and paid by the states through thousands of offices throughout the United States. Once the claim is filed, the state's unemployment office verifies the claim by sending inquiries to the former employer, who must respond, either verifying or disputing the circumstances surrounding the individual's claim. Usually, an agency representative will make an initial determination of eligibility that either party may dispute. Appeals are generally held before a referee. The referee may confirm, change, or reverse the initial award or denial of benefits. Appeal of that decision is to an agency review panel that examines written documentation. Further appeals can be made to the civil courts.

The unemployment insurance system begins with the assumption that an individual who loses his or her job is entitled to receive benefits. Once the former employee files a claim and it is approved, it is up to the employer to contest the claim for benefits and prove that the individual is not eligible. For many employers, it is not worth the trouble. Even though high turnover means higher unemployment insurance rates, employers often do not want to commit the resources needed to appeal. In some states as many as 90 percent of the claimants who are discharged by their employers are awarded benefits, and fully one-third of those who voluntarily quit are successful in getting unemployment benefits. Even when employers do appeal, they often lose because they do not have work rules, or if they have work rules, they fail to apply them consistently and fail to document previous disciplinary steps.

JOBLESS WORKERS NOT APPLYING FOR BENEFITS

More than one-half of those persons who meet the official definition of unemployment do not file for unemployment insurance benefits either because they think they are not eligible or because they are optimistic about finding a job. The proportion of unemployed individuals receiving unemployment insurance has dropped steadily over the past 40 years. Recipiency rates—the number of persons receiving unemployment insurance benefits (from administrative data) divided by the total number of unemployed persons (from current population survey data)—have provided a consistent measure of the unemployment insurance program's scope. Recipiency rates averaged 49 percent in the 1950s, 42 percent in the 1960s, 40 percent in the 1970s, and 33 percent in the 1980s. The rate reached a low point of 28.5 percent in 1984, and since then it has stayed above 30 percent, reaching a recent high of 35.1 percent in 1996.[2]

OTHER INCOME REPLACEMENT OPTIONS

Although workers' compensation, Social Security disability insurance, and unemployment compensation provide the most substantial amounts of replacement income when an employee is out of work, there are other options for individuals:

- Private disability insurance.
- State disability programs.
- Withdrawals from pension plans for emergency purposes.
- Food stamps.
- Veteran benefits for veterans who become unable to work because of a disability.
- Supplemental Social Security for low-income disabled persons.
- Medicare provides assistance to disabled persons when an injury or illness prevents them from working.
- Disaster benefits for persons who have lost their jobs because of disaster.

NOTES

1. U.S. Census Bureau, *Money Income* (Washington, DC: U.S. Department of Commerce, 1999).
2. Stephen A. Wandner and Andrew Stettner, "Why Are Many Jobless Workers Not Applying for Benefits?" *Monthly Labor Review* 123, no. 6 (June 2000): 21–33.

BIBLIOGRAPHY

Anderson, Patricia M., and Bruce D. Meyer. "The Effects of the Unemployment Insurance Payroll Tax on Wages, Employment, Claims, and Denials." *Journal of Public Economics* 78, no. 1/2 (October 2000): 81–107.

Browning, Martin, and Thomas F. Crossley. "Unemployment Insurance Benefit Levels and Consumption Changes." *Journal of Public Economics* 80, no. 1 (April 2001): 1–23.

Burnell, Judith P. *Survey of Workers' Compensation Laws.* Downers Grove, IL: Alliance of American Insurers, 2001.

Considine, Mark. *Enterprising States: The Public Management of Welfare-to-Work.* Cambridge, England: Cambridge University Press, 2001.

Cullen, Julie Berry, and Jonathan Gruber. "Does Unemployment Insurance Crowd Out Spousal Labor Supply?" *Journal of Labor Economics* 18, no. 3 (July 2000): 546–73.

Engen, Eric M., and Jonathan Gruber. "Unemployment Insurance and Precautionary Saving." *Journal of Monetary Economics* 47, no. 3 (June 2001): 545–80.

Fredriksson, Peter, and Bertil Holmlund. "Optimal Unemployment Insurance in Search Equilibrium." *Journal of Labor Economics* 19, no. 2 (April 2001): 370–400.

Gomes, Joao, Jeremy Greenwood, and Servio Rebelo. "Equilibrium Unemployment." *Journal of Monetary Economics* 48, no. 1 (August 2001): 109–53.

Hock, Dave. "Back to the Basics: In Managing Workers' Compensation Insurance Costs, the Fundamentals Still Apply." *Compensation and Benefits Management* 17, no. 3 (Summer 2001): 10–16.

Jordan, Laura. *Various Workers' Compensation Questions.* Hartford, CT: Connecticut General Assembly, Office of Legislative Research, 2000.

Kansas Department of Human Resources, Division of Employment Security. *Employer Handbook for Unemployment Insurance: An Information Booklet*. Topeka, KS: Kansas Department of Human Resources, Division of Employment Security, 2000.

————. *Unemployment Insurance: Employer Handbook*. Topeka, KS: Kansas Dept. of Human Resources, Division of Employment Security, 2000.

North Dakota Workers Compensation. *An Employer's Guide to Workers' Compensation*. Bismarck, ND: North Dakota Workers Compensation, 2001.

Mangan, Doreen. "Your Family's New Income Protector." *Medical Economics* 77, no. 23 (December 4, 2000): 93–8.

Marx, Lynn. *Workers' Compensation Benefits*. Hartford, CT: Connecticut General Assembly, Office of Legislative Research, 2001.

————. *Workers' Compensation and Social Security Retirement Benefits*. Hartford, CT: Connecticut General Assembly, Office of Legislative Research, 2001.

May, Eric M. *Workers' Compensation Practice Manual*. Washington, DC: District of Columbia Bar, 2001.

Ohio Bureau of Workers' Compensation. *Claims Information When You Need It Most*. Columbus, OH: Ohio Bureau of Workers' Compensation, 2001.

————. *Managing Costs: What Employers Should Know About Workplace Safety, Claims Management, Rehabilitation Services, Cost-Control Programs, Fraud Detection*. Columbus, OH: Ohio Bureau of Workers' Compensation, 2001.

————. *Self-Insurance: What Employees of Self-Insuring Employers Should Know About Timely Reporting, the Claims Process, Medical Payments, Payment of Benefits, Rehabilitation Services*. Columbus, OH: Ohio Bureau of Workers' Compensation, 2001.

————. *Workers' Compensation Guide for Self-Insuring Employers and Their Employees*. Columbus, OH: Ohio Bureau of Workers' Compensation, 2001.

Oregon Department of Consumer and Business Services, Worker's Compensation Division. *Terms and Abbreviations for Workers' Compensation*. Salem, OR: Oregon Department of Consumer and Business Services, Worker's Compensation Division, 2001.

Palca, Lewis P. "Reality Check: Common Misperceptions About Workers Compensation." *CPCU Journal* 54, no. 1 (Spring 2001): 46–50.

Patterson, Jim, and Vince Zanca. *Unemployment Compensation: Taxes, Claims, Appeals Manual: In Plain Dollars and Sense*. Baton Rouge, LA: Louisiana Association of Business and Industry, 2001.

Pennsylvania Bar Institute. *Tough Problems in Workers' Compensation*. Mechanicsburg, PA: Pennsylvania Bar Institute, 2001.

Pennsylvania Trial Lawyers Association. *Workers' Compensation Practice Tips*. Philadelphia: Pennsylvania Trial Lawyers Association, 2001.

Poynter, Chris, and Barry Williams. "Income Replacement: It's Not Just Disability Anymore." *LAN: Life Association News* 93, no. 2 (February 1998): 106–10.

"Recent Developments in Workers' Compensation Law." *Tort and Insurance Law Journal* 36, no. 2 (Winter 2001): 665–86.

Renton, Nick. "Workers' Compensation: Time to Rethink the Options." *IPA Review* 53, no. 2 (June 2001): 19–22.

Shapiro, David. "Income Solutions Get a Face Lift." *National Underwriter/Life and Health Financial Services* 104, no. 50 (December 11, 2000): 15–16.

"Study by the Hartford Finds Significant Savings in Prompt Reporting of Workers' Compensation Claims." *Insurance Advocate* 111, no. 20 (May 13, 2000): 37.

Texas Department of Insurance. *Workers' Compensation Insurance: Questions and Answers*. Austin, TX: Texas Department of Insurance, 2001.

U.S. Census Bureau. *Money Income*. Washington, DC: U.S. Department of Commerce, 1999.

Wandner, Stephen A., and Andrew Stettner. "Why Are Many Jobless Workers Not Applying for Benefits?" *Monthly Labor Review* 123, no. 6 (June 2000): 21–33.

Welch, Edward M. *Worker's Compensation in Michigan: Law and Practice*. Ann Arbor, MI: Institute of Continuing Legal Education, 2001.

13 COMPENSATION ADMINISTRATION IN LIBRARIES

Good management consists in showing average people how to do the work of superior people.

—JOHN D. ROCKEFELLER

LIBRARY COMPENSATION

Libraries are like many other organizations in that more than half of their budgets are committed to the fixed costs of salaries. The cost of personnel does not often go up and down with the ups and downs of funding. It is possible to reduce supplies expenditures or cut the materials budget, but it is very difficult to reduce salary expenditures. One might think that the subject of salary administration would be straightforward because of a host of formal procedures governing pay. When the majority of employee salaries and working conditions in libraries were governed by the FLSA, the administrator could more easily manage personnel costs. Salaries went to a small number of exempt personnel. Today, the vast majority of staff employees are classified into exempt positions, as are all of the librarians. Clearly, the management of white-collar, or exempt, salaries requires care and attention.

In a small library, the director may be charged with dealing with salary matters as part of the job. In a larger library, the director may delegate these issues to supervisors, subject to review and approval. In the largest libraries, directors more than likely delegate the task to personnel managers with specific guidelines. There are problems with salaries regardless of the size of library, however. How do you know that individual salaries are really fair? Some supervisors, for example, have an inclination to take care of deserving candidates. Some are stingy and others exceedingly generous when it comes time to determine salaries. Under a new supervisor, a former star performer may become a highly paid mediocre performer, based solely on someone's opinion. Not being a salary expert, the director ponders a number of questions:

- Are we paying our employees too much?
- Are we paying our employees too little?
- Are we paying employees on the same basis in all departments of the library?
- Do the staff members believe that is true?
- Are we attracting and retaining the kind of employees we need, or are we losing good people because of poor salaries?
- Are we getting motivational power from our salary program—especially from salary increases?
- Is our salary program in control, or is it running free?
- Are salary procedures taking too much time?
- Does the salary system encourage or impede promotions and transfers?
- Are salary costs predictable for budgeting purposes?
- How can we keep salary costs under control?

SALARY POLICY

Every library, as part of a larger organization, has a salary policy. In some instances, the policy is unwritten. The advantage of the unwritten policy in a small library is that the director can hire people and give salary increases according to a personal knowledge of the staff and their performances. A written policy may consist of rules governing such things as hiring salaries, the amount and timing of salary increases, and a payment for jury duty. The advantages of the written policy are consistency, clarity, cost control, fairness, legality, and predictability.

An important aspect of a written salary policy is that it provides a means of controlling cost and ensures, or at least helps ensure, consistent treatment of employees. Inept salary management can lead to legal difficulties as well as severe morale problems. The following is one example of a written salary policy.

Library Salary Policy

1. Rationale: This library is able to compensate adequately only if staffed with employees who contribute to its success through

   - superior ability to perform their jobs,
   - dedication and interest in performing their jobs, and
   - assistance in helping one another perform their jobs.

2. Objective: Salaries shall be such as to attract, retain, and develop employees who have the ability to ensure the library's success and thereby the success of all its employees.

3. Salaries shall be internally equitable.

- An objective system of evaluation shall be used to determine the relative levels of positions; these levels shall be expressed in "salary grades."
- Each position shall be assigned to a salary grade on the basis of a job description and an evaluation.
- For every grade, there shall be a "salary range" progressing from a minimum to a maximum.
- In exceptional cases, to attract scarce skills, a position may be assigned a red-circle range; the evaluation itself shall not deviate from the provisions of the evaluation system.
- Each regular full-time employee shall be paid at least the minimum of the salary range for the position filled.

4. Salaries shall be externally competitive.

- Salary levels in the library shall be periodically compared with those in other libraries in the area.
- Salary ranges shall be adjusted as necessary to ensure that they are competitive.
- Employees shall receive individual salary increases to maintain their position in the salary range for the job performed.

5. Salaries shall be individually motivating.

- Each employee shall be given a written copy of the job description and job-performance standards.
- There shall be a system for supervisory appraisal of individual performance against job requirements.
- The employee shall participate with the supervisor in such appraisal, shall be informed of its results, and shall be given a copy of the written appraisal and a statement of needs or opportunities for performance improvement.
- Employees shall have periodical opportunities for merit salary increases depending on quality of performance.
- Each time job descriptions are revised, positions shall be reevaluated to ensure the maintenance of internal comparative relationships.

6. In order that the salary policy may achieve its objectives, each employee shall be provided with

- job description and job-performance requirements,
- salary grade for the position,
- salary range corresponding to that grade, and
- salary increase guide corresponding to various levels of performance.

JOB EVALUATION

In most libraries, the salary of a staff employee depends, at least in part, on the nature of the job. If only one or two jobs are involved, it is relatively easy to find out what other libraries are paying for that kind of work. In larger libraries, jobs are classified according to a job-evaluation plan. The evaluation is done to determine the relationship among the various salaried jobs, or positions, in the organization: not among the people in the jobs but among the positions they fill. Chapter 3 discusses job evaluation in detail. If done professionally, job evaluation provides the basis for relationships between jobs in an organization and provides for career advancement for the incumbents.

Job evaluation is a skill that requires not only training in the system but also experience in its use on many jobs. Attempting to apply it without such training cannot produce reliable results. The impartial evaluator looks at any job in the context of many others. The employee and the supervisor are apt to look at the job differently and sometimes claim that the evaluation is too low. It is entirely possible, however, that the evaluation of the job is not too low but that the incumbent has abilities that exceed those job requirements. At other times, the supervisor may claim that the evaluation gives the incumbent too high a grade. One must remember that the evaluation is of the job, not the incumbent.

SALARY STRUCTURE

Job evaluation reflects the internal relationships among jobs, and those relationships must be reflected in the salary structure—the higher the evaluation of a position, the higher the salary. The salary structure, including salary ranges, determines what an individual is paid.

When offered a job, the new employee is offered a starting salary. At this point, the person can choose to accept the position at this salary or reject it. During that person's stay with the organization, salary increases in the form of across-the-board or merit pay may be expected, as are promotions to higher-graded positions. This situation is multiplied by the number of employees, making the administration of salaries predictable. As noted in chapter 3, for the orderly administration of salaries, organizations should follow two general principles:

1. There shall be a set of rules setting forth exactly how individual salaries are to be determined and how increases are to be granted.
2. All salaries and changes shall conform to the rules.

Unfortunately for salary administrators, there is a third commonly used rule: people will make ad hoc exceptions to both rules. Among the common problems are exceptions at hiring, red-circle salaries, below-minimum salaries, concentration, and range overlap. See chapter 3 for a more detailed discussion of these problems.

SALARY SURVEYS

You want to know how your salaries compare with other comparable libraries. Are they in line with policy? Are they high enough to retain your best employees?

What should you offer to a new library stack supervisor? Or a beginning librarian? What is going on in the outside world of library salaries? Questions like these are answered through library salary surveys, which help employers stay in touch. Surveys may be company initiated or they may be routinely conducted by library organizations such as the ALA or the ARL. One type of survey is a request directed to a number of employers asking them to report actual salaries for a list of identified jobs. Another, more limited type of survey occurs when an employer needs information on the going salary for a specific type of job. The third type seeks information on general practice. Some sample questions:

- How frequently do you increase salary ranges?
- What was the average percentage range increase in each of the last five years?
- What is the percentage spread between minimum and maximum of your lowest- and highest-level positions?
- Do you give general increases? If so, how many and what percentage?
- Do you plan to give another general increase? When?
- In the last year, what percentage did you average for general range increases, for merit increases, and for promotions?

As with everything else, you should take care when using the data from surveys. Because titles alone do not always tell the story, you need to be careful not to compare your positions with other positions based solely on titles. Your survey needs to be extensive enough, definitive in its position descriptions, and reflective of your library characteristics in order to be useful.

SALARY INCREASES

Salary increases almost always result in discussion among those who receive them. The employer and the employees are likely to look at them from different viewpoints. For the employer, a salary increase is an immediate increase in costs that does not often result in a noticeable improvement in productivity. In reality, an increase is often a reward for good work in the past year, not to motivate employees for next year. Seldom do merit increases result in accompanying improvements in profits in industry and certainly do not result in cost savings in the public sector. It does not make much sense to relate merit increases to increased productivity—"I'm checking out 50 percent more books, so I need a 50 percent increase in pay!"

For employees, the salary increase is needed to support increased costs of living—it is expected. As we go through school, we receive report cards telling us how we are doing and get nearly automatic promotions from one grade to another. In the workplace, we expect that new hires will be paid less than someone with years of experience. Even though the new hire may be more productive than the experienced worker, we know that the new employee will receive appropriate increases later. A salary increase is a part of the unwritten bargain between employer and employee.

TYPES OF SALARY INCREASES

The types of increases given to employees are usually dictated by higher-level administrators or even legislators. The following are among the types of salary increases that may be given.

- Cost-of-living increase. Also called salary curve adjustment, inflationary, market adjustment. Cost-of-living implies that the increase will help employees keep up with increasing costs. The truth is that employees seldom get real cost-of-living increases and that what is needed by one employee is not the same as needed by another (for example, someone with four school-age children may have a greater need than a young single male).
- Merit increase. Should be used to reward performance. A merit increase that is too small is often viewed as insulting.
- Tenure increase. Earned for remaining with the employer.
- Progression increase. In certain types of jobs, employees progress from entry level to a top level.
- Promotional increase. Reward for moving to a higher-level position.
- Reevaluation, reclassification increase. Increase awarded when a staff position is reclassified to a higher level.
- Temporary increase. When a lower-level employee fills in for an absent employee at a higher level.
- Bonus. A one-time increase in salary that is not added to the base salary.
- Negative increase, or decrease. If you give decreases, be certain you have a policy that is consistently followed.

PROBLEMS WITH PAY INCREASES

Critics of merit-pay plans say they are often poorly designed and administered. Useful performance criteria have often been absent or too difficult to develop for professional and managerial employees. Time requirements also have discouraged adequate administration, including goal setting, performance contracting, and appraisal. The dynamic nature of many jobs makes this approach almost impossible to carry out. The administration of competition for rewards has been another disaster. The amount of money involved is often inadequate to make the process worth the effort. In some instances, the awarding of merit while reductions in force were being carried out made the process more difficult. The nature of many higher-level jobs requires group cooperation and interpersonal influence, making individual merit-pay determinations unreliable.

Individual merit pay is often administered in a way that adds the merit to base pay, having the effect of a continuous multiplier on salaries. It is understood that yesterday's reward will have little incentive value for today or tomorrow, yet most merit-pay plans continue to reward the person for yesterday's performance. This also has the effect of minimizing the value of seniority. By contrast, the awarding of merit as a bonus has the effect or requiring the high performer to do it again in the next recognition period. The downside of bonuses include the difficulty of determining what performance ought to be rewarded, the problems of bias and favoritism, and the misuse of bonuses in place of market or cost-of-living adjustments, and their prohibition by law in some states. Many of these problems are also inherent in the process that adds merit pay to the base.

From the employees' point of view, there could be no problems with salary increases unless those increases are too low or someone else gets an increase they do not deserve. Salary increases can do a lot to retain desirable employees if done properly, which means fairly—as in fair in the eyes of the employees. Employees discuss their salaries, and if their salary administration is seen as unfair, they will be very unhappy even if they receive nice increases. It is essential that salary administrators have written guidelines and adhere to them.

In many libraries, few promotions occur. As a result, employees stay in their positions for long periods of time and rise to the top of their salary ranges. Many library employees see their skills as nontransferable. This leads naturally to a sense that one cannot get ahead. It also increases the library's personnel budget without requiring higher levels of contribution from staff.

Overgenerosity can be a problem among supervisors who tend to be generous with performance-appraisal ratings and salary increases. There is the feeling that it makes for a happy, productive workforce and that it pays off in the long run. Another common outcome is that the generous supervisor is offset by the stingy supervisor or one who gives big increases to some and small increases to others. The problems arise when employees begin to compare notes. Poor communication between supervisors and employees often result in misunderstandings about raises. Poor performance should be addressed directly, just as should superior performance.

Beyond cost questions, salary administration has a direct effect on morale, on performance, on behavior, on library climate, and on your library's ability to build and sustain a productive staff. Unless you check occasionally for fairness and equity in your salary policies, then your library can become afflicted with morale problems. You must also be certain that you are operating within the law.

PROFESSIONAL COMPENSATION

Professionals are those employees who regularly perform nonroutine assignments requiring originality, discretion, independent judgment, innovative abilities, and analytical skills. Their jobs normally require specialized and prolonged courses of intellectual instruction. They normally hold, at a minimum, an undergraduate degree in a specialized area. Their work normally involves the solution of complex, technical problems that vary widely and may have a broad range of interpretations. They devote a minimum amount of their time to directing the work of others, although they may also be supervisors of other librarians and staff. In libraries, these individuals are the librarians and the group of staff engaged in reference work, original cataloging, selection, instruction, and higher levels of supervision. In larger libraries, this group includes accountants and computer personnel.

The design of compensation programs for these employees is a problem area for many organizations. These employees are easily able to identify with other professionals who have similar credentials and work for themselves or other organizations. They develop fairly accurate perceptions of the kinds and the quality of work their peers are performing in other kinds of work settings and of the compensation and noncompensation rewards these peers are receiving. From their perception-based measurements, either they achieve greater satisfaction from their current jobs or they become dissatisfied with their jobs or work environment.

The professional personnel frequently, to obtain greater income, move into positions of management that are related to their own areas of specialization. The result is sometimes the loss of a good researcher, computer specialist, teacher, or public services person and the gain of an incompetent manager. In many instances, the individual does not enjoy managerial work and would prefer to be working their professional specialty.

On the other hand, the success of libraries depends on its professional personnel. In many libraries, 80 percent or more of the staffing are professionals. It is incumbent on the library administration to select competent managers and provide training where necessary. Compensation for librarians is typically dealt with in the same manner as teaching faculty. If the organization has a professional or exempt group, librarians are included if they do not have faculty status. Professional staff members are typically included with nonexempt staff for the purposes of compensation.

COMPENSATION GOALS

Budgets are an important part of compensation administration. Creating a compensation budget requires trade-offs among basic pay policies—how much to allocate to short- versus long-term incentives, performance-based pay increases versus seniority, and direct pay versus indirect pay or benefits. Budgeting also involves trade-offs between how much to devote to compensation versus other human resource expenditures such as training and development and other organizational priorities.

Consider what could happen if pay decisions were made without a formal compensation system. Total decentralization of compensation decision making, carried to the extreme, would result in chaos. Employees would be given any number of pay rates by supervisors. The objectives of individual employees and their managers might be met but overall the result would be that employees would be treated inconsistently and unfairly. Ideally, any compensation management system would be goal directed and would achieve equity, efficiency, and compliance. Properly designed pay techniques such as job evaluation, surveys, performance appraisals, and merit systems help managers meet these compensation goals. Sometimes these pay techniques become ends in themselves rather than focusing on the overall goals. Managers complain that these techniques are more a nuisance than a help. If poorly designed and executed, they may be correct. All library administrators have to ask themselves whether these activities are well designed and further the goals of equity, efficiency, and compliance. Employees and their supervisors must believe that the organization has an effective compensation system and that fairness is its goal.

COMPENSATION CONTROLS

Pay systems have two basic processes that serve to control pay decisions: pay techniques and budgeting. Pay techniques, including job analysis and evaluation, range minimums and maximums, compa-ratio, performance appraisals, and pay-increase guidelines, serve to guide and regulate managers in their pay decisions.

- Job analysis and evaluation procedures require manager signatures and ensure that new positions are placed with jobs requiring similar skills and abilities.
- Range minimums and maximums in the salary schedule prohibit managers from setting salaries or awarding increases that place a salary outside of the range. The maximum salary represents the highest value the library places on positions in each grade and represents an important cost control. Individual skills and abilities possessed by employees often exceed what is required of a job, and managers attempt to pay more to keep the employee whose skills are more appropriate for a higher-level position. The salary range places limits on what can be paid for each job.
- Compa-ratio is often calculated to assess how managers actually pay employees in relation to the midpoint of the salary range (see chapter 3 for a more-detailed discussion).

Compa-Ratio = Average rates actually paid / Range midpoint

A compa-ratio of less than 1.00 means that, on average, employees in that range are paid below midpoint. A compa-ratio greater than 1.00 means that, on average, the rates are higher than midpoint. If the pay policy is intended to pay employees at midpoint, or market, then the compa-ratio is a compensation control that provides target salaries.

- Performance-appraisal procedures require manager signatures and serve to place individuals in similar categories with respect to the past year's performance. The size of salary increases is often tied directly to these evaluations. The procedures are usually designed to discourage supervisors from giving everyone the same rating.
- Salary-increase guidelines prescribe for managers the amounts and timing of pay increases. These guidelines are designed to ensure consistent treatment of employees by different managers.
- Formal appeals processes provide another control, helping ensure that employees' concerns about inequitable treatment are voiced and addressed.

Compensation is a significant part of the operating expenses of all libraries, and controlling these expenses is one of the goals of a formal budgeting process. Budgeting helps to make sure that future financial expenditures are coordinated and controlled. The budget becomes a plan within which managers operate and a standard by which expenditures are evaluated. The budgeting process provides the controls needed to assure that the compensation plan meets the library's pay objectives.

PAY SATISFACTION

To this point, the discussion has focused on how pay systems work and how to control costs. Libraries should also be interested in whether employees are satisfied with their pay. Dissatisfaction with pay can be detrimental to organizational effectiveness and may indirectly contribute to increased costs in the form of absenteeism and turnover. When pay dissatisfaction is related to perceptions of inequity, employees may simply reduce their efforts. When employees feel that they cannot find comparable positions outside of the library, resignation is not an option. Employees dissatisfied with their jobs and their lives have the potential of affecting their coworkers' satisfaction and can become difficult employees to manage.

Before dissatisfaction with pay can be effectively addressed, the conditions that lead to pay satisfaction and dissatisfaction must be understood. What a person actually receives in compensation is important to pay satisfaction, but it may mean little until it is compared with what a person wants to receive and expects to receive. Pay satisfaction is related to many factors, including who employees compare themselves to or whether individuals are in a position that does not require the level of education or skills they possess.

Managers can avoid some of the problems of pay dissatisfaction by hiring individuals who are likely to be satisfied with the pay levels and to consider the changing expectations of employees. Individuals who are attending classes or training programs expect to receive some form of increased compensation, either through promotion or merit. Managers can work on improving working conditions, autonomy, or the amount of interesting work for individuals who work on improving their skill levels. Managers can also have a negative impact on employee pay satisfaction through their actions with regard to appraisals. Unequal treatment or simple ignorance of the pay policies can lead to pay dissatisfaction among employees. At times, managers make matters worse by failing to gain acceptance of pay-increase decisions.

Many employees know relatively little about the compensation paid to others, either within or outside of their library. Most of the lack of knowledge on the part of employees stems from the relative secrecy of pay information, even in public institutions, where the salaries of all employees are public record. In fact, many institutions place salary information on reserve in libraries so it is readily accessible. Perhaps libraries should consider training sessions for managers and employees on how pay is determined.

INTEGRATING MANAGEMENT BY OBJECTIVES AND MERIT

This work has attempted to provide information on a wide range of pay techniques and salary issues. The appraisal system influenced by management by objectives (MBO), described in chapter 5, is the author's preferred appraisal system.

As previously noted, merit plans do not relate well to this type of goal-oriented appraisal, and pay plans are often unrelated to organizational goals. A method of determining merit using a goal-based appraisal system can integrate merit and MBO.

For example, the supervisor and employee agree at the beginning of the evaluation year that the degree to which seven goals are accomplished will be assessed at the end of the year. This is the *intended weight*. The supervisor and the employee meet at the end of the evaluation year to agree on the degree to which those goals were accomplished. This is the *accomplished weight*. The library uses a system of "exceeds expectations," "meets expectations," and "unsatisfactory" as requirements for merit ratings. Multiplying intended weight (I) by accomplished weight (A) results in a percentage value, which equates to a rating.

The goal accomplishment form reproduced in table 13.1 can be completed as part of the goal setting step in the appraisal process. At the beginning of the year, the employee and supervisor agree on I.

At the end of the year, the employee and supervisor agree on goal accomplishment (A) at the scheduled appraisal meeting. The example in table 13.2 shows how the intended weight and accomplished weight translate into a merit rating.

In this example, the employee and supervisor have agreed at the beginning of the year that goal 1 will count toward 20 percent of merit. The goal was accomplished (100 percent) and resulted in 20 percent of merit. The employee and supervisor agreed that goal 2 was only 33 percent accomplished, resulting in 3 percent of merit. In this example, Employee A earned a "meets expectations" and the merit increase assigned to that rating. In no cases can individuals earn more than 100 percent of merit. As in all systems, an honest assessment by employees and supervisors

Table 13.1. Goal Accomplishment Form

Translating Goal Accomplishment to Merit Rating
Employee_____

Goal Number	Intended Weight (I)	Accomplishment Weight (A)	I × A
1	____%	____%	____%
2	____%	____%	____%
3	____%	____%	____%
4	____%	____%	____%
5	____%	____%	____%
6	____%	____%	____%
7	____%	____%	____%
Totals	100%	____%	____%

Unsatisfactory = 0%–59.9%
Meets expectations = 60%–89.9%
Exceeds expectations = 90%–100%

Table 13.2. Sample Completed Goal Accomplishment Form

Translating Goal Accomplishment to Merit Rating
Employee A

Goal Number	Intended Weight (I)	Accomplishment Weight (A)	I × A
1	20%	100%	20%
2	10%	33%	3%
3	10%	50%	5%
4	5%	100%	5%
5	20%	60%	12%
6	20%	100%	20%
7	15%	100%	15%
Totals	100%	543%	80%

Unsatisfactory = 0%–59.9%
Meets expectations = 60%–89.9%
Exceeds expectations = 90%–100%

of the intended weights and the accomplished weights is absolutely critical to successful appraisals.

TRUST AND COMPENSATION

As in other organizations, the primary leverages in any library are fear and trust. Movement from fear to trust is an indication of a successful organization. Over the long run, increasing trust results in increased productivity and creativity. Organizations that move from fear to trust as a means of accomplishing work have the following basic features:

- They move from a bureaucratic depersonalization to greater interpersonal relationships and personalization.
- They move from a closed to an open management system.
- They move from an external appeal to motivation to building in rewards for greater self-determination.
- They move from dependency to greater independence and interdependence.

In order to establish trust, an organization must demonstrate that it treats employees with equity and fairness. It must deal with employees in a manner that is protective of their dignity and security, and it must develop a compensation system that can be relied on to do what the organization says it will do. If employees are told that they will be given merit (if merit is available) if they accomplish their objectives, the library must award merit according to its plan. That means that everyone charged with completing assessments and making recommendations must complete those tasks. And everyone has to be consistent in their application of the rules for assigning salary increases. Everyone, including the director—especially the director. Trust disappears quickly if the top administrator fails to follow agreed-upon procedures.

It is impossible to carry out an effective and efficient compensation plan in the library if trust is absent from the work culture. If the predominant emotion is fear—of layoff or capricious termination, of unfair treatment in pay matters, or of personal powerlessness—it will be extremely difficult to manage effectively. Who wants to work in such an environment?

Mutuality of trust is, at least in part, brought about by example. Managers and administrators who encourage meaningful work relationships and honesty in interpersonal dealings can develop a trusting environment. Basing performance appraisals and salary increases on goals and demonstrated accomplishments instead of personality or what happened yesterday goes a long way in establishing such an environment. Employees are also more likely to trust their supervisors if they know that the latter can control the situation or at least has support at the next managerial level. And finally, all of this is facilitated by open communications.

Management of the library's compensation system is made more challenging because of constant change. Many forces are constantly at work that affect individual and group wage levels, job content, and the effectiveness of various pay methods. As job content changes (usually higher level), salaries may escalate. Many pressures on salaries come from attempts by individuals to satisfy their needs or personal objectives. Supervisors have been known to try to keep salaries down in an attempt to be cost conscious or to look good to the boss. Others have attempted to curry favor with those they supervise by obtaining the largest pay increases possible for each of them. Legislative bodies, boards, and administrators may demand that the library reduce its personnel costs or may punish it by withholding salary increases. In short, compensation management has many challenges.

Librarians, staff, and administrators should become familiar with the various aspects of pay techniques and compensation in order to understand how these decisions are made and possibly, to affect these changes.

BIBLIOGRAPHY

Berman, Evan M. *Productivity in Public and Nonprofit Organizations: Strategies and Techniques*. Thousand Oaks, CA: Sage, 1998.

Berry, John N. "The Compensation Crisis: Librarianship's Chronic Salary Depression." *Library Journal* 125, no. 3 (February 15, 2000): 100.

Flagg, Gordon. "We've Buttered Our Bread, Must We Lie in It? State of Professional Salaries." *American Libraries* 31, no. 3 (March 2000): 31.

Fletcher, Meg. "Years of Comp Cost Declines Likely Ending." *Business Insurance* 35, no. 23 (June 4, 2001): 3–5.

Harvard Business Review. *Harvard Business Review on Compensation*. Boston: Harvard Business School Press, 2002.

Heneman, Robert L. *Business-Driven Compensation Policies: Integrating Compensation Systems with Corporate Business Strategies*. New York: Amacom, 2001.

Kearney, Richard C., and Evan M. Berman. *Public Sector Performance: Management, Motivation, and Measurement*. Boulder, CO: Westview Press, 2000.

Larue, James. "Can't Get No Satisfaction: Library Pay in the 21st Century." *American Libraries* 31, no. 3 (March 2000): 36–8.

Lawler, Edward E., Susan Albers Mohrman, and Gerald E. Ledford. *"Strategies for High Performance Organizations*. San Francisco: Jossey-Bass, 2000.

"Majority of Workers Are Dissatisfied with Pay." *HR Magazine* 46, no. 6 (June 2001): 35–7.

Mosley, Shelley "How to Survive a Classification Study." *Library Journal* 123, no. 17 (October 15, 1998) 48–50.

Organ, Dennis W. "What Pay Can and Can't Do: Little Impact on Job Performance." *Business Horizons* 43 no. 5 (September/October 2000): 1.

Schneider, Karen G. "All the Basic Issues Come Back to—Money." *American Libraries* 31, no. 3 (March 2000): 35.

Tropman, John E. *The Compensation Solution: How to Develop an Employee-Driven Rewards System*. San Francisco: Jossey-Bass, 2001.

GLOSSARY

Information about money has become almost as important as money itself.

—WALTER WRISTON

Accountability. Used in job analysis to denote the end results to be achieved by the employee.

Across-the-board increase. An increase in wages given to the majority of workers. Also known as a *general increase*.

Actual hours. The actual number of hours worked in a period by an employee.

Actuarially sound. A pension fund is considered "actuarially sound" when the amount in the fund and the current levels of contributions to the fund are sufficient, on the basis of assumptions made concerning interest and other factors, to meet the liabilities already accrued and accruing.

Actuary (pensions and insurance). A person trained in mathematics, statistics, and legal-accounting methods and the sound principles of operation of insurance, annuities, and pension plans.

Administration. Commonly used term indicating the top levels of management or their functions. Occasionally used in an opposite sense to mean the routines of lower management levels.

Administrator (pension). The trustee of a jointly administered labor management pension (for the purposes of the Federal Disclosure Act). In its usual meaning, it denotes the person or organization that performs the routine clerical operations of the plan.

Aggregate funding method. A method of accumulating money for future payment of pensions whereby the actuary determines the present value of all future benefit payments, deducts from this value whatever funds may be on hand with the insurance company or trustee, and distributes the cost of the balance over the future on a reasonable basis.

Agreement increase. An increase in pay given to all workers or to a majority of workers as a result of contract negotiations.

Amortization. Paying off an interest-bearing liability through a series of installment payments.

Annualize rate. Transforming an investment rate of return for a period greater than or less than one year to a rate in terms of 12 months.

Annuity. Periodic payments made to a pensioner over a fixed period of time or until the pensioner's death. To purchase an annuity means to pay over a lump sum or make periodic payments to an insurance company. In return, the insurance company guarantees to provide certain periodic payments to the participant as long as the participant lives beyond the first due date of the annuity.

Approved pension plans. Those plans that qualify for certain tax exemptions under provisions of the Internal Revenue Code and regulations of the Commissioner of Internal Revenue.

Authority. 1) The right to take independent action. 2) The right to direct the actions of others. As applied to functional or staff authority, it is the right to direct another unit of the organization only with regard to the functional specialty of the directing party.

Automatic wage adjustment. Automatically increasing or decreasing wages in accordance with some specific plan.

Automatic wage progression. Automatically increasing wages after specified periods of service. Also called *length-of-service increase.*

Average earned rate. An hourly rate of pay arrived at by dividing hours worked into the equivalent earnings paid for a calendar quarter for use in the next quarter. Excludes overtime and other payments not considered to be earnings.

Average hourly earnings. Hourly pay determined by dividing hours worked per pay period into the total wages paid for the period.

Average straight-time hourly earnings. Hourly pay determined by dividing the hours worked per period into the total straight-time (excluding overtime) earnings for the period.

Balance sheet. An organization's financial statement showing assets, liabilities, and capital on a given date.

Base wage rate. The hourly rate paid for a job performed at a standard pace. Does not include shift differentials, overtime, or incentive premiums. Also called *base rate*.

Benchmark. A standard with characteristics so detailed that other classifications can be compared as beginning above, below, or comparable to it.

Beneficiary. A person named to receive benefits from an insurance policy, pension plan, will, or other source.

Blue-collar workers. Description that includes skilled and semiskilled craft workers, unskilled laborers, and their immediate supervisors, who are usually paid on an hourly basis.

Bona fide occupational qualification (BFOQ). The phrase used in Title VII of the Civil Rights Act of 1964 to allow an exception to the equal employment law. BFOQ exceptions are rare and do not include race or color.

Bonus earnings. Extra compensation in addition to regular wages.

Bootleg wages. Wages above market rate that an employer must pay in a tight labor market to attract and hold skilled workers.

Call-back pay. Payment given to employees who are called back to work after their regular working hours.

Call-in pay. Guaranteed pay for workers who report to work at the usual time and for whom there is no work.

Check-off. The deduction of union dues or assessments from employees' pay for the purpose of turning them over to the union.

Class of positions. A group of positions that are alike enough in duties and responsibilities to be called by the same descriptive title, to be given the same pay scale, and to require substantially the same qualifications.

Class-series. A grouping of job classes having similar job content but differing in levels of skill, responsibility, knowledge, and qualification requirements.

Comparable worth. The concept of measuring a job's value to an organization, important in determining rates of pay for jobs having different job content and making different requirements on the jobholder.

Compensatory time. Comp time. Time off given in lieu of overtime. Must be given in the same workweek.

Consumer price index. A listing of price changes in a selected list of products and services in representative cities prepared by the U.S. Bureau of Labor Statistics.

Controller. An individual who is responsible for accounting and the control of expenditures. Also called *comptroller*.

Cost-of-living adjustment (COLA). Pay adjustments based on changes in price indexes published by the U.S. Bureau of Labor Statistics.

Cost-of-living index. Average changes in the cost of goods purchased by consumers against the cost during some base period.

Criterion. A standard or measure used to appraise an employee's job performance.

Division of labor. The assignment of tasks or responsibilities to an individual or a group within an organization.

Downgrading. The demotion of an employee to a lower-rated job.

Efficiency. A ratio that compares actual performance with a standard, as in performance rating.

Effort. The will to perform productive work.

Employee benefits. Tangible compensation, other than wages, given to employees.

Environment. The external conditions affecting an individual or a group.

Equal pay for equal work. The principle that regardless of age, sex, color, or religion, an individual should be paid the same wage for the same type of work.

Escalator clause. Provision in a labor agreement for making wage adjustments upward or downward in accordance with cost-of-living fluctuations.

Exempt employees. Executive, professional, and administrative employees and others who perform specific duties, earn above a specified minimum, and are exempt from the overtime pay requirements and other protections afforded by the Fair Labor Standards Act.

Factor comparison. A job-evaluation plan in which relative values for each of a number of factors of a job are established by direct comparison with values established for the same factors on selected jobs.

Factor Evaluation System (FES). A method developed by the Office of Personnel Management (formerly the U.S. Civil Service Commission) to evaluate and classify positions. Nine well-defined factors, with multiple levels in each factor, are the basis for position analysis.

Fair day's work. The amount of work performed by a person or a group of persons that is fair to both the organization and the person, concerning wages paid.

Family of jobs. The grouping of two or more classes of jobs that have related or common work content.

First-line supervisor. The manager closest to nonsupervisory employees in the organization. Also called *frontline supervisor*.

Fixed-benefit retirement plan. A type of plan providing retirement benefits in a fixed amount or at a fixed percentage.

Flat-benefit plan. A plan providing benefits unrelated to earnings.

Fringe benefits. *See* **Employee benefits.**

Function. A specific activity performed by an individual or a group.

Garnishment. A legal action whereby a portion of an employee's wages are attached by a creditor to pay a debt.

Golden handcuffs. Compensation components earned over a period of time that assist in retaining an employee.

Golden umbrella. Compensation components payable to an employee upon dissolution of the organization or termination of the job.

Green-circle rate. Rate of pay less than the minimum for that pay grade.

Group bonus. A payment based on the performance of a group of workers operating as a unit.

Guaranteed annual wage. A plan that guarantees a minimum income to employees annually.

Guaranteed wage rate. The rate of pay an employer guarantees for incentive work.

Halo effect. The tendency of one factor in a performance appraisal to influence the rating of other factors.

Human resources department. Or *human resources division*. A staff concerned with securing and maintaining the staffing for the organization. Functions include employment, compensation, training, safety, health, and other activities related to employee-employer relations.

Human resources director. The staff executive in charge of human resources administration.

In-basket exercise. A specific type of work sample test often used in managerial selection. Individual is given a basket of work to respond to, using all possible resources.

Incentive. A reward that compensates the worker for performance above standard. A wage incentive is used to induce effort above normal.

Job. A collection of duties and responsibilities that, when considered as a whole, constitute the assignment of one or more individuals.

Job analysis. The process of observing and appraising a job and then recording the details of the work so it can be evaluated. Also known as *job study*.

Job bidding. Method of allowing employees to bid for or apply for job vacancies.

Job description. A summary of the most relevant features of a job in terms of the general nature of the work involved. It describes the work, not the individual who performs the work.

Job duties. A group of work activities or tasks that, when taken together, describe major responsibilities of the job.

Job evaluation. A procedure for determining the relative worth of various job duties.

Job responsibility. A major purpose of an employee's work activity.

Job specification. That part of the job description that includes the required qualifications of the jobholder.

Keogh plan. A retirement plan designed for self-employed individuals and their employees.

Key class. Selected occupations about which data can be collected to provide the basis for setting pay.

Line. Employees directly involved in the delivery of services for the organization. Compare *staff*.

Management by exception. The practice of confining an executive's attention to matters commensurate with rank and ability. Accomplished by delegating authority and detail responsibility to others.

Management by objectives (MBO). A formal program in which the supervisor and subordinate mutually agree on the achievement of certain desired objectives and in which the performance of the individual is measured by accomplishment of those objectives.

Median. The middle value in a distribution, with an equal number of values above and below it. Important in evaluating salary figures.

Merit increase. A wage increase based on the individual worker's merit.

Merit rating. A method for appraising the work of an employee. Used as a basis for pay rating, promotion, or work reassignment.

Midpoint. The salary midway between the minimum and maximum of a pay range.

Mutual rating. The rating of each person by everyone in the immediate work group. Also called *360 rating*.

Nonexempt employees. Workers subject to the provisions of the Fair Labor Standards Act.

Organization. A systematically assembled group of individuals brought together for the accomplishment of a common goal. Also the process of arranging the units of a group and assigning responsibilities to group members.

Organization chart. A diagram depicting the structure of an organization, including the names of the units and the employees with their titles, their relative ranks, and the interrelationships of the units.

Organization structure. The relative rank and relationships between units as shown on the organization chart.

Output. The total production of a process or worker for a specified unit of time.

Overtime. Time worked by an employee in addition to regularly scheduled hours in excess of the legal maximum number of hours.

Pay adjustment. The revision of pay rates, which may be either across-the-board such as cost of living or spot adjustments in prevailing rates.

Pay compression. Upward movement of pay rates that reduces the differentials between jobs at different grades.

Pay grades. The designation assigned to a pay range.

Pay plan. The schedule of pay ranges and a list of the assignments of each class in the classification plan to one of the ranges.

Pay range. Salary rates having minimum, maximum, and intermediate rates and assigned to particular positions or classes of positions.

Pay step. The levels within a pay range.

Pay survey. The gathering of wage and salary data paid by other employers for comparison purposes.

Performance-appraisal rating. A method for evaluating the contributions of an employee with respect to the job. This rating serves as a basis for merit increases and promotions.

Periodic review. A plan for regularly reviewing the status of an employee or reviewing the contents of a job.

Pink-collar workers. Workers who occupy jobs in which 70 to 80 percent of the incumbents are female.

Point rating system. A method of job evaluation in which point values are assigned to each job factor. The wage rates for specific jobs are then determined by comparing the total points with the point values and wages of specific jobs. Also called *point method, point system.*

Position analysis. A form of job evaluation.

Premium pay. Pay over and above the regular wage rate for work performed outside or beyond the regularly scheduled workday, such as Sundays, holidays, night shifts, and so on.

Promotion. Advancement of an employee to a higher job classification.

Range spread. Difference between the minimum and the maximum pay rates of a given pay grade.

Rate range. Range between the minimum and the maximum hourly rates for a particular job classification.

Real wages. Purchasing power of money received as wages.

Red-circle rates. Rates of pay that are above the maximum rate for a job.

Right-to-work laws. State laws prohibiting any type of union security arrangement whereby union membership is a requirement of the job.

Salary. Compensation for a given period of time, such as weekly, monthly, or annually, as opposed to an hourly wage.

Seniority. Rights and privileges afforded employees based on length of service.

Service. Work done for others.

Shift differential. Extra pay given to employees who work on shifts other than the regular day shift.

Staff. Employees who provide assistance or services to other employees rather than producing the basic goods or services of the organization. Compare *line*.

Straight time. Regular wage rate for work performed during the regularly scheduled workday.

Supervisor. Any person who directs the activities of immediate subordinates. Title often applied to a group leader who heads a section within a department.

Take-home pay. Wages minus required deductions, including taxes.

Turnover. The number of persons hired within a stated period to replace those who leave.

Underutilization. Employment of minorities or women at a rate below their percentages in the relevant labor market.

Upgrading. *See* **Promotion.**

Validation. Verification that an employment test or selection procedure actually predicts job performance.

Wage differentials. Differences in wage rates for similar jobs because of hours of work, working conditions, and so on.

Wage level. Average of all wage rates paid to workers in an occupation, an industry, or a group of industries.

Wage rate. The amount paid to the employee per hour.

Wages. Compensation paid to hourly workers.

White-collar workers. Nonmanual workers such as office, clerical, sales, or administrative personnel.

Workers' compensation. State laws requiring employers to provide employees with insurance protection from work-related disabilities.

Worth. Value measured by its qualities or by the esteem in which it is held.

INDEX

importance of, 7–8
interruption of, 209
Compensation administration. *See*
Compensation management
Compensation controls, 7
budgeting, 230–31, 231–32
pay techniques and, 231
Compensation decisions, policy development and, 7
Compensation laws. *See also* Fair
Labor Standards Act (FLSA,
1938)
age discrimination and, 203–4
child labor laws and, 189–90
Civil Rights Act (1964), Title VII,
198–99
disabled workers and, 202–3
discrimination and, 199–200
Equal Pay Act, 197
ethnic discrimination and, 200–201
history of, 189
jury duty, witness duty, voting time,
and, 204–5
merit decisions and, 206–7
merit pay and, 79
minimum wage, 194
national origin discrimination and,
204
overtime and, 194
performance appraisals and, 205–6
prevailing wage laws and, 197
religious discrimination and, 204
requirements for exempt positions,
194–97
sex discrimination and, 201–2
sexual orientation and, 202
underpayment and, 197
wage-hour law violations and,
192–93
wages and salaries and, 190
Compensation management, 3–4, 10,
223–35
budgeting and, 230–31
controls and, 231–32

goal accomplishment forms and,
233–34
integrating MBO and merit, 232–34
job evaluation and, 225–26
pay satisfaction and, 232
professional compensation and,
229–30
salary increases and, 227–29
salary policy and, 224–25
salary structure and, 226
salary surveys and, 226–27
trust and, 234–35
Compensation system, 1–4. *See also*
specific systems
Compensatory time (comp time), vs.
overtime, 193, 194
Competency-based pay system,
100–102
CompGeo.com, Online Standard Reports of, 167–68
Computer professional, as FLSA exempt employee, 191–92
Concentration, 62
Consistency, performance appraisals
and, 87–88, 89
Contributory indirect compensation,
182–83
Costs. *See also* Compensation controls
of indirect compensation, 184
labor, 46–47
Current performance, individual wage
determination and, 59–60

Data resources
for faculty salaries, 160
government, 166
Dean, in administrative organization,
10
Deferred income, 176–77
Demographic information, of librarians, 122, 160
Dental/vision/hearing aid plans,
178
Department heads, 11

Reasonable accommodation, 200,
202–3
Red-circle salaries, 61–62
Reevaluation, of jobs, 57
Reference groups, for wage-policy
decisions, 6–7
Regulations, merit pay and, 79
Religious discrimination, 204
Responsibilities factor, 20
Resume-building exercise, 89–90
Rockefeller, John D., 223
Roosevelt, Franklin D., 97, 137
Russell, Bertrand, 189

Salaried employees, as exempt employees under FLSA, 190–92
Salaries. *See also* Librarians' salaries
compared to wages, 8–9, 190
free-market economy and, 4–5
staff, 163–64
teaching faculty (2000–2001),
158–59
using outside job offers to improve,
168–69
Salary increases
compensation management and,
227, 231
problems with, 228–29
Salary index. *See* Compa-ratio
Salary management
below-minimum salaries and,
62
concentration and, 62
exceptions at hiring and, 61
problems and risks of, 61–63
range overlap and, 62
red-circle salaries and, 61–62
rules for, 61
Salary ranges, 231
and grades, 45–46
overlap between, 52–53
progression through, 60–61
Salary review, for librarians and
library faculty, 126

Salary schedule
compa-ratio and, 54–57
with fourteen grades (sample),
54fig., 55–56table
Salary structure
broad-banding, 53
compensation management and,
226
conventional, 52–53
conventional vs. broad-banding,
57–58
forces affecting, 57
Salary studies, to gain pay equity,
161–62
Salary surveys
compensation management and,
226–27
developing one's own, 168
Internet, 167–68
of library support staff (*Library
Mosaics*), 165–66
market surveys, 166
selecting, 166
Salary Wizard, 167
Self-directed 360 assessment, 90–94
Seniority, merit pay and, 71
Service Contract Act (1965), 197
Severance pay, 176
Sex. *See also* Gender
wage discrimination based on,
142–43
Sex discrimination, 201–2
Sex-segregated jobs, 142
identifying, 143–44
Sexual orientation, 202
Short-term disability/accident/sick-
ness plans, 175
Sick leave, 175
Simplified employee pension plans
(SEPs), 177
Skill-based pay system, 46, 49–51,
100
compared to competency-based
pay system, 102